A Brief History of
International Relations

This book is part of the Peter Lang Political Science, Economics, and Law list.
Every volume is peer reviewed and meets
the highest quality standards for content and production.

PETER LANG
New York • Bern • Berlin
Brussels • Vienna • Oxford • Warsaw

Kathleen Brush

A Brief History of International Relations

The World Made Easy

PETER LANG

New York • Bern • Berlin

Brussels • Vienna • Oxford • Warsaw

Library of Congress Cataloging-in-Publication Data

Names: Brush, Kathleen, author.
Title: A brief history of international relations:
the world made easy / Kathleen Brush.
Description: New York: Peter Lang, 2019.
Includes bibliographical references and index.
Identifiers: LCCN 2019006237 | ISBN 978-1-4331-6757-7 (hardback: alk. paper)
ISBN 978-1-4331-7659-3 (paperback: alk. paper)
ISBN 978-1-4331-6758-4 (ebook pdf) | ISBN 978-1-4331-6759-1 (epub)
ISBN 978-1-4331-6760-7 (mobi)
Subjects: LCSH: International relations—History.
Classification: LCC JZ1305 .B78 2019 | DDC 327.09—dc23
LC record available at https://lccn.loc.gov/2019006237
DOI 10.3726/b15851

Bibliographic information published by **Die Deutsche Nationalbibliothek.**
Die Deutsche Nationalbibliothek lists this publication in the "Deutsche
Nationalbibliografie"; detailed bibliographic data are available
on the Internet at http://dnb.d-nb.de/.

© 2019 Peter Lang Publishing, Inc., New York
29 Broadway, 18th floor, New York, NY 10006
www.peterlang.com

In memory of Marion Brush (1927–2017),
Jimmy Brush (1955–2017), and George Brush IV (1973–2019).
And to John Bianchi, a steadfast supporter by my side.

CONTENTS

INTRODUCTION

Every week there are puzzling reports of events involving China, Russia, the United States, Europe, and the Middle East. They may not seem so baffling if media reports explained that the events are all part of an ongoing competition for global supremacy. This book's objective is to make the world seem less perplexing by delivering essential context that facilitates connecting and grasping global events. Contextualization focuses on three areas: (1) the competition for global supremacy (1453–1945), (2) the *20th-century* transition from giant empires to 193 nation-states, and (3) a shortage of qualified national leaders.

It strikes many as a shocking revelation that in the early 20th century the Chinese, Russians, Turks, and Europeans were still ruling most of the world and battling for global supremacy. Empires conquering, and subjugating populations sounds like the ancient history of gladiators fighting starving tigers, not something so recent that it provides simple explanations to many of today's headlines, like Islamic unrest, obstinate China, Russian intransigence, European xenophobia, and American meddling.

What's behind Islamic militants spewing venom toward "western imperialists?" The competition for global supremacy, the transition to nations states, and a shortage of adept leaders that are global citizens. It wasn't long ago that Islamic empires were riding roughshod over Christian empires—the western imperialists. But in 1923 Muslim empires were gone, and Christian empires were "overseeing" their lands, which included allocating land for a new Zionist nation. For Muslims, these outcomes were mortifying, but it's been worsened by political and religious leaders opportunistically interpreting history to cast Muslims as innocent victims of western Christian hegemons. Hence the venom.

In the 21st century, China's rise has been inexorable; at some point it was inevitable. For centuries the Chinese Empire cut a daunting figure on the world stage. Then it suffered a Century of Humiliation (1839–1949) at the hands of Russian, Japanese, and European empires. Since 1949, China's leaders have taken no prisoners. They have been executing strategies, some successful and some clearly not, to minimally re-dominate the world's largest continent, home to 60 percent of the global population.

The Russian Empire shared the global limelight until its dissolution in the early 20th century. In the interwar years Russia, as the lead nation in the Soviet Union, was re-ascending. When World War II (WWII) ended it sat higher than it ever had on the global pecking order. It was positioned to redevelop an empire-like commanding presence on the world stage, but to do this, its leaders had to disregard the new zeitgeist of a world of sovereign nation-states providing fundamental freedoms for all. Soviet success lay in showcasing communism's superiority to the democratic and capitalist systems used by western powers. Forty-six years later the showcase was a joke, and the Soviet Union lost its superpower perch and its empire. Their primary adversary had been the United States, a puny colony when Russia was a vast empire. Ouch. After the Cold War, Russia re-emerged again. It had all the appearances of round two with the western powers. The USA bore a bullseye.

In the early 21st century membership was soaring for some anti-immigrant parties in European nations. Conjuring up memories of WWII's very dark period of racism, many Europeans were surprised and horrified. But for centuries racism pervaded Europe's global colonial empires and relations with non-European empires. Histories involving discrimination have a very long half-life.

The conversion from empires to nations occurred just in the nick of time. Early on competitors fought for religious converts. During the *uber* contests of WWI and WWII, there was no hint of moral purpose. Concentration camps, the vivisection of prisoners, and the murder and rape of millions of civilians reflected a competition for global supremacy that had gone too far. The global zeitgeist of massive imperial powers annexing tracts of land as large as continents and subjugating hundreds of millions of indigenous people had to end before it was too late.

Altering the course of history was a decision taken by WWII's primary Allied Powers: China, the Soviet Union, the United Kingdom, and the United States. (France was later added to this group of decision makers.) A principal vehicle for transitioning the world from empires to nation-states was the newly created United Nations (UN), an organization where new and old nations alike committed to respect sovereignty and protect equal freedoms for all people. The most powerful roles at the UN were allocated to the primary Allied Powers and France. Political giants dominating the world during the Era of Empire (1453–1945) were positioned to do it again in an Era of Nation-States (1945–?), with two material changes. The United States was in, and an Islamic power was out.

In the Era of Nation-States colonial populations had the opportunity to self-determine independence. Ready or not they flocked to be free from the subjugation of foreign empires. Annually for the next fifty years three sovereign nations,[1] on average, were added to the global atlas. In 1945 there were fifty-seven nations.[2] In 2018 there were 193.

Declarations of independence were joyous events as the yoke of subjugated rule was finally over. But the euphoria was short-lived. People had been so focused on dispensing with the imperialists they failed to adequately contemplate their state of preparedness. And they were not prepared. There was no shortage of men stepping up to the plate to be national governors. There were so many wannabes; coups were as common as elections. Many new national leaders arrived in office and refused to leave outside a coup or a coffin. Instead of building infrastructure and institutions, many used national treasuries like personal piggy banks.

The Cold War was another problem. Divisions among the former WWII Allied Powers shattered the UN's effectiveness and reignited the competition for global supremacy. Between 1947 and 1991 pro-democracy western powers including France and the United Kingdom but led by the US global-power neophyte engaged in proxy wars with the advocates for global communism led by the Soviet Union and China.

The Cold War tread comparatively lightly on Muslim-majority nations, but this hardly left them conflict free. The controversial creation of Israel, as a homeland for Jewish people amid Muslim nations, instigated successive Arab-Israeli and Iran-Israeli wars.[3] In 1979 there was a new source of conflict. Shiite Iran and Sunni Saudi Arabia commenced a proxy war for the leadership of Islam, the Middle East and North African (MENA) region, and the entire community of Muslims. It was reminiscent of a return to the 16th to 18th-century battles between the Safavid and Ottoman empires.

An estimated 20 million people died from Cold War-related conflicts. Most were from new nations that were vulnerable to the influence of global powers. In the Arab-Israeli and Iran-Israeli conflicts, there were over 100,000 fatalities and millions became refugees. Casualties from the Iran-Saudi proxy wars are unknown. What is known, is where there was conflict there were setbacks to nation-building.

When the Cold War ended, pundits imagined that finally, global peace was at hand, there would be global ideological unity behind democracy and capitalist-weighted systems, the UN would resume its enumerated responsibilities, and countries would focus on nation-building. These were the naive thoughts of people unfamiliar with the ongoing competition for global supremacy. The world has never been united on democracy and capitalism or fundamental freedoms for all, in agreement with the roles of the UN, or even the replacement of empires by nation-states.

But there would be no return to empire. The world had turned a corner. The Soviet Union was the last hurrah of empires, and it did not turn out well.

Nation-building continued to face enormous challenges. The responsibilities for oversight allocated to the United Nations were dogged by disunited former Allied Powers and the Organization of Islamic Powers. A void of global supervision was replaced with regional oversight by familiar global powers. China, the European Union replacing Europe's empires, Iran and Saudi Arabia for the Islamic empires, and Russia were rebuilding spheres of influence in areas where people followed similar religions, spoke similar languages, and shared common histories. These were the same areas ruled by their predecessor empires. Aftermaths of the competition for global supremacy created a means for the grandest competitors of the Era of Empire to perpetuate global power in the Era of Nation-States.

The influence these nations/unions have on their respective spheres has been impressive. The global influence of the United States has also been impressive. But rarely does influence exceed that from sovereign leaders. Sovereigns' control national resources and ultimately decide on the relationships with foreign powers. They manage national success or failure. Their collective track records are abysmal. Initially, this was foreseeable. Neither the empires nor the UN were running national leadership academies. A continuation of so much lousy national leadership decades later is harder to reconcile. There is nothing that prevents sovereign nations from developing qualified leaders.

Nineteen forty-five was a pivotal year in world history and not just because WWII ended. This is when the world began transitioning from the Era of Empire (1453–1945) to the Era of Nation-States (1945–?). The Era of Nation-States is historically speaking brand new. The world is filled with start-up nations built upon the aftermaths of empires by many inexperienced and misguided leaders. Examining these premises offers context to connect and simplify world events. Instead of events being hard to fathom, there is an easy path to make them understandable. Grasping high-level issues, like why some nations are rich and others poor, and why some nations see discrimination as bad and others see it as useful for organizing society can be streamlined. Insights into the nuances of relationships between China, the EU, Russia, Iran, Saudi Arabia, and the United States can become increasingly evident.

At a more granular level there is context to grasp things like: Why does the United States attract so many poisonous barbs from nations in Latin America? What possesses Russia to create havoc in western democracies? Why did Islamic militancy begin rising when the Cold War ended? Why can't nations in Eastern Europe escape the clutch of Russia? Why do many small nations in eastern Asia live in trepidation of rising China? Why do so many take exception to Western European statesman as the pontificators of peace? And, why was the UN's mission as a peacekeeper doomed at inception?

Organization of the book

There are two central sections: The Era of Empire, and the Era of Nation-States: Becoming Nation-States. The first section focuses on the competition for global supremacy taking place between 1453 and 1945 and the aftermaths. The competitors were the Chinese, European, Islamic and Russian empires. Each left behind enduring aftermaths with significant consequences for the Era of Nation-States.

Before the second section begins, an epilogue covers cardinal events that occurred during the very unclean cutover from the Era of Empire to the Era of Nation-States. This offers additional context for the Era of Nation-States.

Section Two: The Era of Nation-States: Becoming Nation-States takes a look at how a sample of countries from the twelve different regions of the world have progressed as independent nations. The influence of empire aftermaths including diverse and discriminated populations, and actions by global powers to rebuild the historical spheres of their predecessor empires figure prominently, but not more so than the role of sovereign national leaders in the twists and turns, and successes and failures of their nations.

One more book is planned to specifically cover the Era of Nation-States. In 1945 there were 57 nations; in 2018 there were 193 divided among twelve regions. New national leaders were in charge of creating self-sustaining economies and governments, and delivering fundamental freedoms for all, while accommodating aftermaths from colonial rule like histories of subjugation, and empire postscripts like the Cold War. These were tall orders for national leaders suitably competent and motivated for nation-building, but most were not. Worse intergovernmental organizations, like the UN created to facilitate nation-building, fell woefully short of plan. Outcomes have included underdeveloped nations, poor qualities of life, armed conflict, widespread discrimination and repression, and the perpetuation of gender subjugation.

Notes

1. A sovereign by definition has ultimate power between its recognized borders.
2. In this book, the term nation refers to a UN recognized sovereign. However, applying this definition in 1945 would leave out nations like Germany, Italy, and Japan because initially the only sovereigns recognized by the UN were those that supported the Allied Powers. In this instance, the reference to fifty-seven nations is an approximate number of independent nations in 1945.
3. With the Soviet Union supporting Arab nations and the United States supporting Israel, some consider these Cold War-related conflicts, but these wars had nothing to do with communists vs. democrats or anti-communists, and they continued after the Cold War ended.

SECTION I

INTRODUCTION

The Era of Empire

"Make no mistake, those who are not willing to confront the past, will be unable to understand the present and unfit to face the future."
—Bernard Lewis, FBA, *The End of Modern History in the Middle East* (2011)

The Era of Empire began in 1453 and ended in 1945. It was an era when European, Islamic, Chinese, and Russian empires engaged in a competition for global supremacy. They conquered, ruled, and subjugated the world's land and people, and left behind indelible marks of their presence.

The Islamic Ottoman Empire instigated the competition. Muslim rulers had been besting Christendom, also known as Europe, for centuries. In 1453 the Ottomans added a *coup de grace* to centuries of humiliation by placing the final nail in the coffin of the Christian Byzantine Empire (330–1453). The Ottoman sultan poured salt into this wound by declaring himself the Master of Kings, an emperor of the world. Then came more salt. He instituted measures to curtail Europe's overland access to the Silk Road and spice trade. This affected European lifestyles and their wallets.

The Ottomans provoked the Christian Russians too. Beginning in 1449 the Ottoman's made Crimea a vassal state. The Crimean Khanate[1] (1449–1783) became a slave *entrepôt* where an estimated 2 million white Christians, mostly Russian, were enslaved and sold in the Ottoman Empire.

The actions of the Ottomans were a giant wake up call to the leadership of the Roman and Orthodox Catholic Churches and Europe's Christian rulers that instigated a competition for global supremacy. The competition was intense at the Eurasian geographical nexus of the European, Islamic, and Russian empires. For centuries, the Chinese Empire was isolated from the competition, but this changed in the 19th century when "barbarians" from the European, Japanese, and Russian empires took advantage of an empire in decline.

WWII was the climax and the anti-climax of the contest for global supremacy. The Chinese, Russian, and Europe's greatest colonial empires, the British and the French, all fought on the same side and won.[2] From a spoils-of-war perspective, it wasn't much of a win. They won bragging rights to the war sounding a wake-up call to the escalating danger of the competition for global supremacy. They also won a superior position at the bargaining table when defining the unwinding of the Era of Empire and essential aspects of the Era of Nation-States. Noticeably absent from a prominent presence in WWII and the bargaining table was an Islamic power.

Below is the story of the Era of Empire (1453–1945) told through events that have shaped and will continue to shape the world. There is no period in history with more profound implications for the world today and tomorrow. This era holds the keys to understanding crucial context underlying: relation-ships among global powers and other nations, conflict between Muslim and non-Muslim and democratic and autocratic nations, discriminatory practices, and why some nations have been able to perpetuate world power. It is the story of the Chinese, European, Islamic, and Russian empires competing to control the land and people of the world.

Notes

1. Genghis Khan and khanates are related. Khan's empire was divided into khanates that were ruled by his descendants.
2. France surrendered to Germany in 1940. The Allied Powers liberated France in 1944.

· 1 ·

ISLAMIC EMPIRES

Islamic empires ruling contiguous expanses of Africa, Asia, and Europe had an extraordinary run. It was in the first Islamic empires, the Rashidun (632–661) and Umayyad (661–750) that Christianity lost much of the Iberian Peninsula (Iberia), North Africa and parts of the Middle East, including Syria and Turkey, to Islam. Millions converted to Islam. Christians tried to halt Muslim advances in the battles of the Crusades (1096–1291).[1] In the end, the Christians were again defeated by the Muslims, and Muslims continued ruling the Holy Land.

The Christian-Muslim conflict that inspired the competition for global supremacy was long in the making. For the Christians, the final straw was delivered by the Ottoman Empire (1299–1922), also called the Turkish Empire. In 1453 the Ottoman's laid waste to what remained of the Byzantine Empire[2] (330–1453), an Eastern Orthodox empire.[3] For the next 150 years, the Ottoman Empire sowed fear throughout Christendom and beyond. They conquered Central Europe's Balkan Peninsula, and Western Europe's Greece, Cyprus, and parts of Italy. In Eastern Europe, they controlled the Crimean Peninsula and parts of Moldova. They also annexed many Muslim polities in the Middle East and North Africa, northern sub-Saharan Africa, and parts of central Asia.[4] The long run of successive conquests finally ended on 9-11-1683 at the gates of Vienna.

The 17th century marked a turning point in the wars against Christian empires. Instead of Christian conquerors, the Ottomans became defenders, making them defenders on two fronts. Wars with the Persian[5] Shiite Safavid empire[6] (1501–1736) had begun consuming them in the 16th century. When the Ottomans made it illegal to practice Shiite Islam in Safavid territory,[i,7] this instigated a major rivalry for leadership of Islam. Several major and minor wars took place, followed by treaties that mostly failed to bring about detente.[ii] Armed hostilities finally ended in the 19th century.

Muslim empires consumed in war made them a tempting target for a rising Russian Empire. The Russo-Persian (Russo-Iranian) and Russo-Ottoman (Russo-Turkish) wars took place from the 17th to the 19th centuries. The Russian Empire's greatest territorial gains came at the expense of these empires.

While the Ottomans, Persians, and Russians were battling in the middle of Eurasia, Islamic expansion was not standing still. The Islamic Mughal Empire (1526–1857) had been making considerable progress expanding in South Asia. By 1707, the Mughals were ruling most of the Indian sub-continent.[8]

In 1744 the Ottomans had another Islamic foe to battle; this one was Sunni, Arab, and within the empire. Arab Muslims accepted Turkish rule as long as it was according to sharia.[9] When the Ottomans adopted secular, cultural practices like European literature, music, painting, and architecture, some Arab Muslims saw these as tasteless or even heretical practices and the root of the Ottoman's declining state. Muhammad ibn Saud and Muhammad ibn Abd-al Wahhab began conquering polities on the Arabian Peninsula on a mission to restore Islamic greatness with an empire based on Islamism. This is where government and society revolve around Islam, much as it had under the Prophet Muhammad in the 7th century.

In 1818 the Ottomans regained control of the lands in the nascent Saudi state. In 1823 the Ottoman's claimed victory over the Persian Shias in the Qajar Dynasty (1789–1925). These were among the Ottoman's last victories. The victory over the Saudis was temporary and the win over the Shias bittersweet. Shiite empires left a legacy of millions of Shiite Muslims in the Middle East, South Asia, Southeast Asia, and Central Asia.

The 19th and early 20th centuries were dreadful for the Islamic empires. The British Empire captured South Asia from the Mughal Empire. Shiite empires lost today's Georgia, Armenia, and Azerbaijan to the Russian Empire. The Ottomans lost: Cyprus, Egypt and the Sudan to the British Empire; Algeria and Tunisia to the French Empire; Libya to the Italian Empire; and Crimea, Moldova, and lands in the Caucasus to the Russian Empire.[iii] The Russian

Empire was also ruling local Muslim polities in Central Asia previously ruled by different Shiite and Sunni empires and kingdoms.

The Ottomans lost Greece, Bulgaria, Montenegro, Romania, and Serbia to wars of independence. The return of these nations to Christendom was not all good news. They were filled with diverse ethnolinguistic Muslims and Christians unhappily living side by side, and the Russian and Austro-Hungarian empires coveted their annexation. The Balkans were a European tinderbox.

The 15th century glory days of Islam socking it to Christendom seemed very far off in the late 19th and early 20th centuries. What remained was the Ottoman Empire, a rump state with severe financial problems. In 1875 they defaulted on over $1 billion of sovereign debt (equivalent to about $2 trillion in 2014 dollars), and Britain became the majority shareholder in the Suez Canal. In 1881 the Ottoman Public Debt Administration was established. Now, Europeans were administering tax collection in the Ottoman Empire. In 1882, Egypt, a powerful administrative division, became a virtual protectorate of the British Empire. In 1914 it became a formal protectorate that had the appearances of a colony of the British Empire.[iv]

Ottoman financial problems seemed insurmountable. The continual loss of land meant the constant loss of taxpayers including the higher-taxed Christians. If Ottoman rulers had modernized the economy, a shrinking population might have been overcome, but they did not. While Europe's industrialized economies were producing and distributing high volumes of manufactured goods, the Ottomans oversaw a contracting agrarian economy.

The insolvent Ottoman rulers had acknowledged the need to modernize their economy, and they had implemented some reforms,[10] but getting from agrarian to industrialized was an enormous challenge that among other things required an educated labor force and massive investments in infrastructure. This was a tall order for a cash-strapped empire where religious leaders managed important economic levers, like education, and interfered with modernization initiatives that they saw as Christian, European, and bad.[v]

There was another enormous stumbling block; the endless intrusions of wars reflexively prioritized defense over economic development. The Ottomans did have one thing working in their favor. The British and French were fearful that the dissolution of the Ottoman Empire would result in many small independent Muslim nations that could damage global stability and limit access to British India. They endeavored to preserve the rump of the Ottoman Empire, but the Ottomans decided to take a double or nothing bet and joined the Germans and other Central Powers in WWI.

Notes

1. The establishment of a new empire with a new religion on previously Christian lands was destabilizing and frightening. This motivated the Crusades.
2. The Byzantine Empire was also called the Eastern Roman Empire. It was the final remnant of the Roman Empire.
3. The official name of the Eastern Orthodox Church is the Orthodox Catholic Church. This can create confusion with the Roman Catholic Church, also known as the Catholic Church. This is why in this book Roman Catholics are abbreviated as Catholics, and followers of Eastern Orthodoxy are identified as Eastern Orthodox, Orthodox, or "something" Orthodox, e.g., Russian Orthodox.
4. See Appendix A for a list of nations included in different regions, e.g., Western Europe.
5. Persian and Iranian are often used interchangeably because Persia was the name of Iran prior to 1935. Some writers refer to the Safavids as the Persian Safavids and others, the Iranian Safavids. There are, however, distinct Persian and Iranian ethnolinguistic groups that lived within Persia and continue to live in Iran. In this book, Persian is used as the ethnolinguistic qualifier for the Shiite empires centered in the future nation of Iran.
6. Shiite empires are more regularly labeled by the ruling family's dynasty, for instance, the Safavid Dynasty. The same is true of many European empires. Europe's empires are also referred to as the House of Something, for example, the House of Habsburg or the House of Bourbon.
7. The Safavids were very successful, but they may have been more so if they had established a military alliance with the Habsburg Empire against the Ottoman Empire. There were numerous unsuccessful diplomatic efforts between Safavid rulers and rulers in the Habsburg Dynasty, including with Charles V, the emperor who came closest to building a pan-European empire.
8. The Mughals were descendants of the Mongols. The Mongols handed the Muslims a rare defeat in the 13th century in the Siege of Baghdad (1258). After this many Mongol rulers converted to Islam.
9. Sharia law is the religious law of Islam. It has three primary components: Hadiths or the verified words of the Prophet Muhammad, sunnah or verified actions of the Prophet Muhammad, and the Quran.
10. Many Tanzimat reforms (1839–1876) introduced secular western practices. They covered politics, economics, and society. Before they were abandoned, they had some successes, but these were generally unpopular reforms.

References

i. "Safavid Empire (1501–1722)." *BBC.co.uk*. Retrieved October 25, 2018.
ii. Bitterlemons.net. "The Myth of 1639 and Kasri Sirin." *The Washington Institute*, May 18, 2006.
iii. Hanioğlu, M. Şükrü. *A Brief History of the Late Ottoman Empire*. Princeton: Princeton University Press, 2008.

iv. Shaw, Stanford, and Ezel Kural Shaw. *History of the Ottoman Empire and Modern Turkey*. New York: Cambridge University Press, 1977.

v. Faroqui, Suraiya, Bruce McGowan, Donald Quataert, and Şevket Pamuk. *An Economic and Social History of the Ottoman Empire*. New York: Cambridge University Press, 1994.

· 2 ·

THE EUROPEAN EMPIRES

In Europe, the competition for empire took two distinct paths: some competitors focused on a intra-European empire and some on overseas colonial empires. The French empires, the House of Habsburg, and later the German empires were the primary intra-European competitors. The Spanish, Portuguese, British, and French were the main competitors for overseas colonial empires. There were, however, other European competitors that ruled a small number of colonies.

The creation of overseas colonial empires was uniquely European. So was the creation of empires that spanned the Old and New Worlds. The Chinese, Islamic, and Russians built their empires by conquering contiguous land polities in the Old World.[1] Only the Europeans built far-flung empires that in the case of Britain included colonies on all six inhabitable continents: Old-World Africa, Asia, and Europe; and New-World Australia, North America, and South America.

Europe's overseas colonial empires

The Ottoman defeat of the Byzantine Empire in conjunction with monopolizing access to the Silk Road and spice trade was a provocation that shook

Europe's commercial and religious establishments from its Middle Ages torpor. For centuries, the Silk Road had been the source of innovations and coveted luxuries that drove profits for merchants and monarchs in Europe. Rulers became motivated to restore access. The pope, Europe's most influential religious leader, was naturally very concerned by the continuing loss of Christians and Christian lands. He prioritized eliminating the remaining Islamic polities from the Iberian Peninsula and expanding the population of Christians.

Portugal and Spain's Roman Catholic monarchs were the primary executors of the pope's priorities. These monarchs also prioritized discovering a maritime route to the Silk Road and spice trade.

In 1492 Spain's Queen Isabella and King Ferdinand ejected the last of the Islamic polities from Iberia. In the same year, they sponsored the Genoese explorer Christopher Columbus to discover a maritime route to the spice trade.[i,2]

Columbus ended up sailing west of target by about 14,000 km (9,000 mi.). Instead of finding a maritime path to the spice trade he landed in the Bahamas. What little the Portuguese and Spanish knew about his "discovery," was enough for each to want exclusive ownership. In exchange for agreeing to convert the indigenous people to Roman Catholicism, the pope in the Treaty of Tordesillas (1494) divided the ownership of the North and South American continents and the Atlantic coast of Africa between Spain and Portugal.[3] This instigated the colonization and Christianization of two plus continents. Some opined that the pope had no idea what he was doing, while others remarked that it had to be divine providence that led the pope to reserve two plus continents for Christianity.

The priority of a maritime route to the spice trade was also achieved. Vasco da Gama, sailing for Portugal discovered a route in 1498. The Age of Discovery was on, and so was a competition for global supremacy that would make the Ottoman's regret adding salt into the wounds of Christendom.

The discovery of the New World changed the competition completely. Instead of battling the militaries of the Ottoman, European, and Russian polities to expand access to precious resources, land, and people, it was simpler and more lucrative to engage in conquests in the New World.

Initially, only Catholic Spain and Portugal could engage in conquests in the New World because the pope had granted them ownership. By the late 16th century, the Iberian monarchs became distracted by wars in Europe, the power of the pontiff was eroding, and the treaties of Tordesillas and Saragossa were no longer honored. A claim to land ownership required building and defending established settlements. In 1604, the French established Acadia, a settlement on the southeast coast of the future nation of Canada. In 1607, the British established their first settlement in the future United States.

After their loss in the French and Indian War (1756–1763), also called the Seven Years War in Europe, France's New-World empire was decimated. Correctly sensing defeat, they pre-emptively ceded the Louisiana Territory to Spain in 1762. They lost their Canadian colonies to Britain, but they saw this as trivial. Voltaire characterized this loss to France's King Louis XV as a "few acres of snow." They did keep some sugar-producing islands in the Caribbean, like Haiti, which was satiating Europe's desire for sugar and coffee, and generating revenue for the French government.

The French lost their establishment in Bengal to the British.[4] At this time Bengal was responsible for 25 percent of global production vs. 1.9 percent in England.[ii,iii, 5,6] The British Empire had not yet established colonies in South Asia, but the British East India Company had established virtual colonies, which now included Bengal, and they were exercising "company rule."

Britain was now the predominant ruler in North America, but not for long. Between 1775 and 1783 the Thirteen Colonies became the first overseas colonies to successfully revolt for independence as the new United States of America. Five years later the British compensated for this humiliating loss by colonizing the third New-World continent of Australia.

In 1800 the French were back in North America. The soon to be emperor, Napoleon Bonaparte, was on a mission to rebuild France's New-World empire starting with reacquiring the Louisiana Territory from Spain. Expanding the empire in North America was the next step. But before expansion there had to be a reconciliation with Haitians that were revolting for independence. After contemplating war with the Americans who had just defeated the British,[7] Napoleon decided to sell the Louisiana Territory to the United States in 1803 and use the money to finance wars to reignite France's quest to rule Europe.

Keeping Haiti remained a priority. Napoleon wanted revenue from sugar to finance wars in Europe. The Haitians weren't cooperating. Free and enslaved blacks and mulattoes were 90 percent of Haiti's population and they wanted an end to their brutal French slave masters. Tortured, mutilated, and roasted alive, half of Haiti's slaves died after a few years of labor.[iv] Motivations for independence increased when Napoleon engaged in one of the earliest documented cases of genocide. He ordered the killing of all blacks over twelve.[v]

In 1804 a small nation of slaves, former slaves, and free descendants of slaves did something Europe would struggle to do for ten years—beat Napoleon and France. They also created the world's first slavery-free republic.

Napoleon's inadvertent impacts on the New World went beyond expanding US territory and instilling fear of a successful slave revolt into every polity in the Americas. When Napoleon deposed the monarch of Spain, he created a void of central authority for the Spanish Empire, placed fear of French rule throughout Latin America (Latam), and set in motion the law of unintended consequences. Avoiding French rule led to the creation of emergency governments and juntas in Latam. In turn, this ignited civil wars between those loyal to the deposed Spanish monarch and those that wanted independence.

The restoration of power to Spain's King Ferdinand VII made some content to return to Spanish rule. In the monarch's absence, things had improved for the colonials. Significant self-governing powers had been constitutionally granted to them. But Ferdinand abolished the constitution and restored an absolute monarchy. All over Latam, battle-tested, self-governing colonies successfully waged wars for independence between 1809 and 1825.[8]

The dissolution of the Napoleonic Empire, also called the First French Empire (1804–1814, 1815) left France anxious to build another colonial empire and restore its stature as a world power.[vi] Its recovery was aided by industrialization that generated money and advanced military technologies. The French had to reckon with the reality that there were no more easy conquests. The United States would defend attempts to re-conquer lands in the Americas, and the British Empire would defend Australia. The easier conquests had moved to the Old World where the agrarian Ottoman and Chinese empires were showing signs of decline. Economically and militarily they were a poor match for Europe's industrializing nations. In 1830 France made Ottoman Algeria a colony.

Industrializing Britain targeted the same empires. In the First Opium War (1839–1842) Britain successfully went head to head against the Chinese Empire and acquired the island of Hong Kong. This loss started the calendar for the Chinese Century of Humiliation. In the Second Opium War (1856–1860) China lost again, and now barbarians from the European, Japanese, and Russian empires, and the United States were infringing on Chinese sovereignty by operating self-governing treaty ports.

Britain's next conquest was the Islamic Mughal Empire (1526–1857). It was an easy conquest. The Mughals had been successful conquerors but they were horrible governors. The empire had become a collection of local fiefs with an economy that resembled something from the Middle Ages.[vii] In 1858 Britain had its crown jewel. British India included the lands of present-day India, Pakistan, Bangladesh, and Myanmar (formerly Burma) and with more than 200 million inhabitants, it had eight times the population of Britain. By the end of the 19th century, the British had colonized most of South Asia. What they had not colonized they were protecting.[9]

The British also took aim at the Ottoman Empire. The highly coveted port of Aden located in today's south Yemen links the Mediterranean Sea to the Indian Ocean. In 1874 it became a British protectorate, and in 1937 became the only European (British) colony in the Middle East.

Britain and France both aimed at China's tributary empire in Southeast Asia. In 1786 the British began making inroads on the Malaysian Peninsula where local rulers were seeking protection from acquisitive neighbors, like Thailand (formerly Siam). In the 19th century Brunei, Malaysia, and Singapore were colonized and became unofficially known as British Malaya. The Indochinese weren't seeking a protector, but they got one. By 1893 France had colonized Vietnam, Laos, and Cambodia (collectively called French Indochina).[10]

The Dutch East India Company had been exercising lucrative company rule in Indonesia for three centuries, but the encroachment of the French and British in Southeast Asia was unnerving. The Dutch converted Indonesia to a colony and expanded their rule to cover the entire archipelago. At this point, European empires ruled all of Southeast Asia except Thailand.

The creation of the German Empire in 1871 brought a new competitor for global supremacy. The German Empire's first Chancellor, Otto von Bismarck, was initially opposed to building a colonial empire. He wanted a strong German state in Europe, and to avoid conflict with the British and French empires. Later he changed his mind. In 1885 Bismarck said, "Colonies would mean the winning of new markets for German industries, the expansion of trade, and a new field for German activity, civilization, and capital." That was a practical reason. Reichstag member, Heinrich von Treitschke, echoed a common but less pragmatic driver of empire. "Every virile people has established colonial power. All great nations in the fullness of their strength have desired to set their mark upon barbarian lands and those who fail to participate in this great rivalry will play a pitiable role in time to come."

Bismarck hosted the Berlin Conference (1884–1885), a meeting of European powers and the Russian Empire to discuss a colonial carve-up of the African continent. Africa was the last expanse of land unencumbered by any major empire. Participants justified this takeover in part on religious grounds;

Islam had already taken over the north of Africa, and they needed to implant Christianity in the south. In part on a desire to abolish slavery, and in part "to initiate the indigenous populations into the advantages of civilization."[viii] Economic motivations were a clear driver, but they had the wooden sound of naked western imperialism. Something better discussed in private.

In divvying up Africa consideration was given to the foreign empires with an established presence in Africa. This favored Britain and France, and the greatest number of colonies were given to them. Smaller numbers were given to Belgium,[11] Italy, Portugal, Spain, and Germany.[12] At the end of the conference only: Ethiopia, a Christian kingdom; Christian-majority Liberia, a former colony of the American Colonization Society (1821–1847); and Muslim-majority Morocco retained their independence in Africa.[13]

Africans were excluded from the carve-up discussions and many wholly rejected this usurpation of land and "white man" rule. Some empires like: the Islamic Sokoto Caliphate of northern Nigeria (1804–1903); Mahdist Sudan (1885–1899), an Islamist state that has been called an ancestor of the Islamic State of Iraq and Syria (ISIS);[ix] the Zulu Kingdom/Empire (1816–1897) of southern Africa; and an independent Ashanti Empire of Ghana (1670–1902) fought hard, if unsuccessfully, to maintain their independence. Many smaller polities negotiated a transfer of power, knowing that fighting an industrialized European power with modern weapons, and trained African mercenary soldiers would incur significant casualties, and they would still lose their sovereignty.

At the turn of the 20th century, the smallest continent, Europe, had amassed colonial empires that spanned all inhabitable continents in spite of enduring endless wars at home. Europeans (whites) or their descendants were the majority populations and governing almost all of the New World and ruling most of the Old World. The competition, however, was not over. The greatest battles for supremacy were still to come, and the importance of being an industrialized empire was about to become crystal clear.

Intra-European empire builders (until 1914)

Ruling Europe was essential to global supremacy, and this made the competition in Europe particularly intense. Continuous wars are part of Europe's history (and also part of Turkish and Russian history). The Ottoman and Russian empires were often belligerents, as adversaries or allies of different European empires. Nearly everyone wanted to rule Europe, and just as many wanted to prevent another from ruling Europe. This seemed to create strange bedfellows, but at the time this was not necessarily so. For much of the Era of Empire "none of the other 'great' European powers—e.g., the British, French, Russian[14] or Austro-Hungarian empires would have taken issue with counting the Ottoman Empire as one among them."[x]

Early on there was an intense rivalry between Europe's Christian empires and the Muslim Ottoman Empire, but that was already fading in the 16th century. When the Habsburgs looked to have a chance of ruling Europe, the Ottomans became the lone Muslim member of a coalition of Christian empires foiling their chances. This showdown was centered in the Holy Roman Empire, a Habsburg polity. It was ground zero for one-hundred years of wars, ostensibly between Protestants and Catholics. Called wars of religion the lineup of belligerents tells a more nuanced motive, like the quest for building or maintaining political power. Roman Catholic France, Eastern Orthodox Russia, and the Islamic Ottomans were aligned with different Protestant principalities battling the Roman Catholic Habsburgs.[15,xi] In the final battle, the Thirty Years War (1618–1648), the mixed-religious coalition defeated the Habsburgs and ended their bid for supremacy of Europe. This finality also severely diminished the power of the Catholic Church and the pope, which eroded the power of every Roman Catholic polity. Roman Catholic monarchs could no longer rely on Papa, the supreme pontiff, to intervene and settle a score.

These were very unusual times in Christendom. The competition for global supremacy was instigated by the challenge that Islamic empires posed to Christianity and Christian polities, but less than one-hundred years later, the most significant challenges Christendom faced came from Christian polities. On the European continent, there was a century of debilitating "religious wars" that could have been called Christian wars. Across the channel, something similar occurred in the British Isles.

In the 16th century England unilaterally separated from the Catholic Church. This created many enemies on the still Catholic continent. Adversarial venom increased when England favorably compared Britain's Protestant faith to Islam. In need of allies, the English seemed to stop at nothing.[xii] Nothing the Roman Catholic French hadn't engaged in twenty years earlier, when they developed a military alliance with the Ottomans to halt the Roman Catholic Habsburgs.

Protestant (Anglican) England, Protestant (Presbyterian) Scotland and Roman Catholic Ireland were all separate kingdoms ruled by a common king. After separation from Rome, they engaged in intra-Christian wars over the question, should the state dictate the religion followed or should there be religious freedom. These were hardly passive conflicts. The Wars of the Three Kingdoms (1639–1651) took the lives of about 2.5 percent of the civilian populations.[xiii]

Europe's so-called wars of religion created opportunities for Tsardom Russia and the Ottoman Empire to expand into Europe, which they did. When the religious wars ended, the battle for Europe continued apace. There were several wars of succession taking place in the first half of the 18th century, including the Spanish, Polish and Austrian. There was so much genetic linking among the Russian and European monarchies, anytime a successor was ambiguous, polities from all over engaged in war. These wars determined who ruled, who was aligned with ruling empires, and who participated in the weighty spoils of war. When spoils included shifting which empires ruled foreign people and places, this created political discontinuities in different parts of the world. European colonies were pawns of the warring empires.

With so many wars in Europe, the nations and people of Europe were pawns too. Sweden's successive conquests in northern Europe made the Polish, Danish and Russians anxious. Too anxious. In the Great Northern War (1700–1721) the Swedish Empire allied with the Ottoman Empire and others to fight Tsardom Russia, the Polish-Lithuanian Commonwealth, the Kingdom of Prussia, Denmark-Norway, and others. In the end Sweden lost its empire, Russia became an empire, Prussia was recognized as a global power, and in short order, Polish-Lithuania lost 30 percent of its land to its Prussian and Russian allies. Wars were how global powers were elevated and debilitated. Wars altered the trajectory of history for the victorious, and the defeated, including their subjugated colonials.

The Seven Years War (1756–1763), later called the first world war, spanned five continents. At stake was the rule of Europe, the New World and more. The primary belligerents were the French and a British-Prussian coalition. France was allied with the Russian and Mughal empires and some European powers. The French lost and suffered diminished authority in the New and Old Worlds, while the win cemented Britain's position as a leading European and colonial power.[16]

In the early 19th century, France resumed its mission to rule Europe (and more) under the leadership of Emperor Napoleon Bonaparte. Napoleon wreaked havoc all over Eurasia and into North Africa. His greatest destruction was reserved for Europe. Here there were 3–7 million casualties. In the end, France lost again. The dissolution of the First French Empire (1804–1814, 1815) left France prostrate.

So unsettling were the Napoleonic wars that the winning powers: the Austrian, British and Russian empires, and the Kingdom of Prussia made provisions in the Concert of Europe to prevent France and any other power from disrupting a balance of power in Europe. This worked, but not for long.

Napoleon's loss took France out of the empire competition completely, but he took others with him. The Habsburgs lost their crown jewel, the Holy Roman Empire (962–1806). For centuries it had been Europe's most powerful political entity. Habsburg rule was now limited to the Austrian Empire, a smallish empire in the center of Europe. Napoleon also debilitated the Spanish and Portuguese empires and weakened his ally, the Dutch Empire. He also plunged a dagger into the sultan of the Ottoman Empire when he became the first Christian ruler to occupy Egypt (1798–1801).[17]

Napoleon ended the competition between the French and the Habsburgs for supremacy of Europe. This hardly finished the competition between the French and the German-speaking. The creation of the German Confederation was another outcome of the Napoleonic wars, and this was an intermediary step on the way to a German empire.[18]

The idea of ruling Europe was abandoned by the French until another Bonaparte was back in charge. In 1870, Napoleon's nephew, Emperor Napoleon III, declared war on the German-speaking Kingdom of Prussia. A year later France was defeated again and now all German-speaking states, except Austria, were united in the new German Empire. The French who had endeavored to keep the German-speaking people weak could take credit for creating a new, powerful German competitor for European and global supremacy. The Germans were not just numerically strong; they were leaders in providing widespread access to education that fueled industrialization and a trained and disciplined military.

By the late 19th century Europeans had their fill of the endless battles for supremacy of Europe that brought unbounded misery, but little else. But there would be no peace. The Germans were educated, armed, productive, and ambitious. They would soon play commanding roles in global wars involving every surviving empire. These wars were deadlier and more destructive than any heretofore in the competition.

Notes

1. Russia had a colony in the US state of Alaska from 1787–1867. They also had small colonies in California and Hawaii, and one in sub-Saharan Africa that they later abandoned.

2. It's not clear if the monarchs knew that Columbus planned to amass wealth from his maritime successes and use the profits to battle for Jerusalem. He wanted to succeed where the Crusades had failed. When Columbus died in 1506, the quest to recapture Jerusalem was no longer a priority.

3. In the Treaty of Saragossa (1529), the borders in the Treaty of Tordesillas were adjusted. Portugal now had control of Asia, and Spain controlled most of the Pacific.

4. Bengal was a vast region that included today's Bangladesh and the Indian state of West Bengal.

5. This is a reference specific to England's production, even though England was already part of Great Britain. Formed in 1707, Great Britain included England, Scotland, and Wales. With the addition of Ireland, the United Kingdom came into existence in 1801. (See Appendix B for a list of formal or informal names for regionally grouped states.) For simplicity, except where a reference needs specificity, when referring to actions and people related to Great Britain or the United Kingdom the terms Britain and British are used.

6. Comparable data for France could not be located. In the 18th century it had about twice the population of England. At this time labor was the primary determinant of production.

7. The French were formally allied with the Americans against the British in the American Revolutionary War (1775–1783).

8. Napoleon also altered the heft of the Dutch Empire. South Africa, then called the Dutch Cape Colony, was one of Holland's most important colonies. But Holland was Napoleon's ally, and they lost this colony to the British at the end of the Napoleonic Wars (1803–1815).

9. Becoming a protectorate was sometimes voluntary because polities were concerned about being invaded and conquered by a disagreeable empire. Other times "agreeing" to be a protectorate was a decision to avoid conquest by the intended protector. A protectorate was in theory different from a colony because they had self-governance. Sometimes theory didn't match practice.

10. The Thais also attacked China's weakness to expand their empire. Cambodia, Laos, and some kingdoms in British Malaya spent 50–100 years between 1779 and 1893 as vassal states of Thailand when it was the Rattanakosin Kingdom.

11. It wasn't Belgium, but King Leopold of Belgium that was given the Congo Free State as his personal property/colony. His abusive rule led to the colony's transfer to Belgium in 1908.

12. In early 1889, the Russian Empire briefly settled a small colony called Sagallo in present-day Djibouti in Africa. After about a month, the French routed the settlers.

13. In 1912 parts of Morocco became protectorates of France or Spain.

14. Even though Russia is partly in Europe, in this book, it is not grouped with the European empires.

15. One job of the Holy Roman Emperor was protecting the Roman Catholic Church. This ruler alone was eligible to be crowned by the pope and rightfully carried the aura of a divine right to rule. Charles V was the last Holy Roman Emperor (1519–1556) to be crowned by the pope.

16. In North America, the Seven Years War is called the French and Indian War. The French loss meant the British were uncontested as the primary colonial power in North America.

17. The Ottomans suffered a humiliating defeat when the fledgling United States beat them in the Barbary War (1801–1805). The United States, however, did not conquer territory, but it did cut the Ottomans off from a source of revenue—ransom from holding ships hostage.
18. At the Congress of Vienna (1814–1815), it was agreed to consolidate thirty-nine German-speaking states, including the Kingdom of Prussia and the Austrian Empire into an association called the German Confederation (1815–1866).

References

i. Delaney, Carol. "Columbus's Ultimate Goal: Jerusalem." *Comparative Studies in Society and History* 48, no. 2 (2006): 260–92.

ii. Cleary, Vern. "The Turning Point: Robert Clive and the Conquest of Bengal." *Modern World History*. Retrieved August 30, 2018.

iii. Rusnock, A. *Vital Accounts: Quantifying Health and Population in Eighteenth-Century England and France*. Cambridge University Press, 2002.

iv. Abbott, Elizabeth. *Haiti: A Shattered Nation*. Penguin, 2011.

v. Ribbe, Claude. *Napoleon's Crimes*. Oneworld Publications, 2005.

vi. Hayes, Carlton J. H. "From Nationalism to Imperialism." *Panarchy.com*. Retrieved May 14, 2018.

vii. Ziegler, Philip. "Decline and fall of the Mughal Empire." *The Telegraph*, May 25, 2003.

viii. Mazower, Mark. "Paved Intentions: Civilization and Imperialism." *World Affairs*, Fall 2008.

ix. Motadel, David. "The Ancestors of ISIS." *The New York Times*, September 23, 2014.

x. Bostanci, Anne. "Why Turkey hasn't forgotten about the First World War." *The British Council*, September 1, 2014.

xi. Dunn, Richard. *The Age of Religious Wars 1559–1715*. New York: W. W. Norton, 1979.

xii. Brotton, Jerry. *The Sultan and the Queen: The Untold Story of Elizabeth and Islam*. Viking, 2016.

xiii. Ohlmeyer, Jane. "English Civil Wars." *Encyclopedia Britannica*, November 2, 2018.

· 3 ·

THE RUSSIAN EMPIRE

Before the Russian Empire, there was Tsardom Russia (1547–1721).[1] Since the translation of tsar is emperor (and also Caesar), this might seem like odd labeling, but in Russian history, the words tsar and emperor are as distinct as Tsardom Russia and the Russian Empire. The permanent boundaries of the Russian nation were created during the Tsardom Russia period.[2] Annexed into Russia proper were lands from the Polish-Lithuanian Commonwealth and the Swedish and Ottoman empires. The Russian Empire, on the other hand, was different. Conquered lands became colonies. Where the two were similar was the presence of a very ambitious ruler, Peter the Great. Tsar Peter was the last ruler of Tsardom Russia (1682–1721). Emperor Peter was the first ruler of the Russian Empire (1721–1725).

Russia entered the competition for empire nearly three hundred years after it began. They were behind, and Peter was anxious to catch up. To expedite expansion, he removed the impediment of a powerful church. Some tsars believed that Russia was destined to become the Third Rome[3]—the successor to the Byzantine Empire. Not Peter. He didn't care about becoming the Third Rome or having a holy mission, and he wasn't amenable to religious leaders compromising his power or vision to create a vast empire run by all-powerful secular emperors. To make his position clear, Peter eliminated the position of patriarch of the Russian Orthodox Church and subordinated the church to the state. All subsequent emperors maintained this arrangement.

Peter's emphasis on the military was something else other emperors adopted, and this was important to the empire's expansion. At a time when Europe's empires cobbled together mercenaries, criminals, and state soldiers to fight wars, the Russians created Europe's first state-sponsored army. The military was a government priority that consumed up to 70 percent of government spending. The Russian military was so strong, the Russians demonstrated that they didn't need to be a leading economic power to be a world power.[i]

The expansion of the Russian Empire began with reconquests in the lands of neighboring Islamic empires. Russian rulers were anxious to settle a couple of scores with the Ottomans. One was for the conquest of the Eastern Orthodox Byzantine Empire, and another was for the subjugation and enslavement of millions of Russians living in Crimea.[4] The timing was perfect because the Ottoman and Shiite empires[5] were preoccupied battling each other.

Eleven Russo-Turkish/Ottoman wars took place between 1568 and 1878. Five Russo-Persian[6] wars took place between 1651 and 1828. These wars gave the Russian Empire its greatest territorial gains including today's Moldova and Crimea in Eastern Europe (EE), and Armenia, Azerbaijan, Georgia and most of Kazakhstan in Central Asia. The borders of Russia proper were also expanded with the annexations of three predominantly Muslim regions in the Caucasus Mountains: Chechnya, Dagestan, and Ingushetia.

The Russian Empire had been essential to freeing Europe from Napoleon's quest for a European empire, but the expansion of their empire was a concern for Europe's powers. In the Crimean War (1853–1856), Christian France, Britain, and the Kingdom of Sardinia, which is part of France, Italy, and Monaco today, aligned with the Ottoman Empire to prevent the Russian Empire from acquiring Ottoman lands. Defeat on Russian soil stunned and humiliated the Russians. Russia's once formidable military was no match for the combined militaries of Europe's industrializing powers.

The Russian military was still powerful relative to other agrarian empires. They set their sights on China. In two separate treaties negotiated in 1858 and 1860, without the need to fire a shot, the Russians acquired Outer Manchuria, a whopping 910,000 km² (350,000 mi²) that included the highly coveted summertime warm water port in Vladivostok and another adjacent 500,000 km² (200,000 mi²). The Russians convinced the Chinese to cede this land in part for protection from the Europeans. This was ironic because the Russian military was no longer a match for the Europeans, and it wasn't from the Europeans that the Chinese needed protection. The Europeans wanted favorable trade with China. It was Russia that wanted China's lands.

Russia also set its sights on neighboring underdeveloped Turkestan[7] which comprised all or part of the present Central Asian countries of Kazakhstan, Kyrgyzstan, Tajikistan, Turkmenistan, and Uzbekistan. For centuries rulers of the Uzbek Empire (circa 1500–1850),[8] other Muslim rulers, and nomadic populations had been looting and enslaving Russians, even when intermittent protection, trade, and non-aggression pacts existed with Russia. The nomads saw jihad as more profitable, and they behaved opportunistically. When the Russian emperor had enough of the double-dealing, the Russian military between 1865 and 1885 had an easy triumph.[ii]

The Russians incorrectly assumed that Japan would be another easy target. In the Russo-Japanese War (1904–1905), Asia's first industrialized nation became the first Asian power to beat a European or Russian empire. It was the Russian Empire's second substantive source of humiliation in fifty years.

The Russian Empire's last conquest wasn't on the battlefield; it was negotiated. The Russians and the British had been long-time rivals for geographically strategic countries in the center of Asia. Their rivalry was called the Great Game. In 1907 with the background of an increasingly powerful German Empire, the two agreed to negotiate the disposition of some contested and coveted areas. This included dividing Iran (then Persia) into zones of control for the British, Russians, and Persians. Per usual great power "diplomacy" the Persians were uninvolved in the negotiations.

Notes

1. Tsardom Russia was also called the Tsardom of Muscovy.
2. Later there were a couple of small annexations that were mostly in the Caucasus.
3. Rome is synonymous with the center of Catholic power. The Roman Empire is considered the first Rome. Constantinople, the capital of the Byzantine Empire, is considered the second Rome.
4. The Russians were not wholly innocent when it came to the business of selling slaves. They traded in Muslim and non-Orthodox Christian slaves.
5. The most prominent Shiite empires/dynasties in the Era of Empire were the Safavid Dynasty (1501–1736) and the Qajar Dynasty (1789–1925). The Russian Empire's most significant victories against a Shiite empire were against the Qajar Dynasty.
6. Many writers use Iranian and Persian as synonyms. Technically they are different. The confusion probably rests with Persia being renamed Iran in 1935. In Persia it was common to call everyone that lived there Persians even though this included many people that

were from the Iranian ethnolinguistic group. Persians are a separate ethnolinguistic group. Most live in Iran today, and they are also called Iranians.

7. Turkestan was the name of a region in central Asia where Turkic languages prevailed. The inhabitants were mostly Muslim.

8. The Uzbek Empire was split into two sometime in the 17th century.

References

i. Hosking, Geoffrey. *Russia: People and Empire (1552–1917)*. Harvard University Press, 1997.

ii. Khodarkovsky, Michael. *Russia Steppe Frontier: The Making of a Colonial Empire (1500–1800)*. Indiana University Press, 2004.

· 4 ·

THE CHINESE EMPIRE

The Chinese Empire was different in many ways from the other major participants in the Era of Empire. One was the configuration of a mainland and a tributary empire. The emperor directly ruled the former but not the latter. The mainland empire was a contiguous overland empire. The tributary empire was dispersed, and at times it reached beyond Asia and into Europe and Africa.

Tributes demonstrated their subordinated status by paying homage to Chinese superiority in the forms of reverence, deference, and payments in cash or kind. In return, the Chinese offered security, for example from Chinese conquest, in addition to insights into their superiority, such as Confucian practices for ordering society and administering the government.

The Chinese Empire was unremarkable in projecting power with tributary relationships. What was exceptional was the geographic vastness, a durability that spanned centuries, and the rationale. Influenced by Confucian principles, the Chinese saw the armed invasion of another state as shameful; their weapon of choice was psychology. They "attacked" by persuading other rulers that it was in their best interest to acknowledge Chinese superiority and to accept Chinese protection. The absence of Chinese interest in administering states filled with barbarians made a foreign ruler's decision to pay tribute easier.

The Chinese were also unremarkable in seeing foreigners as barbarians. It was common for people to view anyone with foreign political or cultural practices as a barbarian. In contrast, the people of the motherlands of empires were civilized. Believing others were uncivilized offered a noble, albeit ethnocentric rationale for conquest—civilizing the barbarians. Where the Chinese were different was, they didn't want to civilize the barbarians; they wanted them to stay away.

There were some exceptions to conquest by psychology. China physically conquered and directly ruled Vietnam, Cambodia, Laos, and Korea for some time prior to the 16th century. When direct rule ended these polities became China's most valued tributary states. China also engaged in armed campaigns to defend and expand the mainland empire, and it unsuccessfully invaded Myanmar on four occasions in the 18th century.[i]

Another way the Chinese Empire was different was the relative acquiescence of the Chinese to foreigners (barbarians) ruling Chinese dynasties, but the arrangement was also unusual. Mongol rulers of the Yuan Dynasty (1271–1368), and even more so the Manchu rulers of the Qing Dynasty (1644–1912) employed Chinese bureaucrats, married Chinese women, and adopted many Chinese practices because they were superior to their own. The assimilation of the Manchus was so extensive, it could be difficult to distinguish them from the Chinese.

The history of most empires went from expansion to contraction. The mainland Chinese Empire was different. It went from expansion to contraction to expansion to contraction to expansion. The grandest growth occurred under the barbarian rule of the Mongols and the Manchus. Between the periods of barbarian rule was rule by the Chinese in the Ming Dynasty (1364–1644). Ming rulers lost some 75 percent of the mainland empire. They did preside during a vast, albeit brief, expansion in the tributary empire. Between 1405 and 1433 a eunuch Muslim mariner by the name of Zheng He,[1] in the service of the Chinese emperor, commanded a navy said to have 3,500 ships that traveled throughout southern and eastern Asia, the Middle East, and Africa, collecting tribute along the way. Most of He's achievements were shelved after his voyages because the emperor was compelled to defend his shrinking mainland empire.[ii]

When the Manchus were in charge in the Qing Dynasty (1644–1912) the mainland empire doubled in size. This was a great achievement that was overshadowed by the Manchus ruling during the Century of Humiliation. The Manchus are not wholly to blame for this period of humiliation. Most bureaucrats were Chinese, and they were opposed to the modern practices others were implementing. They characterized the industrialization taking place in the European and Japanese empires as western, inapplicable, inferior barbarian practices that would disrupt their ordered society. In the Chinese Empire, bureaucrats and farmers sat at the top of society, and merchants were near the bottom. With industrialization, the privileged position of bureaucrats would sink, while those of merchants would rise. The military would also gain capabilities making them a rival source of power.

Seeing industrialization as bad ended up being a lethal mistake. In the 19th century, the Chinese Empire was under attack, and no amount of psychology was going to repel barbarians with modern armaments. The Century of Humiliation occurred because the Chinese could not defend their empire. They lost their tributary empire in Southeast and Eastern Asia to the European and Japanese empires. In the First Opium War (1839–1842), also called the Anglo-Sino War (British vs. Chinese), the Chinese Empire ceded Hong Kong to the British. After the Second Opium War (1857–1860) in the Treaty of Tientsin, known to the Chinese as the unequal treaties, the Chinese lost Outer Manchuria to the Russian Empire and agreed to something extraordinary; conceding some sovereignty to barbarians. Some European countries, Russia, Japan, and the United States operated treaty ports without Chinese oversight.

China might have given a better fight in the Second Opium War if it hadn't been combatting multiple rebellions. In one "uprising," the Taiping Rebellion (1850–1864), estimates of the dead range from 20–100 million making it the deadliest war in the 19th century.

With massive internal rebellions and losses to barbarians on their home turf, the emperor was ready to acquire modern weapons and expertise from barbarian sources, but there was insufficient time to prevent the most sobering source of humiliation. In the mid- to late-19th century Japan ended its feudal structure and centralized power, industrialized, and militarized. They were on a mission to be a great power, and this meant building an empire. According to Wolfram Eberhard in A History of China (2006), the Japanese emperor's mission was officially called the Imperium of the Yellow Race, and this included conquering China. In the First Sino-Japanese War (1894–1895) the victorious Japanese acquired Taiwan, the Liaodong Peninsula, and southeastern Manchuria, and they occupied Korea. The Chinese had little regard for the Japanese, and now they handed them an exceptional defeat.

The Chinese were being beaten by barbarians at every turn while enduring a severe drought, and things were about to get worse. A series of uprisings directed at the barbarians called the Boxer Rebellion took place between 1899 and 1901. The boxer's indiscriminate attacks on foreigners motivated a powerful backlash. The European, Russian, and Japanese empires and the United States formed a military coalition to end the rebellion. Thinking their bodies were impervious to bullets, the boxers were no match for large militaries firing penetrating bullets with modern weapons. Now, the Chinese were saddled with extraordinary war debts that left the empire in receivership. Worse, it was being managed by western barbarians.

To add insult to injury, the Russo-Japanese War (1904–1905) came three years later. The Russian and Japanese empires fought over land in the Chinese Empire, and they fought in the mainland empire. Russia was occupying most of Manchuria in northeastern China, but Japan wanted this land and prevailed.

Japan's triumphs in China bolstered the emperor's confidence in his mission. If the contest had been solely between China and Japan, the Japanese might have won, but it wasn't. Others saw the Japanese Empire as getting too powerful. The European and Russian empires and the United States had their eyes on China for different reasons, and they thwarted Japan's success. Korea was different; it became a Japanese colony in 1910.

Being occupied, protected, and defeated by barbarians amid internal rebellions and economic turmoil was not the outcome of virtuous rulers, and being virtuous was key to a dynasty's continued rule in the Chinese Empire. In 1911 the Chinese Revolution overthrew the emperor, but this time there would be no new dynasty. The Qing Dynasty was China's last empire. China became a republic, and Sun-Yat-Sen became the provisional president, soon to be replaced by a self-proclaimed emperor, warlords competing for power, and a long and bloody civil war that was temporarily interrupted to fight the common enemy of Japan during WWII.

Note

1. It was a common practice during the Ming Dynasty to enslave and castrate the young boys captured in war. This was Zheng He's fate.

References

i.   Dai, Y. "A Disguised Defeat: The Myanmar Campaign of the Qing Dynasty." *Modern Asian Studies*, 38 no. 1 2004: 145–189.

ii. Brook, Timothy. *The Troubled Empire*. The Belknap Press of Harvard University, 2010.

· 5 ·

THE UNITED STATES

The United States was not a competitor for empire. So why is it covered here along with the behemoth Chinese, European, Islamic and Russian empires?

The United States predecessor, the Thirteen Colonies, was part of the British Empire from 1607 to 1776. In 1776 it became the first overseas colony of any empire to declare and permanently keep its status as an independent nation-state. American history during the Era of Empire is the tale of a fledgling start-up nation that defied conventions and became a world power with a strength comparable to an empire. Some say it became an empire, and others say if it was, it was a puny empire.[1]

Some actions interpreted as empire-like could be explained as defensive measures to expand the reach of their borders to prevent empire conquests or re-conquests. Many nations did the same for the same reason, including Tsardom Russia, China, Spain, Canada, Germany, Iran, Italy, Japan, the United Kingdom, China, and Saudi Arabia. Americans were under no illusions that the perpetually warring empires of Europe and Russia were going to permit the wobbly United States sitting on a vast store of unknown potential the chance to live in peace. National leaders decided the best offense was a good defense. A belief permeated the United States that it had a Manifest Destiny to expand its borders from the Atlantic Ocean to the Pacific Ocean and south to the Caribbean Sea and the Gulf of Mexico.[2]

Controlling all of this land was complicated by the long-time residents and owners of the land—the Native Americans. Marginalizing Native American tribes became part of a defensive strategy. Many tribes had aligned with the British during the Revolutionary War and then again during the War of 1812, adding to the stereotype that Native Americans were dangerous. When the Native Americans had their land taken from them, they fought back, and the stereotype became stronger. The alignment of some Native Americans tribes with the Americans during wars with Britain, the rational response of Native Americans to losing their land, and the many helpful Native Americans were inconvenient truths muddying the motive of civilized people defending themselves from the uncivilized.[i] Defense against the uncivilized was an opportunistic rationale for conquest, common to all empires.

The greatest threat Americans were defending against was not, however the Native Americans; it was the European empires. The Monroe Doctrine was another defensive measure to prevent European empires from re-conquests in the Americas. The United States applied this doctrine when it facilitated the ejection of Europe's empires from Mexico (1867) and Venezuela (1903). In 1902 the Canadian Prime Minister said the policy was essential to Canada's security.[ii,3]

The operationalization of Manifest Destiny and the Monroe Doctrine were instrumental to the United States remaining relatively free from the inter-empire conflicts consuming the European, Russian, Islamic, and Chinese empires. This paid an enormous dividend. In the early 20th century the United States was the world's leading manufacturer and economy.

The United States may have hoped to stay isolated from the warring empires, but during WWI the German Empire was baiting the United States and threatening its land. It participated in WWI as an Allied Power alongside the British, French and Italian empires on the condition that the people and lands of the losing empires would be given a choice to become independent. The United States was using its new-found muscle to put an end to the spoils-of-war driving the competition for empire.

During WWII the United States became the leader of a movement to end the competition for empire. In the WWII conferences attended by Soviet Premier Joseph Stalin, UK Prime Minister Winston Churchill, and US President Franklin Delano Roosevelt (FDR), FDR prioritized the creation of the United Nations, an intergovernmental organization that would oversee the peaceful transition from empires to nation-states.[iii]

Was the United States an imperial power? Both sides can be argued. Less debatable is that it was clearly an ardent anti-imperialist that used its considerable influence to end the competition for global supremacy. And undebatable is that in the early 20th century the United States became a power as formidable and influential as any empire. This is why the United States is covered here with the other empires.

Notes

1. After the Spanish-American War (1898), the United States colonized the Philippines, Puerto Rico, Guam, and uninhabited Wake Island. The Philippines, Puerto Rico, and Guam were permitted to self-determine their destiny after WWII. Only the Philippines chose independence. Some categorize Liberia as a US colony, but it was a colony of the American Colonization Society, a private organization whose objective was to relocate free US blacks to Africa. After WWII, the UN assigned responsibility to the United States for the UN Trust Territory of the Pacific Islands which included the Northern Mariana Islands, the Marshall Islands, the Federated States of Micronesia, and Palau. (These four polities had formerly been colonies of both Spain and Germany and also part of a Japanese League of Nations mandate.) All are now independent but the Northern Mariana Islands, which has voluntarily declined independence and forged closer ties with the United States.
2. Manifest Destiny was also presented as a God-given mission to expand liberty and economic opportunities across North America.
3. Later applications of the Monroe Doctrine were more intrusive and widely criticized. Still, the United States never used this doctrine to annex territories.

References

i. Utley, Robert M., and Washburn, Wilcomb E. *Indian Wars*. Houghton Mifflin, 2002.
ii. Dzuiban, Stanley. *Military Relations Between the U.S. and Canada*. Center of Military History, United States Army, 1959.
iii. Schlesinger, Stephen C. *The Act of Creation: The Founding of the United Nations*. Westview Press, 2003.

· 6 ·

WWI AND WWII

The late 19th-century characterization of the newly independent states on the Balkan Peninsula as a tinderbox was prescient. This was ground zero for WWI (1914–1919), where the Central Powers fought the Allied/Entente Powers. The primary Central Powers were the Austria-Hungary, Ottoman and German empires, and Bulgaria. Austria-Hungary and the Ottomans were hoping to ride on the coattails of the militarily and economically stronger German Empire, share the spoils of war and reverse the malaise or decline of their empires.

The Ottoman Empire's position was curious. The French and British empires had been continuous, albeit at times overbearing, supporters of the Ottomans since the Crimean War (1853–1856), a war where the British and French prevented the loss of Ottoman territory to the Russian Empire. But the Allied Powers also included the Ottoman's arch nemesis, the Russian Empire, and the Germans made the Ottomans an offer they could not refuse. The Kaiser wanted Muslims to engage in mass uprisings (jihad)[1] in British, French and Russian colonies in Central Asia, sub-Saharan Africa, South Asia, and Southeast Asia.[i] In exchange for the Ottoman caliph declaring jihad against the Allied Powers the Germans bankrolled much of the costs for the Ottomans to fight the war and train their soldiers.

It was soon apparent that the caliph did not command the allegiance of the community of Muslims, let alone the Muslims in his empire. By 1916 there were armies of Arab Ottomans fighting against the Turkish Ottomans. These Arabs were uninterested in a revival of power for the Ottoman Empire. They wanted to end Turkish rule and create an Arab-ruled empire. They aligned with the Allied Powers motivated by the British government's support for an Arab empire.

Other Muslims also fought against the Central Powers and at times directly against Ottoman Muslims. More than 1.2 million Muslim soldiers from British India, French North Africa, and the Russian Empire fought for the Allied Powers.[ii–iv]

There was too much turmoil at home for the Russian Empire to stay an Allied Power. In 1916, Muslims in Central Asia were revolting against discriminatory practices, including forced labor. Then came the Russian Revolution (1917), the abdication of the emperor, and civil war (1917–1922) in the new Russian Federation.

The leader of the Russian Federation, Vladimir Lenin was vocal in his hatred of imperialism and his desire to break ties with the Allied Powers. His goal was to exit WWI and protect Russia from German aggression. To do this, in the Treaty of Brest-Litovsk (1918), he agreed to: give Estonia, Latvia, and Lithuania in Central Europe (CE) to Germany; return areas of Armenia to Russia's arch-adversary the Ottoman Empire; and pay 6.6 billion marks (at the time about $1.1 billion) in reparations. Many saw Russia's exit as Lenin stacking the deck for a Central Powers victory. This perspective discounted the impact of the United States becoming an Allied Power nearly a year earlier.[2]

The Americans didn't want to enter WWI; in 1914 President Wilson declared neutrality. In January 1917, the Germans went two provocations too far. They announced the resumption of unrestricted submarine warfare and sent a telegram to Mexico (the Zimmerman telegram) proposing the return of Texas, Arizona, and New Mexico in exchange for Mexico becoming a German ally.

The Allied Powers were victorious, and the empires of the losing Central Powers were disbanded. The end of Austria-Hungary was the end of Habsburg rule that began in 1279. For hundreds of years the Habsburgs had ruled vast swathes of the European continent, now they were part of history. The contiguous three-continent-spanning Ottoman Empire that began in 1299, Islam's most powerful empire, killer of Christendom's Byzantine Empire and instigator of the competition for empire was also part of history. The Russian Romanov's 200-year run ended during the war, but not before incurring an estimated

7–8 million casualties (killed and wounded). The German Empire that exploded onto the scene in 1871 was no more. Unrelated to WWI, the Chinese Empire ended its 2,000 plus year run just before the war. In 1919 the only major empires left standing were European and the nascent Japanese empire.

The winning British, French, and Italians suffered enormous losses. France counted an estimated 6 million casualties (dead and wounded), the British Empire 3 million, and the Italian Empire 2 million. US casualties were about 200,000.[v] If the treaties of war operated per usual the victors could expect compensation for their losses in the forms of spoils that would expand their empires and pay for damages.

Spoils had motivated the empires to engage in wars for centuries, and they drove all but one Allied Power. The United States entered the war with the agreement that the people living in the losing empires would have the right to self-determination. The United States precipitated an extraordinary break with history. Treaty terms after WWI were not per usual.

During the treaty negotiations Britain, France, and Italy tried to dispense with this US-imposed condition, to no avail. The Italians had entered the war in exchange for significant territorial gains enumerated in the Treaty of London (1915). Instead, they received a handful of small territories that were adjacent to Italy. China entered the war hoping to reclaim German concessions in China. To their horror, Japan received them in addition to the League of Nations[3] South Pacific Mandate, which covered Germany's Pacific Island colonies. This was disappointing to the Japanese because they wanted to annex them. The Japanese were also angered because the Treaty of Versailles would not include a clause on racial equality. As an industrialized empire, the Japanese believed the western powers should see them as equal. The British and French had their eyes on prime lands in the Ottoman Empire, some of which held the promise of plentiful stores of oil. In anticipation of winning the war the British and French had divvied up the region in 1916 in the secret Sykes-Picot agreement. Had this occurred, Middle Easterners would have been subjugated to Christians; people Muslims had subjugated for centuries. Instead the British and French had to settle for temporarily exerting influence in the Middle East as overseers of League of Nation mandates charged with facilitating independence.[4]

Some reparations were paid by Germany, mostly to France.[5] Among other members of the Allied Powers, the Arabs who were led by Emir Faisal at the peace conferences made out relatively well, although they did not see it that way. Instead of an expansive Arab state that they believed had been promised to them by the British in exchange for Arab support during WWI, Faisal became the leader of another smaller than envisioned Arab state, Iraq.[6]

Among the Arabs, Ibn Saud probably fared the best and he didn't even support the Allied Powers. He did, however, agree not to infringe on protected British interests on the Arabian Peninsula.[7] Saud and his British protector (1915–1932) had been developing a warm relationship that would soon generate enormous dividends for Saud.

Across the Middle East instead of colonization by European empires or immediate independence, lands were allocated with guarantees of protection and assistance to prepare for independence. MENA also got something they had not asked for; the allocation of land for a future Jewish homeland.

Disappointed parties should have been expected. The victors had endured enormous sacrifices and hardships, and incurred debilitating debts—not to liberate millions of people from the Ottoman, German, and Austria-Hungary empires, some of which had killed and raped their citizens. Now some New World ideologue that only had a real presence in the war when it was almost over, albeit a decisive presence, and suffered 2 percent of the total Allied Power casualties was calling the shots.

It turned out the New World ideologue wasn't really calling the shots. Disappointed parties fought back, and others seized the moment of WWI fatigue, wide-spread anger at conquering empires, and anxiety from the Great Depression (1929–1939). Popular leftist revolutions instigated by the Russian Revolution and the leadership of Vladimir Lenin, and rightest fascist revolutions were organized. One thing led to the next and the world experienced the grandest condensed period of empire conquests in history.

The organizer of the first fascist regime, Italy's Benito Mussolini, came to office in 1922 vowing to build the Italian empire in part denied after WWI. After the Second Italo-Ethiopian War (1935–1936), Italy added Ethiopia to Italian East Africa. In 1939 Italy annexed Albania.

By 1925, with the protection of the British Empire, Ibn Saud had created an Arab state three times larger than it was in 1915. Included in this was the forcible annexation of the Kingdom of the Hejaz in 1925, which included Islam's two holiest cities, Mecca and Medina.[8] With the caliphate disbanded by Turkey in 1924, Saudi Arabia claimed the mantle of Custodian for the Two Holy Mosques in Mecca and Medina and attained a position of leadership among the global community of Muslims.

Next up was Japan. Emperor Hirohito (1926–1989) who had been given divine status following the Meiji Restoration (1868) had at his disposal soldiers akin to holy warriors. With the Republic of China engaged in a civil war, he saw the opportunity to advance Japan's mission, once described as the Imperium of the Yellow Race but now marketed as the Greater East Asia Co-Prosperity Sphere. In 1937 the Second Sino–Japanese War commenced, and Japan began occupying large swathes of China and fortifying the islands in the South Pacific Mandate.

The greatest malcontent with the outcome of WWI was probably Germany. Their anger was exacerbated by an unfair allocation of blame in the Treaty of Versailles, but it accumulated with some devastating events in the interwar period. The wreckage from WWI made it easy for the global influenza pandemic (1918–1919) to spread,[vi,vii] and cascading effects from the Great Depression worsened economic instability. In Germany, annual inflation approached 30,000 percent monthly between 1920 and 1923. In Austria, it reached 10,000 percent between 1921 and 1922.

Germans were receptive to someone promising to change their status from losers to winners. Adolph Hitler's message of Germany as a ruler of the world resonated. Fascist Chancellor Hitler's path to global rule required a racially pure Third Reich. Without protest from the Austrians, Hitler annexed Austria in 1938, and in 1939 the German-speaking portion of Czechoslovakia (the Sudetenland).

The Russians were not happy with the outcomes of WWI either. It was humiliating to withdraw and to concede so much to the Germans. A few years after WWI ended, Vladimir Lenin, the leader of the new Soviet Union re-annexed Armenia, Azerbaijan, and Georgia from Central Asia (CA). In spite of all appearances of imperialism, Lenin defended these actions as "geopolitical protection against capitalist imperial depredations." When Joseph Stalin incorporated these republics, the Soviet Union's faux anti-imperial stance officially ended.[viii] And then he removed all doubt.

Joseph Stalin was not oblivious to the threat posed by Hitler; he had read Mein Kampf and was aware of the plan to expand east into Soviet lands, but the Soviet Union was economically debilitated, and Stalin saw an opportunity to reinvigorate a Russian/Soviet empire by steering clear of the impending war with Nazi Germany.[9] In the Molotov-Ribbentrop Pact (1939) Stalin and Hitler pledged mutual non-aggression in addition to shamelessly dividing the newly independent sovereigns of Finland, Poland, Romania (included Bessarabia, today's Moldova), and the three Baltic nations (Estonia, Latvia, Lithuania) into Russian and German spheres of influence.

Eight days later, Germany invaded Poland. Two days later, France and Britain along with its dominions Australia and New Zealand declared war on Germany. WWII began, and the grandest battle for global supremacy was on.

In 1940 Hitler, Hirohito, and Mussolini united as the Axis Powers. Three fascist/ultranationalist totalitarian leaders with no regard for others and equipped with the latest innovations in military technology was an exceedingly dangerous combination.

In 1940 the Allied Powers lost France. For the next four years, France was divided into a German-occupied portion and a "free" portion. The latter, called Vichy France, was officially neutral but collaborated with the Nazis, including hosting concentration camps for "undesirables," and providing access to Jewish populations in France's Middle Eastern mandate.

After the fall of France, it was the British Empire as the lone Allied Power vs. the Axis Powers, but this was about to change. On June 22, 1941, Germany violated the Molotov-Ribbentrop Pact and invaded the Soviet Union. Now, the Soviets joined the Allied Powers. On December 7, 1941, the Japanese bombed Pearl Harbor, Hawaii, USA. The next day the United States declared war on Japan. Three days later Hitler declared war on the United States. Now Britain, the Soviet Union, and the United States were the Big Three Allied Powers.

For some time, the Axis Powers racked up impressive results, controlling much of Eurasia, and making a mockery of the French and British empires' ability to protect their colonies. The Japanese Empire occupied every British and French colony in Southeast Asia, and much of China.[10] The Third Reich was controlling much of Western, Central, and Eastern Europe, and parts of the Middle East.[11]

By 1945 all Axis Power occupations and annexations were reversed. Marked as morally bankrupt, Germany and Japan were occupied until 1952. Italy lost their small empire, but they were otherwise spared the fate of their former allies, in part because they surrendered in 1943 and declared war on Germany.

WWII was very different from WWI and most wars from the perspective that the war-dead were predominantly civilians. Of the 50–55 million killed in the war, 30 million were civilians. Another 19–28 million civilians died from starvation and disease.

Large portions of Europe and Asia were in shambles. What would a WWIII do to the world? The hope was that the world would not find out. The trajectory of a competition among industrialized empires mass-producing increasingly deadly weapons was evident. Equally evident was the growing dissatisfaction with European colonial rule. The agreements concluding WWII didn't just end the war; they concluded the Era of Empire. A new era of nation-states was set to begin.

Conferences held during WWII hammered out the details of a world configured by nation-states. Some forums had forty and fifty participating Allied states representing every region of the world. The plan focused on dissolving the empires, preventing a reoccurrence, maintaining peace, and facilitating nation-building.

During the conferences, it was clear that there could be no *uber* ruler, but there needed to be rules, and it was imperative that nations honor their commitments to the rules. The ink was barely dry, and it was plain that many commitments were hollow. Two years later the Cold War commenced, and the optimism that accompanied the inauguration of the Era of Nation-States was shattered by the reality that the competition for global supremacy had merely changed forms.

Conclusion—The Era of Empire

Between the 15th and 20th centuries the grandest of competitions took place; a contest for the world's land and people. The Islamic, European, Russian, and Chinese empires ruled virtually every square meter of land on the planet as territories, colonies, tributes, mandates, or protectorates. Centered in the Old World were the Chinese, Russian, and Islamic empires. The European empires weren't centered at all. Their reach extended across every continent in the Old World and they cornered the New-World's three continents.

When the competition began, the goal of religious supremacy featured prominently between the Christian and Islamic empires. In time, economic power took priority over religion. The industrializing motherlands of Europe's Christian empires had a clear advantage over the agrarian Islamic, Chinese and Russian empires.

Later, industrialization was the undoing of the European empires. In WWI advanced military technologies fueled a new level of death and destruction in the quest for empire, only to be outdone by innovations available in WWII. WWII was different again; there was a new benchmark for depraved indifference to human life. Murderous, barbaric practices illustrated how far the competition had strayed from religious and moral motivations.

The winning powers of WWII agreed that the competition for empire had to end. The plan was to transition to dozens of sovereign nations. Key to the transition was the oversight of a newly created intergovernmental organization, called the United Nations (UN). The UN was the recipient of enormous responsibilities, including maintaining peace, preventing the re-emergence of empires, and holding nations accountable for delivering fundamental freedoms to all.[12] It all sounded too good to be true, and it was.

Notes

1. Jihad literally means struggling and it can pertain to internal, external, and personal struggles. The reference here is to a struggle with an external power to defend Islam using force if necessary. This is also known as a holy war and jihad by the sword.
2. It was easy to conceal the potential impact of the United States because the arrival of millions of American troops took nearly a year.
3. The League of Nations was the predecessor to the United Nations.
4. The British were able to make Cyprus a Crown Colony, but they had effectively been ruling Cyprus since 1878 with the consent of the Cypriots and the Ottomans.
5. The Treaty of Versailles assigned full responsibility for the war to Germany. It was required to pay 132 billion gold marks in reparations. Actual payments amounted to 21 billion gold marks, which was 16 percent, or about $5.3 billion.
6. Initially, Faisal was the King of Greater Syria (1920), but the French expelled him. In 1921 he became King of Iraq, which was under British control.
7. The Treaty of Darin (1915) was between the United Kingdom and Ibn Saud as leader of Nejd (the central region of the future Kingdom of Saudi Arabia). Britain agreed to protect and recognize the evolving Saudi state in exchange for Saud leaving the future nations of Kuwait, Qatar, Oman, and the United Arab Emirates (UAE) alone.
8. The Kingdom of the Hejaz was ruled by the Sharif of Mecca, who was responsible for giving the Arab Revolt legitimacy. Angry at the failure of Britain to honor an Arab kingdom at the end of WWI he refused to agree to anything with the Allied Powers, including a treaty with the British to defend the Kingdom of the Hejaz.
9. Two months before Germany invaded the Soviet Union in 1941, Stalin also signed a neutrality pact with Japan.
10. Thailand, a Japanese ally, annexed parts of Cambodia Laos, Malaysia, and Myanmar during WWII.
11. Vichy France, a puppet state of Nazi Germany controlled Vichy French Syria and Lebanon. These were the lands of the French Mandate for Syria and Lebanon. The British liberated and occupied the mandated lands in 1941.
12. According to the UN's International Covenant on Civil and Political Rights, fundamental freedoms include but are not limited to freedom of religion and speech, protection from exploitation and arbitrary actions of the state, and a right to education.

References

i. Warren, James A. "How the Ottomans Ruined the 20th Century." *Daily Beast*, April 14, 2015.
ii. Quinn, Ben. "The Muslims who fought for Britain in the First World War." *The Guardian*, August 2, 2014.

iii. Davies, Franziska. "Muslim Soldiers in the Russian Army." *International Encyclopedia of the First World War.* Retrieved April 24, 2018.

iv. "Algeria, WWI, WWII and Indochina (1914–1954)." *Invalides.org.* Retrieved April 24, 2018.

v. "World War I Casualties." *Centre-robert-schuman.org.* Retrieved December 15, 2018.

vi. Ansart, Severine, Camille Pelat, Pierre-Yves Boelle, Fabrice Carrat, Antoine Flauhalt, and Alain Jacque Valeron. "Mortality Burden of the 1918–1919 Influenza Pandemic in Europe." U.S. National Institute of Health, May 2009.

vii. Phillips, Howard. "Influenza Pandemic." *International Encyclopedia of the First World War.* Retrieved June 19, 2017.

viii. Hensman, Rohini. "The Revolution and Russian Imperialism." *TheWire,* November 11, 2017.

THE AFTERMATHS OF
EMPIRE—AN INTRODUCTION

The competition for global supremacy had many world-altering aftermaths. Organized religions were permeated across the globe, there were alterations in population diversity and patterns of discrimination, empire languages proliferated, empire political systems became familiar, many victorious winners and vanquished losers were produced, intergovernmental organizations were created, and a foundation was laid for the revival of historical global powers. Aftermaths made forgetting the Era of Empire impossible.

When the Era of Empire began the four major organized religions: Buddhism, Christianity, Hinduism, and Islam were established on 2¼ continents. When it ended, they were present on all six inhabited continents.

The empires operated like giant population mixers and changed the world from collections of homogenous to heterogeneous populations. They also stratified these increasingly diverse populations, institutionalizing discrimination against select populations.

In all the empires, but those in Europe, political systems were hereditary, autocratic, and greatly overlapped church and state until the end. Europe's were that way until *near* the end. The Era of Empire's made autocratic rule familiar. In 1453 the world was a tower of babel, in 1945 most people spoke one of nine empire languages as a first or second language.

The empires weren't in the business of preparing colonies for independence. In the closing years of the era, intergovernmental organizations (IGOs) were created to facilitate nation-building and an environment of ongoing stability. This included the United Nations (UN), IMF, and the World Bank.

When the competition for global supremacy ended in 1945, left behind were many winners and losers. But losers had no opportunity for a rematch to reclaim lands and people. This did not mean they became good losers and accepted their defeat.

The aftermaths of empires have greatly influenced the world we live in, for better or worse. A separate chapter exploring each aftermath follows.

· 7 ·

POLITICAL SYSTEMS

Aftermaths of Empire

The empires ruled with hereditary monarchies using autocratic political systems with significant overlap between church and state. Rulers exercised complete control of land, labor, and capital.

Athenian democracy, a product of the BC period, was an aberration; autocratic governments were the rule. A small democracy window opened in the 13th century. England's Magna Carta tried to reign in their all controlling monarchs by constitutionally limiting power. The actual impact was limited. Still, the seeds of democracy were planted. The rulers, however, did not nourish them. Monarchs relied on the simplicity of inherited rule, control over the economic factors of production (land, labor, and capital), subjugated populations, and censorship of opposing positions. They would be destroyed by any type of bottoms-up rule like democracy or *laissez-faire* capitalism.[1]

Hereditary systems provided continuity of rule. A member of the House of Osman always ruled the Ottoman Empire, and members of the Imperial House of Yamato invariably ruled the Japanese Empire. In some empires, successful challengers initiated a new dynasty of hereditary successors, for example, the Qing Dynasty (1644–1912) followed the Ming Dynasty (1368–1644) in the Chinese Empire, and the House of Brunswick (1714–1901) followed the House of Stuart (1603–1642, 1660–1714) in the British Empire. The Russian Empire was a little different. It was forever controlled by the Romanov family even though rulers weren't consistently Russians or Romanovs.

Church overlapping state has existed as long as religion, but in this era, overlap could be significant, even in the Chinese Empire, which lacked a church. Overlap was essential to order. The legitimacy of rulers and rules came from a perception that rulers were selected or descended from heaven, God, or her messengers. A general belief held that rulers had a divine right to rule. They provided the link between heaven and earth. Absent a source of legitimacy for the ruled—like being elected, being chosen by God was persuasive. Enforcing the notion of a divine right to rule were religious leaders who existed in a *quid pro quo* relationship with secular rulers. It was a cozy relationship that delivered reciprocal legitimacy.

Hereditary rule was meant to be a real plus for the people because their rulers were born and bred to rule. Numerous nightmarish reigns tell a more nuanced story, but heredity was not the only problem. Rulers were all powerful, exercising complete control over people and resources, and doing this under the notion that they were selected by or descended from God; everything they did or ordered could be construed as God's will. Autocrats chosen by God was a perfect combination for despotic and corrupt rule.

In 1534 England's King Henry VIII, from the House of Tudor, was the first English monarch to claim a divine right to rule. Divine-right Henry, seeing the kingdom's financial accounts as his own, spent the Crown into bankruptcy, ruthlessly dealt with his opponents, and had two of his wives beheaded. Charles Dickens said of Henry's rule: "The plain truth is, that he was a most intolerable ruffian, a disgrace to human nature, and a blot of blood and grease upon the History of England."

The Ottoman Caliph Murad IVth (1612–1640) was a killing machine. He oversaw or personally executed tens of thousands of people. Beheading was his favorite method. Murad was known to murder or have people murdered on a whim. Rule breakers, excluding the rulers, or in this case Murad, didn't have a chance. Murad outlawed the consumption of coffee and alcohol and had partakers executed on the spot. Murad loved his coffee and alcohol and died of cirrhosis of the liver when he was twenty-seven.

Japan's Emperor Hirohito's mission of an imperium of the yellow race turned Japanese soldiers into holy warriors fighting a holy war. This created a situation similar in some respects to the soldiers in the Crusades honoring the pope's mission to retake the Holy Land, albeit several hundred years earlier. Like the Crusaders, Japanese soldiers had a reputation for brutality that was justified as God's will. Italian writer Umberto Eco wrote: "People are never so completely and enthusiastically evil as when they act out of religious conviction."[i] "Surrender was officially forbidden in the Japanese military."[ii] Civilians had the same prohibition. Mass suicides by civilians who were at risk of being captured were not uncommon. Death expressed total obedience to a perceived divine Hirohito.[iii]

In the Chinese Empire, up until 1905, divine-right emperors could punish lawbreakers with "nine familial exterminations." This imposed a death sentence on nine categories of the accused's relatives. The history of divine-right Romanov rule has been characterized as "a story of conspiracy, drunken coups, assassination, torture, impaling, breaking on the wheel, lethal floggings with the knout, sexual and alcoholic excess, charlatans and pretenders, flamboyant wealth based on a grinding serfdom, and, not surprisingly, a vicious cycle of repression and revolt."[iv]

Considerable lives of unearned luxury, despotism, corruption, immorality, power conspiracies between church and state, wanton disregard for the laws of the land, and illusions of grandeur at the people's expense were some of the reasons the masses would sacrifice their lives for revolutionary change.

The overlap of church and state created more problems than legitimizing the acts of unrestrained rulers. Sacred texts could become incontrovertible laws. This was a recipe for marking time because these laws didn't evolve, although they could be opportunistically interpreted which wasn't necessarily an improvement. Allegiance to Confucian practices was at the root of the inglorious dissolution of the Chinese Empire. The Chinese failed to industrialize, and Confucian practices, like prohibiting the accumulation of personal wealth which was seen as a selfish and greedy practice, were deterrents to industrialization.

When Ottoman rulers realized they had to industrialize to arrest the empire's decline, they expanded educational curriculums and access to education. But education was controlled by religious leaders, and they insisted on consistency with their interpretation of sharia. Science that conflicted with creationism was out, but so were subjects deemed Christian, which included many secular subjects.[v] Religious leaders were more concerned with religious conformity than modernity that could save the empire or improve the quality of life for the masses.

It wasn't always this way. The Islamic Golden Age, an Islamic renaissance, began in the Abbasid Caliphate in the 8th century. It was an age where Muslims, Christians, Jews, Persians of different faiths, and pagans cast off by the Byzantine Empire worked together in Baghdad's House of Wisdom to advance secular and religious knowledge. This took place when Christian religious leaders practiced intolerance and believed that education contradicting scripture was dangerous.[vi] During the Islamic Golden Age, Islamic society was sophisticated and civilized; Christendom was not.[vii]

The Mongol siege of Baghdad in 1258 ended the Golden Age, and the Ottoman Empire did not revive it. Beginning in the 14th century, it seemed like Muslims and Christians were trading places. In the Ottoman Empire sacred texts were used to guide the government and society. Non-Muslims were enslaved or lived in separate millets, and faced discrimination. Education was religious, and access was restricted. The European Renaissance (14th–17th centuries), the European Enlightenment (17th–18th centuries), the Thirty Years War (1618–1648) where Catholics and Protestants were killing each other for the right to choose a religion, and the Glorious Revolution (1688) contributed to ending Medieval Europe and starting Europe's modern period. Now, there were lively discussions about minimizing overlap between church and state and challenging the divine right to rule, in addition to democratic governance practices, industrialization, and laissez-faire capitalism that called on governments to end their hold on the economy.

Discussions led to revolutions that ultimately brought enormous changes to the political and economic systems used by many governments. Following the American Revolution (1775–1783) the newly independent United States pioneered an early form of republican, democratic government that placed separation between church and state and employed laissez-faire capitalism. The French Revolution's siren calls for similar changes quickly followed and reverberated in smaller revolutions throughout Europe. These revolutions spurred absolute monarchs everywhere to reinforce their power. But they could only hang on for so long. Silencing the increasingly educated, wage-earning industrial workers was impossible. A path had been paved toward democracy and capitalism.

These pivotal changes to the government and the economy were not making headway in the Chinese, Ottoman, and Russian empires.[2] Autocratic, all controlling, hereditary monarchies with overlapping church and state, and agrarian economies stayed until nearly the end. They were also not taking place in the colonies of European empires. Like the empires, rule was characteristically top-down, paternalistic, and all controlling.[viii–x] There were a handful of British colonies, like Canada and Australia, that were given a semi-independent Dominion status[3] in the 18th and early 19th centuries and they followed in the footsteps of Britain's democratic governance.

At the very end, the Chinese Revolution (1911), and the Russian Revolution (1917) ended their rule by hereditary monarchies with overlapping church and state. In their successor states, the People's Republic of China and the Soviet Union, there would be significant changes to their governing systems. Both adopted a communist political and economic system. These were non-royal, all-controlling autocratic systems that had no use for church in the state. Their leaders hailed communism as a superior and benevolent alternative to democracy and capitalism. Between the decades of colonialism, the Great Depression, and deprivations during the world wars, there was no shortage of destitute people in new nations keen to adopt superior benevolent systems.

In the Ottoman successor states, any system that denounced religion was out. Many took the familiar autocratic path used by the Ottomans. Some like Saudi Arabia would have rulers that seemed to carry a quasi-divine right to rule that conveyed a source of legitimacy. Most autocrats had no allusion of a divine right to rule. Instead, many gained legitimacy with something akin to, or in fact a police state.[xi]

Generally, the successor states to Europe's empires would end up being more predisposed toward democracy when given a chance to choose a political system, but decisions outside "neo-European" colonies,[4] like Australia, Canada, New Zealand, and the United States were often short-lived.[xii] They may have lasted longer, but replacing democratic systems with non-communist autocratic systems during the Cold War occurred with little resistance from the United Nations or the motherlands of their former empires; the supposed advocates for democratic systems from the First World. Without resistance, it was an easy decision to change to autocratic systems with their control over land, labor, and capital. They are much simpler to implement and manage. They also offer many of the same perks enjoyed by Murad IV, Henry VIII and other absolute monarchs, like untold riches for national leaders and their supporters, immunity from prosecution for even despotic behaviors, and longevity in office, premature deaths, like Murad's, notwithstanding.

Notes

1. The Catholic Church was also opposed to democracy and in particular separation of church and state.
2. The progression toward democratic forms of government in Europe suffered major setbacks in the interwar years. Most nations abolished their legislative assemblies. Only Britain, Finland, the Irish Free State, Sweden, and Switzerland stayed true to democracy.
3. All British colonies were dominions of the British Empire, but only a handful were semi-independent Dominions with a capital D.

4. Neo-European colonies had majority populations that were European or descendants of Europeans.

References

i. Eco, Umberto. *The Prague Cemetery*. Houghton Mifflin Harcourt Trade, 2010.

ii. Fisher, Max. "The Emperor's Speech: 67 Years Ago, Hirohito Transformed Japan Forever." *The Atlantic*, August 12, 2012.

iii. Bartlit, Nancy, and Richard Yalman. "Japanese Mass Suicides." *Atomic Heritage Foundation*, July 28, 2016.

iv. Beevor, Anthony. "'The Romanovs: 1613–1918' by Simon Sebag Montefiore." *The Financial Times*, January 15, 2016.

v. Abu Bakr, Tahir Abdurraham, Abdul Hakim Abdullah. "Western Educational System-Confusions and the Islamic System of Education: An Analysis on the Implications of Educational Dualism in Nigeria and Malaysia." *Proceeding of 3rd Global Summit on Education, Kuala Lumpur, Malaysia*, March 2015.

vi. Renima, Ahmed, Tiloune, Habib, Estes, Richard, J. "The Islamic Golden Age: A Story of the Triumph of the Islamic Civilization." In Tiliouine, H., Estes, H., Richard J. (Eds.), *The State of Social Progress of Islamic Societies*, pp 25–52. Springer, 2016.

vii. Frankopan, Peter. *The Silk Roads: A New History of the World*. Bloomsbury, 2018.

viii. Achebe, Nwando, Adu-Gyamfi, Samuel, Alie, Joe, Ceesay, Hassoum, Green, Toby, Hiribarren, Vincent and Kye-Ampadu, Ben. *History Textbook: West African Senior School Certificate Examination*, 2018. wasscehistorytextbook.com.

ix. Szczepanski, Kallie. "Comparative Colonization in Asia." *ThoughtCo.com*, March 8, 2017.

x. Shani, Giorgio. "Empire, Liberalism and the Rule of Colonial Difference: Colonial Governmentality in South Asia." *Ritsumeikan Annual Review of International Studies* 5 (2006): 19–36.

xi. Strauss, Bob. "A Brief History of the KGB." *Thoughtco.com*, December 16, 2017.

xii. Lee, Alexander, and Jack Paine. "Did British Colonialism Promote Democracy? Divergent Inheritances and Diminishing Legacies." *Rochester.edu*, August 28, 2016.

· 8 ·

THE PRESENCE OF RELIGIONS

Aftermaths of Empire

The four major organized religions: Buddhism, Christianity, Hinduism, and Islam existed long before the Era of Empire began. The youngest, Islam was founded in the 7th century. When the era commenced, there were millions of followers of all four faiths in Old World Asia and Europe, but there were also millions following indigenous and other eastern religions. When the era ended, the major organized religions dominated all six inhabited continents.

The empires most committed to religious expansion were the European and the Islamic, and both were enormously successful. No empires fought to expand or preserve Buddhism or Hinduism, and these religions lost presence.

Christianity was the biggest winner. When the competition began all Christian nations were in Europe but Ethiopia in sub-Saharan Africa (SSA), and Armenia in Central Asia (CA).[1] When it ended, the three New World continents were also overwhelmingly Christian, and sub-Saharan Africa had a Christian majority.

The expansion of Islam was also impressive. When the competition began, Islam had already made substantial inroads in the Middle East and North Africa. During the competition, it expanded further into Africa, South Asia (SA), Southeast Asia (SEA), and Central Europe (CE).

In the Era of Nation-States, more than 80 percent of nations would have a Christian or Islamic majority. Hindu and Buddhist-majority nations would represent another 5 percent. Most others had syncretic eastern religious majorities.[2]

Christianity—expansion, contraction, and dispersal

When the Era of Nation-States commenced, Christian majorities were present in more than half the countries and colonies of the world. Expansion was primarily the work of missionaries from the European empires. Missionaries from Belgium, France, Italy, Portugal, and Spain spread Roman Catholicism. Those from Britain,[3] the Netherlands, and Germany[4] spread Protestantism. The Russian Empire was the only Eastern Orthodox empire, but its commitment to expansion was relatively moderate.

Europe's empires

In the New World colonial empires, the expansion of Christianity was routine. European conquerors and Christian missionaries arrived together, or missionaries followed close behind. Catholic priests traveled with Christopher Columbus on his second voyage to the New World in 1493. Still, converted indigenous people ended up being a small fraction of the Christian populations. Most were immigrants from the Old World that brought their different denominations of Christianity with them and then procreated new generations of Christians.

In English-speaking North America the combination of British, French, Dutch and Spanish empires created future nations with a mix of Roman Catholicism and different branches of Protestantism. One contributor to Christian diversity in this region had the unusual origin of being an outcome of Christians facing persecution in Europe. Religiously intolerant European states reclaimed homogeneity by having unwanted Christians migrate to colonies in ESNA, and in particular to the Thirteen Colonies.

Consistent with the land for converts agreement struck with the pope in the Treaty of Tordesillas, the Spanish and Portuguese oversaw the development of an entire region of Roman Catholics in Latam. In Oceania (O), Britain was the principal colonizer, and Protestantism became the predominant faith. Europe's conquests followed by missionaries, and the arrival of millions of Christian immigrants led to three New-World Christian-majority continents.

The expansion of Christianity was pretty routine in Old World sub-Saharan Africa too. In the 15th and 16th centuries, the Portuguese set up trading posts and colonies in western and southern Africa, and Roman Catholic missionaries arrived to convert indigenous populations.[5] Christianity, however, retained a minor presence for centuries; the majority continued following indigenous faiths. Europe's colonization of the region in the late 19th century brought Europe's Christian missionaries in force, although some missionaries, who were mostly African-Americans, came from the United States. The latter met with resistance from Europeans who suspected them of promoting an end to colonialism.[i]

Ultimately, sub-Saharan Africa became a Christian-majority region. Because indigenous religious practices were culturally embedded, it was common for Christianity to be practiced in a syncretic form. As a rule, the former colonies of the Belgians, French, Portuguese, and Spanish (Equatorial Guinea) would have syncretic Roman Catholic majorities and former colonies of the British or Dutch (South Africa) syncretic Protestant majorities. The exceptions to this rule were some French and British colonies in the north where Islam had been simultaneously making inroads. Here there was a healthy mix of Christianity and Islam, and both were practiced in syncretic forms.

The expansion of Christianity was not routine when the European empires arrived in Old World Asia in the 19th century. It was clear that most people were content with Islam, Hinduism, Buddhism, and other eastern religions. Some intrepid missionaries attempting conversions found it could be a dangerous undertaking. This was fine because expanding Christianity had seized to be a primary goal of empire expansion.

Portugal and Spain achieved the greatest conversion successes in Old World Asia, but they established colonies more than two centuries before the British, Dutch, and French and they forced many conversions. Large populations in Goa, India in South Asia (SA), Macau in Eastern Asia (EA), Timor-Leste in Southeast Asia (SEA), and the Philippines (SEA) converted to Christianity.

In the Old World, Christianity experienced some losses. Between the 14th and 16th centuries, the Ottomans conquered the Balkan Peninsula. Over time the benefits of converting to Islam in combination with a prohibition on proselytizing any faith but Islam led to unaddressed Christian (mostly Eastern Orthodox) attrition in the Balkans. There may have been more attrition, but the Ottomans saw Slavic people, historically a slave class, as undesirable Muslims.

Around this time the Christian population was also experiencing losses in Western Europe (WE). For about one hundred years Christians were killing Christians in and around the Holy Roman Empire. War deaths and famine during the Thirty Years' War (1618–1648) took the lives of an estimated 3–11 million Christians or 4–15 percent of the population of Europe. Some principalities lost more than 50 percent of their populations.

The dead did not die in vain because the desire for religious freedom that instigated the war made progress. Instead of one official religion, Roman Catholicism, it was now permissible for a polity to designate certain branches of Protestantism as the official faith. The outcome was significant attrition in Roman Catholicism and considerable expansion in Protestantism. In time different Protestant denominations became majority religions in polities in the north of Western Europe, except in Ireland. Ireland along with Belgium, France, Spain, Portugal, and Italy remained overwhelmingly Roman Catholic.

Where Europe's empires conquered, conversions to Christianity followed. Success was greatest when indigenous populations were large and unaffiliated with organized religions. This qualified sub-Saharan Africa as the region where missionaries had their greatest success. However, Christianity's greatest triumph was in the three New World continents where European immigrants seeking an end to religious persecution and superior economic opportunities carried their religions with them and created New Christendom.

Russian Empire

In Tsardom Russia (1547–1721) some tsars saw themselves as divine-right rulers of the Third Rome with a mission to preserve and expand Eastern Orthodoxy. This was not the case in the Russian Empire. Peter the Great aborted the mission. He had no use for a holy mission, although the divine-right to rule came in handy. His mission was to build a vast empire.

Some Russian emperors professed a commitment to expanding Russian Orthodoxy, and they supported missionaries reaching into conquered lands, but expansion was just not a major priority. An illustration of the feebleness of any pledges is the celebrated achievement of missionaries bringing Russian Orthodoxy to the sparsely populated Russian colony in the future US state of Alaska. Most emperors did, however, have an interest in reconquering or freeing areas (and Orthodox Christians) in the Balkans that had been lost to the Ottoman Empire.

This lack of interest in expanding Eastern Orthodoxy was not synonymous with being indifferent to religion. When the Russian Empire began in 1721, it was near exclusively Eastern Orthodox. Conquests in Crimea, Central Asia, and the Caucasus introduced significant Muslim populations that stayed Muslim. The Ottomans didn't want to convert Slavic people to Islam, and the Russians didn't want to convert Muslims to Eastern Orthodoxy. In part, this was said to be due to a fear of revolt. There was though a lack of trust or affection for Muslims. This is evident in the Russian transport of Muslims to the Ottoman and Persian empires, and also into Russian and Soviet territories in Central Asia.[6]

The acquisition of large Jewish populations from conquests in the Polish-Lithuanian Commonwealth also offered opportunities for conversion. This did not occur for reasons that are as varied as the policies for managing the Jewish population over the history of the Russian and Soviet empires:[ii] policies that led most Jews to emigrate in the 19th and 20th centuries.

When the Russian Empire dissolved in 1917 the presence of Eastern Orthodoxy had not expanded beyond the reach obtained by the Byzantine Empire (330–1453); instead, it contracted. It remained the predominant religion of Eastern Europe, and the majority religion in Greece and Cyprus in Western Europe. In the Balkan nations (CE), Orthodox Christianity maintained a healthy presence in some states, but some Orthodox converted to Islam. This also occurred in Cyprus. In the early 20th century there was a net increase in the Central European Orthodox population, but not the global population. Motivated to end campaigns to cleanse religious diversity in former Ottoman lands, the League of Nations encouraged Christians to migrate to Europe and Muslims to Turkey. In total 5–7 million Christians and Muslims cross-migrated.

The Russian Empire looked like an Orthodox expansion machine compared to the Soviet Union. The Soviets were definitely not indifferent to religion. Millions abandoned Orthodox Christianity (and other religions) when the official religion became atheism. Public displays of religion could result in a one-way ticket to a Siberian labor camp, or worse. The Soviets though minimized temptation. Between 1927 and 1940 an estimated 200,000 clergy were killed, 41,000 churches and mosques destroyed, and 12 million Christians martyred.[iii]

Among empires, the Soviet Union's religious aftermath is unique and simple to explain. It suppressed all religions and encouraged the rise of irreligion in Central Europe (CE), Eastern Europe (EE), and Central Asia (CA) for 44–70 years.

Islam—expansion, contraction, and dispersal

How and when Islam spread varied by region. The highly motivated con-quering armies of empires that encouraged or forced conversions[7] were the greatest source of Islamic expansion. There were four powerful empires/groups responsible for significant conversions. Three were Sunni and one was Shia: the Sunni Arabic-speaking empires, the Sunni Turkish-speaking Ottoman Empire, the Sunni Turco-Mongol Mughal Empire, and the Shiite Persian Safavid Empire.

The most expansive episode took place under Arabic-speaking Sunni empires in the 7th century. This is when the Middle East and much of North Africa converted to Islam. Many were converting from Christianity.

Arab empires brought Islam to Christendom's Iberian Peninsula in the 8th century. This was, however, reversed by the 15th century. Around the 15th century, the Ottoman Empire was introducing Islam to conquered lands on the Balkan Peninsula in Central Europe. Success was limited by design. The sultans had reasons for minimizing their conversion campaigns. Politi-cally, there was the risk of war from an angered Christian empire. Econom-ically, the Christians paid higher taxes, and they were also a source of slave labor. Socially, these Christians were mostly ethnic Slavs, and the Ottomans didn't want Slavic Christians to be Muslims. The Slavs had a long history as a European slave class, and they were undesirable as Muslims.

In the birthplace of Hinduism and Buddhism, traders introduced Islam to South Asia but mass conversions, many forced, took place during the Mughal Empire (1526–1857). South Asia became the region with the world's largest Muslim population.

Conquering Islamic empires were mostly Sunni until the 16th century.[8] In 1501 the Ottomans outlawed Shiite Islam in the lands of the Persian Safavids. That same year Shah Ismail began building the Shiite Safavid Empire. By 1504 he had conquered the lands and converted, often by force, Sunnis across lands that later became part of today's Iran.[iv,9] Later Ismail and his successors conquered and converted significant populations of Sunni Muslims in other areas within the Middle East, Central Asia, and South Asia.

Traders introduced Islam to Southeast Asia. Traders and Arab nomads introduced Islam to people in Central Asia, but a number of Islamic empires including the Sunni Timurid (1370–1507), Shiite Safavid (1501–1736), the Sunni Ottoman (1299–1923), and the Sunni Mughal (1526–1857) played more significant roles in converting the Central Asian region to Islam. Over time many converted from Sunni to Shia and vice versa depending on the religion of the current ruler.

The Russian Caucasus region is adjacent to the region of Central Asia. People of the Caucasus with the guidance of Muslim, religious, resistance leaders encouraged conversions from Christianity or indigenous religions to Islam. A rejection of Christian Russian rule motivated them, and so did the thought that Muslims outside the region would help them defeat the Russians. The latter didn't occur, but Islam remained.[v]

Islam was brought to many remote areas by Sufi orders or brotherhoods. Sufis precipitated conversions in remote areas of sub-Saharan Africa, Central Asia, the Caucasus in Russia, Albania (CE), Xinjiang province in China (EA), and Brunei, Indonesia, and Malaysia in Southeast Asia.

The role of Sufi orders in the 20th century in sub-Saharan Africa is noteworthy. Sufi orders arrived to challenge Christian missionaries that had recently arrived *en masse*. The highest concentrations of Muslims identifying as Sufis,[10] which is about 25 percent, is found in this region. Sufis are least common in MENA where some Muslims see their practices as heretical.

In Eastern Asia, it was only in China where Islam achieved some amount of success, and it came by an altogether different route—a non-Islamic empire. The rulers of the Yuan Dynasty (1279–1368) were Mongols. They encouraged Muslims to move to China because they saw them as more trustworthy than the conquered Chinese. Chinese Muslims became known as the Hui,[vi] and they are one of fifty-six recognized minorities in China.

Islam also reached all three New World regions, and it too came by a different route. Following the abolition of slavery, Muslim (and Hindu) indentured servants, mostly from India and Indonesia arrived to work on plantations. This is how Trinidad and Tobago in English-speaking North America, Suriname, and Guyana in Latam, and Fiji in Oceania acquired significant Muslim minorities.

Islam did suffer setbacks along the way. Wars between the Sunni Ottoman and Shiite Safavid empires beginning in the 16th century led to many Muslims dying, and energy being zapped away from inter-faith conversions and toward intra-Islamic conversions. Something similar occurred in the 18th century when conquering tribes[11] of an emerging Saudi state were spreading Wahhabism on the Arabian Peninsula. Sunni Muslims had the option to convert or die. Non-Sunnis were considered heretics or infidels, and cleansed, converted, or tolerated as second-class citizens.

There were also losses when the Ottoman, Mughal, and Safavid empires went into decline between the 18th and 20th centuries and lost territories to other empires. The Russian and Chinese empires annexed Muslim lands, and the European and Russian empires colonized, occupied, or protected Muslim lands.[12] However, except for the Russian Empire, the others are not known for converting or cleansing Muslim populations.[13,14] In the 19th century, the Russian Empire oversaw ethnic cleansing of the Circassians and other Muslims in the Caucasus.[15,vii] Human-made famines took a toll on Muslims in the Kazakh Autonomous Soviet Socialist Republic (ASSR) between 1932 and 1933,[16,viii] and in the Tatar ASSR between 1921 and 1922. Muslims were also forced to migrate from some Balkan nations following the successful prosecution of wars for independence from the Ottoman Empire. In the process, an estimated 300,000 died.[ix]

The expansion of Islam had its greatest successes in Asia and Africa. But every region has at least one nation with a majority or significant Muslim-minority population (>8 percent). Only in Western Europe did this occur in the Era of Nation-States.

Overall, conversions by Sunni Muslim sources were the most successful. Muslims are 80–90 percent Sunni and 10–20 percent Shia.[17,18] The Sunnis did have many more empires and traders and a nine-hundred-year head start. Out of forty-nine Muslim majority nations, four have Shiite majorities: Azerbaijan, Bahrain, Iran, and Iraq. The other forty-five have Sunni-majorities. Most Muslim-majority nations have a mix of Sunni and Shia, with the highest Shiite percentages found in Greater Persia.[19,20]

Hinduism—contraction and dispersal

There were no empires in this era with a mission to expand Hinduism. Instead, some empires and agents facilitated its contraction. The greatest contraction took place under Muslim rule in South Asia. During eleven centuries of repeated bouts of sharia-sanctioned persecution and conquest, estimates for murdered Hindus range from 60 to 400 million.[x,xi] This episode of violence is commonly referred to as the Hindu Holocaust.[xii] By the 19th century Islamic traders, local sultanates, and Islamic empires succeeded in virtually extinguishing Hinduism outside Bali, Indonesia and the Indian subcontinent where India and Nepal maintained Hindu majorities.

European empires ruled the Indian sub-continent and Indonesia, but they did not play a role in the contraction of Hinduism. The British did facilitate the geographic dispersal of Hindus as indentured servants and free laborers into British colonies all over the world. These movements created significant Hindu-minority populations in the future independent nations of Mauritius and South Africa in sub-Saharan Africa, Myanmar and Malaysia in Southeast Asia, Fiji in Oceania, Trinidad and Tobago in English-speaking North America, and Guyana and Suriname in Latam.

Buddhism and other eastern religions—expansion and contraction

Buddhism's expansionary period took place before the Era of Empire began and so did much of its contraction. Expansion initially took place by Buddha, monks, and nuns converting people in India. Then it expanded internationally, often along the Silk Road where Indian traders facilitated conversions. Later contractions also took place on the Silk Road when Muslim traders converted Buddhists to Islam. Buddhism was able to develop durable roots in parts of Eastern, South, and Southeast Asia. The Chinese Empire helped to do this.

The Chinese Empire didn't have a religious mission, but it was influential in spreading Buddhism in a syncretic form along with other eastern religions within its mainland and tributary empires. Religions generally categorized as eastern include Buddhism, Confucianism, Shintoism, Taoism, Zoroastrian, and East Asian-derived animist or indigenous religions like ancestor worship.

For some time, Neo-Confucianism, a syncretic mix of Buddhism, Confucianism, Taoism, and ancestor worship, was the "official" faith in the mainland Chinese Empire, Korea, and Japan. Before the arrival of Neo-Confucianism, some Confucian practices, like the hierarchy of the family, and a reverence for education, were already culturally embedded in areas within Eastern and Southeastern Asia. If these sound-like odd religious practices, it's because Confucianism is not a transcendent religion; it's a civics religion that provides guidance on social and ethical behaviors.

Shintoism is indigenous to Japan. During WWII aspects of State Shinto[21] like worship of the Japanese emperor were forced on the colonies and lands occupied by the Japanese. After WWII State Shinto was not practiced anywhere and Shintoism returned to its indigenous roots.

Judaism—contraction and dispersal

Judaism might appear to be a major organized religion. It is an organized religion, but with less than 0.05 percent of the world's population as followers, it is not a major religion. But, in history, it punches over its weight.

From the beginning of the Era of Empire, the relatively small Jewish population featured prominently. Jews that didn't convert to Christianity were officially expelled from the Spanish Empire in 1492. Around this time, Jews were also expelled from German-speaking lands in the Habsburg Empire. Many fled to the more tolerant Poland and the Ottoman Empire. Quite a bit of Poland, including areas heavily populated by Jews, was annexed by the Russian Empire. In the late 19th and early 20th centuries, the discriminatory treatment of Jews here sent many fleeing. Most went to the United States, and Central and Western Europe, but some became part of the first migration to Palestine.

Central and Western Europe turned out to be the worst place for Jews to migrate. The German Empire's Final Solution (1941–1945) exterminated 6 million Jews. Some Jews successfully emigrated to the United States and the Mandate for Palestine, but they were a fraction of those murdered.[22]

In Europe, the history of discrimination against the Jews resulted in the Jewish Question. The question was how to manage the negative perceptions of the Jews. After WWI, the answer became the allocation of lands from the former Ottoman Empire for a future independent Zionist state. This land became the League of Nation's Mandate for Palestine. After WWII, creating this state took on an urgency, and Israel became an independent nation in 1948. This answer was very unwelcome throughout MENA where Jews were strongly encouraged to migrate to Israel, virtually eliminating Jewish diversity in MENA outside Israel. It was also in 1948 that Stalin began purging Jews from the Soviet Union. Later, it became quite difficult for Jews to leave the Soviet Union, but this changed in the 1980s. This was when 1.6 million Russian/Soviet Jews and their relatives emigrated. Many chose to go to the United States,[xiii] where the track record for peace was better than Israel.

The global Jewish population in 1933 was about 15 million. This was also its population in 2018.

*****

Without empires, there might still be thousands of unique indigenous religions. Instead, Christianity dominates the continents of Europe, North America, Oceania, and South America. Christianity and Islam share Africa, and Islam is the most popular religion in Asia, although it is not a majority religion because India has a Hindu majority and China has an irreligious majority.

When the Era of Empire commenced, forty-four of today's nations had Christian majorities. When the era ended, Christian majorities populated the lands for one-hundred-twelve current and future countries.[23]

Islamic expansion was already well underway when the Era of Empire began. When it ended, there were forty-nine near contiguous current and future Muslim-majority nations that span 14,000 km (8,500 mi.) from east to west and 6,500 km (4,000 mi.) from north to south. Muslim-majority nations, or in the case of China and Russia, administrative regions, are present in every Old-World region except Western Europe. In the New World, there are a few significant Muslim-minorities in relatively small nations.

The expansion of Christianity and Islam all over the world brought a level of cross-nation religious and cultural uniformity that did not previously exist. Followers of like religions share common beliefs about good and bad behaviors, and rewards and punishments in the present or hereafter. The expansion also created two globally dominant religions that have some very different beliefs in addition to several future nations with diverse religious populations. Most of these future nations had histories of religious conflict from slavery, massacres, forced conversions, and other forms of discrimination. In combination with varying belief systems, this set the stage for in-state religious disunity.

The expansion, contraction, and dispersal of organized and eastern religions are among the most powerful, expansive and durable aftermaths of the Era of Empire. It is an aftermath with local and global implications. The independent state of Israel as the answer to managing the negative perceptions of the Jewish people created another durable aftermath with global implications.

Notes

1. Armenia is a country where there is still debate on its status as a European or Asian country.
2. Religions generally categorized as eastern include Buddhism, Confucianism, Hinduism, Shintoism, Taoism, Zoroastrian, and East Asian-derived animist or indigenous religions like ancestor worship.
3. The British spread Anglicanism. It is often categorized as Protestant, but also classified as a hybrid-Catholic faith.
4. Some German missionaries were Roman Catholic.
5. In the 16th century, the Portuguese were also helpful in preventing the loss of the Christian Kingdom of Ethiopia to Muslim conquest.

6. Some Muslims were obviously trusted because they were nobles ruling large Russian serf populations.

7. The Quran forbids forced conversions. But what constitutes forced? It was common for Muslims to tolerate monotheists (People of the Book) if they paid the land use tax and the *jizya*, which was a dhimmi head tax paid in exchange for Muslim protection. The payment of these taxes often involved a humiliating ceremony and for the reluctant torture. If someone converted to Islam to end these taxes and the humiliating ritual, is this a voluntary or forced conversion? Most Muslim writers say voluntary and non-Muslim writers say forced. This debate notwithstanding, some conversions were forced.

8. One notable exception is the Shiite Fatimid Caliphate (909–1171). Conversion success for this caliphate was limited, and much of it reversed by successor Sunni empires.

9. Forcible conversions were justified as necessary to create a common culture to strengthen and defend the empire against the Ottomans.

10. Sufis can be Sunni or Shia. They are variously said to practice mystical, ascetic, or folk forms of Islam.

11. The word tribe has been virtually banned from some cultures as a racist term, but in many non-western cultures, it is a standard reference for different ethnic sub-groups. In the spirit of global political correctness, the term tribal-ethnic group is used, except where a reference is specific to a tribe.

12. Iran was briefly (1907–1917) partitioned into Russian, British, and Persian spheres of control. Officially the British and Russians were neither protectors nor colonizers, but they were also not to usurp control beyond their sphere. The Russians repeatedly violated the Anglo-Russian Convention of 1907.

13. There were massacres of Muslims in the Chinese Empire, but ostensibly this was because they were engaging in rebellion, rather than for religious reasons. The Japanese also massacred Hui during WWII, but it is unclear if this related to religion.

14. In the 15th century, the Spanish Empire became the first empire in this era to engage in cleansing Muslim populations. During the Spanish Inquisition (1478–1834) Muslims (and Jews) from the Iberian Peninsula were forced to convert or emigrate. Death was one outcome for those that refused or rebelled.

15. The Circassians were originally Christian, but many converted to Islam supposedly as a means to solicit support from the Ottoman Empire against a conquering Russian Empire.

16. An estimated 1–1.5 million Kazakhs and 500,000 to 2 million Tatars died from human-made famines.

17. According to Pew Research, it has become common for Muslims in regions once part of the Soviet sphere (Central Asia, Central Europe, and Eastern Europe), in addition to sub-Saharan Africa to identify as "just Muslims."

18. Estimates of Sufis, who are Shia or Sunni, are generally said to be unreliable.

19. Greater Persia also called Greater Iran refers to areas in Central Asia, Eastern Europe, the Middle East, and South Asia where Iran's cultural influence is strong.

20. Lebanon was not part of Greater Persia, but it has a significant Shiite minority.

21. Americans created the name State Shinto to refer to Shintoism as a combined political and religious system.

22. Many more Jews would have liked to migrate during WWII, but welcome mats were in short supply, and between 1939 and 1951 there were no refugee conventions to distinguish between immigrants and refugees. The United States was one nation that welcomed Jews, but at this time it had an immigration policy with restrictive quotas. There were also controversial issues related to Jews as possible German spies.

23. This includes Christian-majority countries that were temporarily atheist while part of the Soviet sphere.

References

i. Engel, Elisabeth. "The (African) American Missionary Movement in Africa in the Early Twentieth Century." *Processhistory.org*, August 29, 2017.

ii. "Russia." *The YIVO Encyclopedia of Jews in Eastern Europe*. Retrieved April 15, 2018.

iii. Nelson, James M. *Psychology, Religion, and Spirituality / Edition 1*. New York: Springer, 2009.

iv. "The Safavid Empire (1501–1722)." *BBC.co.uk*. Retrieved April 18, 2018.

v. Halbach, Uwe. "Islam in the North Caucasus." *The Archive of Social Sciences and Religion*, July-September 2001.

vi. Hays, Jeffrey. "History of the Hui and Hui Islam." *Facts and Details.com*. Retrieved October 26, 2018.

vii. Richmond, Walt. "Russia's Forgotten Genocide." *History News Network*, March 18, 2013.

viii. Oliver, James. "Stalin's Holodomor in Kazakhstan, or a very brief guide to 'The Goloshchekin Genocide.'" *Euromaiden Press*, February 2, 2015.

ix. Chatty, Dawn. *Displacement and Dispossession in the Modern Middle East*. Cambridge University Press, 2010.

x. Lai, K. S. *Growth of Muslim Population in Medieval India (A. D. 1000–1800)*. Delhi: Research Publications, 1973.

xi. Ferishta, Muhammad Qasim Hindu Shah Astarabadi and Jonathan Scott. *Firishta's History of Dekkan*. (Vol 1). Jonathan Scott, translator, London: John Stockdale, 1794.

xii. Elst, Koonraed. "India's Holocaust." *HinduismToday.com*, March 1999.

xiii. Montalbano, William. "Israel Troubled by Jews 'Dropout' Rate." *Los Angeles Times*, June 2, 1988.

· 9 ·

INCREASING DIVERSITY
AND DISCRIMINATION

Aftermaths of Empire

The diversifying of populations counts among the most expansive and enduring empire aftermaths. When the era commenced, the world was composed of homogenous indigenous societies. Homogeneity was maintained by cultural practices, basic modes of transport, and laws that encouraged people to find marriage partners, raise their families, and attend religious services in their communities. It was a formula for eliminating religious and ethnic diversity and discrimination. When the era ended the world consisted of heterogeneous societies where discrimination was prevalent.

During the Era of Empire diversity skyrocketed from the conquest and annexation of lands and diverse people, and tens of millions freely or forcibly traveling to foreign lands to escape religious persecution, for reasons of government security or policy,[1] to work, or serve prison sentences. In some colonies, populations became overt composites of descendants from Africa, the Americas, Asia, and Europe.

Many populations suffered terribly from the discriminatory practices of the empires, but for slaves from Africa, New World indigenous populations, and the Jewish people the outcomes measurably increased or decreased their presence in parts of the world. There were though many populations that experienced the very worst of discriminatory practices: massacres, expulsions, forced emigration, slavery, indentured servitude that resembled slavery, genocides, population transport, and ethnic cleansing.

Enslaving conquered people following wars of conquest was a traditional behavior throughout history.[2] It counts among history's many highly regrettable traditional behaviors. During the Era of Empire, however, hundreds of conquests in Africa were specifically carried out to meet the demand for more slaves, in particular, to work conquered lands in the Americas. Descendants of African slaves became the majority or minority populations in dozens of nations in the Americas.

New World indigenous populations were mostly victims of white man's diseases for which they had no immunities, but many perished from inhumane labor practices and defending their lands. The decimation of indigenous populations followed empire conquests on each of the three New-World continents.

Empire-defined borders also introduced diversity. At the start of the Era of Empire, boundaries were as fluid as a polity's ability to defend them. Loosely defined borders generally enclosed small territories of homogenous populations. The empires changed this. With little regard for the final composition of communities, and any histories of ethnic or religious conflict borders were defined to organize, administer, and defend colonies, territories, mandates, or protectorates. Being defensible required size, and this often meant amalgamating diverse religious and ethnolinguistic groups.

A lack of information is a common excuse for combining some populations with histories of conflict. However, so many border decisions were made without the input of indigenous populations, such as occurred in Africa, this excuse rings hollow. There were also times when borders were defined by empires just before a colony's independence when information on the ethnic composition and bonhomie was extensive. This was the case when defining borders for India and Pakistan. Still, forethought was noticeably absent to the implementation of the boundaries. The consequences were grave, cascading, and long-lasting.

Everywhere diversity was introduced, and it mattered little how it was instigated, discrimination followed. At the time it wasn't thought of as discrimination because this was an unrecognized concept. It was readjusting the hierarchical stratification of society to maintain order, with the motherland of empire's "superior" population on top ensuring the order of everyone else.

Introducing and diminishing populations, the means to add and subtract them, and altering social hierarchies left many aftermaths for future nations.

Diverse populations with histories of conflict and lingering memories of all manner of discriminatory practices are aftermaths that are particularly powerful. (Covered in a separate chapter is gender discrimination.)

Islamic empires

Religion was always center stage in the Islamic empires, and this was true of practices that altered diversity and influenced discrimination.

The Ottoman Empire reached into expanses of Africa, Asia, and Europe, encompassing the homelands of the founders of Christianity, Islam, and Judaism. Half the Ottoman population did not follow the official Sunni religion, and this half was considered untrusted. This meant they had to be managed.

The Ottomans acquired millions of followers of Eastern Orthodoxy when conquering the European lands of the Byzantine Empire. One technique for managing these untrusted populations was to mix them with the trusted Sunnis. Some untrusted Christians were transported into Anatolia (most of present-day Turkey), and some became slaves.[3] With minor exceptions,[4] Christians were subjugated. Taking their place were victorious and trusted Muslim soldiers rewarded with the booty of a Christian home and fertile land, Muslim peasants in need of land, and Muslim government administrators.

Another large conquered Christian population was the Armenian Catholics. Like the Eastern Orthodox, the Armenians were subjugated, but both of these Christian sects were permitted to live in millets with their religious leaders and laws. This privilege also extended to Jews, some of which had voluntarily come to live in the Ottoman Empire during the Spanish Inquisition.

Millets are often extolled, particularly by Muslim writers, as symbolic of religious tolerance in the Ottoman Empire. In comparison to Europe's religious intolerance, abundantly in evidence during the Spanish Inquisition (1478–1834) and the Thirty Years War (1618–1648), the point is well taken. But it's useful to put tolerance into context. Millets are an early implementation of multiculturalism based on religion, and "tolerance" had limits. These were subjugated populations that paid burdensome taxes and endured public humiliation. Non-Muslim writers are likely to present the millets as vehicles to perpetuate inequality and discrimination, isolate the infidels and keep them under the thumb of Islamic rule. The perceptions of both Muslim and non-Muslim writers are justified.

Ottoman tolerance is debatable, but there is little disagreement that the Ottomans did not trust Christians in the same manner as Sunni Muslims. Some Christians, the Slavic Christians, were so odious the Ottomans avoided conquering some Slavic lands. This opened up an opportunity for the Ottoman's future arch nemesis, the Russian Empire that was surely later regretted.

Ottoman tolerance became a moot discussion point in the late 19th century. From 1894–1896 and then again in 1909 Christian Armenians were victims of Turkish massacres that killed from 50,000 to 300,000.[5,i] Things became even worse for Christians when the Young Turks came to power in 1913. Endeavoring to create a homogenous Turkish-speaking Sunni Muslim state in Anatolia, they saw religious diversity as a problem in need of a solution. Their behaviors and motives have been compared to Hitler in his quest for a pure Aryan nation. They perpetrated cleansings or genocides[6] on Christian Bulgarians (1913), Christian Armenians (1914–1917), Christian Assyrians (1914–1923), Christian Greeks (1914–1923), and Kurdish-speaking Yazidis.[7] In total, an estimated 3.5 million Christians were eliminated or about 80 percent of the empire's total, and 20 percent of the population of Turkey. The Young Turks came close to achieving their slogan "Turkey for the Turks."[ii]

The tolerance that had been afforded, or previously provided to Christians and Jews was surely envied by religious groups that were untrusted and did not have separate millets. After conquest in the 16th century, the Kurds adopted Islam. At first, they were treated like other Sunnis but when they refused to abandon the Kurdish language for Arabic in the 17th century they were categorized and treated as untrusted without the protections of a millet.[iii] The worst discrimination against Muslims was directed at the Shias who were viewed as heretical Muslims. At one point they were banned from the empire.

Tolerance in the Mughal Empire is not a hotly contested topic because, excepting some enlightened rulers, this empire displayed a rare level of intolerance for the beliefs and followers of Hinduism and Buddhism. Both were considered polytheistic faiths,[8] and in Islam, polytheists are guilty of Islam's most serious sin, shirk. Hindus and Buddhists underwent voluntary and forced conversions, and many were murdered.

"The Islamic conquest of India is probably the bloodiest story in history. It is a discouraging tale, for its evident moral is that civilization is a precious good, whose delicate complex of order and freedom, culture and peace, can at any moment be overthrown by barbarians invading from without or multiplying within."[iv] Buddhists and Hindus were targets of state-sponsored religious violence[9] and their shrines and temples were destroyed.[10] Some describe the murder of Hindus in terms of genocide or holocaust, but it was rationalized by the Islamic conquerors as a "religious duty to smite non-believers."[v]

In 1501 the Ottomans outlawed Shiite Islam in the lands of the Persian Safavids. This motivated Shah Ismail to build an empire where Twelver Shias and only Twelver Shias could practice their faith in peace. Non-Twelvers were voluntarily or forcibly converted or killed. Shah Ismail created a very inelegant solution for ending religious discrimination within his empire.

Something similar occurred in building the first Saudi state. The Saudi state's two founders Mohammed bin Saud, and religious leader Abd al-Wahhab were on a mission to purify Sunni Islam. Apostates, heretics, and infidels were out. The idolatry practicing Shiite and Sufi Muslims were considered heretical and their practices not even Islamic. Like other non-Muslims, they converted, were isolated, forcibly expelled, or killed.[vi,vii]

The impact of the Arab slave trade on diversity and discrimination was significant. It commenced during the first Islamic empire (7th century). The enslavement of conquered non-Muslims was legal under the newly devised Islamic law. This was hardly an innovation; many religions sanctioned slavery against non-believers. However, in this case, it spurred the trade in slaves.

Between the 7th and 20th centuries millions were forcibly removed from their homelands during the Arab slave trade. (The Atlantic slave trade is considered separately.) Various estimates made from minimal records place the number enslaved during this trade at 20–200 million with 10–20 million sold, and 10–190 million dying before being sold.[11,viii] Two common causes of death were castration and infanticide. Castration was common for black slaves,[12] and only 1 in 6 to 10 survived.[ix] The rationales for castration were to limit temptation and procreation.[x] Infanticide was a near certainty for the babies of black female slaves serving as concubines or sex slaves for their lighter skinned Muslim owners.[xi] Murdering mulatto infants were "a mere matter of course, and without the least remorse or dread."[xii]

Most slaves were black Africans, but some were east and central Asian, Turkish, Persian, and European. Slaves sold in the Ottoman Empire between the 14th and 19th centuries were 15–40 percent European.[13] This coincides with Ottoman conquests in the Balkans in the 14th to 16th centuries when there was mass enslavement of Christians.[xiii,14] Similarly, it coincides with the presence of the Crimean Khanate in Eastern Europe (EE), a vassal state of the Ottoman Empire between 1449 and 1783. This khanate was a slave *entrepôt* that supplied an estimated 2 million white Christian Russian, Polish, and Lithuanians as slaves. Another 1–1.25 million, mostly from Italy, Spain, and Portugal were enslaved and sold by Ottoman/Barbary pirates in the 18th and 19th centuries.[xiv]

The Arab slave trade gained extra vigor in the 19th century when European empires outlawed the trade. Brazilians had unmet demands, and the French wanted slaves for their sub-Saharan plantations in Mauritius and Reunion.[15] Demands for slaves were also increasing in the Middle East to support farming and fishing, in addition to the more traditional roles as soldiers and domestic servants. Zanzibar (SSA), a 19th-century slave entrepôt, ruled by Omani Arabs filled many requests,[xv,xvi] but like other slave traders, they relied on local African leaders for a continuous supply of slaves.[xvii,16]

The Arab slave trade endured much longer and processed many more slaves than the Atlantic slave trade, but little tangible evidence was left behind in the primary market, the Middle East. Surviving European Christian slaves returned to Europe when manumitted or otherwise freed. For black slaves, the combination of castration, infanticide and encouraging manumitted slaves to return to Africa limited any enduring presence. What is left, is an unforgettable chapter in history.

The Arab slave trade created historical chapters in Africa with many indelible aftermaths from heinous forms of discrimination, lost tribes, large mulatto populations in slave entrepôts, the use of females as sex slaves, and local African rulers fulfilling demands for slaves on other continents.

Other diversity and discrimination practices in the Islamic empires also left pronounced aftermaths. Europe, the continent once called Christendom had an entire region, the Balkan Peninsula carrying the historical scars of subjugation, enslavement, and religious conflict. Similar scars from a very-ghastly colonial period, but involving Hindus and Muslims, was bequeathed to South Asia.

The Shiite-Sunni situation in the Middle East is more nuanced. Sunni discrimination against Shias could be horrid, but in Shiite empires, discrimination against Sunnis was equally grave. Discrimination against Shias was, however, more enduring.

All the major Islamic empires had significant impacts on population diversity, and discriminatory practices. This has left many aftermaths, and chief among them is intra-faith and inter-faith discrimination and conflict.

Chinese Empire

Like so many things in the Chinese Empire, the introduction of diverse populations and patterns of discrimination were different. This was the most homogenous empire. The expanse of the mainland Chinese Empire stayed within the eastern and east-central portions of the Asian continent. Conquered populations were almost exclusively adjacent Mongoloid ethnolinguistic groups. Uniquely, all conquered people, regardless of their ethnicity and language, were considered Chinese. Everyone else was a barbarian.

In the 19th century, a small population of barbarians began living in the empire. They became an easy scapegoat for the empire's declining state. During the Boxer Rebellion (1899–1901) "boxers" targeted barbarians in addition to Chinese Christians framed as barbarian agents. Tens of thousands were murdered. A coalition of barbarian powers (European, Japanese, Russian and American) suppressed the rebellion.

One downside of the everyone-is-Chinese policy was that diversity was never addressed, and serious conflicts erupted among different ethnolinguistic groups. This occurred in the Taiping Rebellion, and 20 plus million died. After the Chinese Empire dissolved, leaders of the Republic of China (1912–1949) knew they had to strengthen defenses against barbarians. But first, they had to end the internal ethnic conflict. They looked to barbarian practices and started thinking about Chinese ethnicity as denoting a common language and culture, similar to Soviet and western thinking. They oversaw a Sinicization process that required all Chinese to adopt the culture and language of the Han, the predominant ethnolinguistic group. When the process was complete "ethnicity and nationalization" became "almost interchangeable."[xviii] The Chinese transformed diversity into cultural homogeneity. The Han ethnic group became 92 percent of the population. Being Han was now synonymous with being Chinese.

The Chinese didn't need additional labor, which eliminated the discrimination problems associated with importing foreign populations. But an inability to provide sufficient labor opportunities in the 18th and 19th centuries encouraged millions of Chinese to emigrate for work, creating a different problem. Chinese indentured servants and free laborers filled needs for labor in European colonies in Southeast Asia, Africa, and the Americas. Most worked in colonies that had been Chinese tributes in Southeast Asia. One thing was clear to these Overseas Chinese;[17] no one else shared a belief in Chinese superiority. Discrimination against the Chinese included subjugation, expulsions, and massacres.

The Chinese were unique in creating sizeable diasporas all over the world that were unrelated to conquests by the Chinese Empire. They were also unique in initially accepting diverse conquered populations as Chinese and then later developing a near-homogenous ethnolinguistic population that spans one-sixth of the world's population. Having a 92 percent homogenous population really limits ethnolinguistic discrimination, although this is not evident for the other 8 percent and anyone else that is a non-Han resident of China. Discrimination against barbarians has a long history in China, and this remains an enduring aftermath.

The Russian Empire

Diversity in the Russian Empire came from conquering contiguous ethnolinguistic groups. Encompassing vast expanses of Asia and Europe, diversity was religious and ethnolinguistic. Ethnolinguistic groups were Slavic, Turkic, Persian, European and Inorodtsy. The latter was a Russian category for people of other origins. Religious diversity was primarily Christian, Islamic and Jewish.

It was people of different religions, not ethnicity that experienced the severest episodes of discrimination, and the worst fell on the non-Christians. Muslims didn't have a chance when the Russians annexed the Crimean Khanate in 1783. The khanate had been a slave entrepôt for the Ottoman Empire. Muslims immediately began relocating to the Ottoman Empire. Of the descendants that stayed most voluntarily or forcibly emigrated to the Ottoman Empire after the Russian Empire's loss in the Crimean War.[xix]

In the 19th century, the empire annexed much of Central Asia, in addition to Chechnya, Ingushetia, Dagestan, and Circassia in the Caucasus.[18] To help manage Muslim populations in Central Asia, Russians were transported in. The solution for managing Muslim populations in the Caucasus was religious cleansing. An estimated 90 percent were cleansed primarily through forced deportations to Iran, Turkey, and Siberia. Many died en route.[xx]

The empire acquired a large Jewish population when parts of Poland were annexed (which at the time included most of Ukraine) in the 18th century. In 1804 legislation was passed that restricted the movement and employment of Jews. Later in the century, things worsened for the Jews. The empire was undergoing a Russian nationalization campaign, and the Jews didn't fit the model. Jews could stay in Russia and face discrimination, which could be severe, or they could emigrate.[xxi] Between 1881 and 1914 more than 2 million Jews left Russia, and 1.75 million went to the United States.[xxii]

The Soviet Union

Diversity and the face of discriminated populations changed in the Soviet Union, but not entirely. The addition of Central Europe's satellite nations to the Soviet sphere brought more religious and ethnolinguistic diversity. There were now greater populations of non-Slavic Europeans, Roman Catholics, and Protestants. Because all people were comrades in the communist Soviet sphere, added diversity was not expected to create new targets for discrimination. An internationalization policy mandated ethnic bonhomie, and the policy on religion was that everyone was atheist.

Official discriminatory practices did not have an ethnic or religious component. Instead, discrimination was directed at anyone that opposed Soviet communism. This generally included people of religion who opposed atheism, wealthy people fighting asset confiscation, and advocates of personal freedoms resisting repression. Under Premier Joseph Stalin (1922–1952), despite the internationalization policy, there was also an ethnolinguistic component because he didn't trust non-Russians. Like opponents, millions were exterminated, imprisoned, or relocated.

Between 1935 and 1949 relocation initiatives transported large populations of Crimean, Finnish, Romanian, Estonian, Latvian, Lithuanian, Polish, and Ukrainians to different locations within the Soviet Union but far from their homes. In their place came the trusted Russians. This changed the ethnolinguistic diversity of all affected republics and satellites and encouraged social discrimination that could not be contained by a Soviet policy demanding ethnic bonhomie.

The imprisonment of government opponents inadvertently became a giant vehicle for diversifying and un-diversifying populations within the Soviet Union. Up to 18 million people[xxiii] of various ethnicities, including Russians, were transported into the Soviet camps and colonies of the gulag labor system. For those that survived their sentences, they were deported or transferred somewhere to work, but never back to familiar lands and people where they could create a base and stir up trouble.

Initiatives in the Soviet Union to un-diversify were just as common as those to diversify. In 1943 and 1944 Stalin oversaw the transport of Turkic Muslims from Crimea and Chechnya to Soviet republics in Central Asia.[xxiv] "The entire Karachai population, Kalmyks, Chechen and Ingush peoples, Balkars, Crimean Tatars and Meshketian Turks were rounded up and expelled; those who could not be moved were shot, their villages burned to the ground."[xxv] Muslims were being punished for allegedly collaborating with the Nazis, an accusation that holds little credibility outside Russia. Nearly 200,000 Muslims or virtually the entire population of these areas were transported. This transport is categorized as ethnic cleansing,[xxvi] or in the case of the Council of Europe, genocide because so many died in the process.

During the Russian Empire, the Ukrainians were considered a trusted population. In Stalin's Soviet Union they were untrusted. In the *Holodomor* (1932–1933) an estimated four million Ukrainians starved to death in a Soviet instigated human-made famine. This was about 13 percent of the population.[xxvii] Several nations have categorized the Holodomor as genocide. The European Parliament categorizes is as a crime against humanity; one of many committed during Stalin's reign.

Germans with business acumens were encouraged to emigrate to the Russian Empire. In Stalin's Soviet Union German-Russians were branded as the enemy. They were held accountable for the unfair terms Russian Leon Trotsky negotiated with German and Austrian diplomats in the treaty of Brest-Litovsk (1918), and then for Hitler's violation of the 1939 non-aggression pact that Stalin had negotiated with Hitler, through their agents Molotov and Ribbentrop. Most of the estimated 2.5 million German-Russians were sent to labor camps in Siberia or Central Asia of which an estimated million plus died from execution or cruel conditions.[xxviii]

After WWII Jewish hatred in Central and Eastern Europe, two regions of the Soviet sphere remained high. In 1948 it worsened. Stalin saw Soviet Jews as a fifth column, and they suffered severe repression and purges. In the 1960s Soviet Jews that had emigrated to Israel and the United States were seen as a real threat to Soviet stability. Now it became impossible for Jews to emigrate. Beginning in the 1980s restrictions were removed, and an estimated 1.6 million Russian Jews and their relatives emigrated. Israel and the United States remained favored destinations, but Germany had also become accessible and welcoming.[xxix]

In total, the reversal of diversity in the Soviet Union was massive. British historian Norman Davies estimated that 50 million in the Soviet sphere died of unnatural non-wartime causes between 1925 and 1953. Other estimates range from 20–100 million.[xxx–xxxii] Stalin ruled during this entire period. One of Stalin's favorite expressions was "a person, a problem, no person—no problem."[xxxiii] These deaths cut across Soviet ethnicities, but Russians bore the brunt of the dead. The combination of WWI, the Russian Civil War, and WWII incurred just as many wartime deaths. Estimates for the Russian Civil

War including deaths due to famine and imprisonment are 7–14 million.[xxxiv] Estimates for WWI deaths are 3.3 million.[xxxv] Including an estimated 9 million military deaths, estimates for deaths by all unnatural causes during WWII are 26.6 million people or 13.5 percent of the Soviet population.[xxxvi] All total this amounts to about 80 million unnatural deaths in the 20th century.

In 1900 the United States and Russia had similar populations. According to the World Bank when the Soviet Union dissolved in 1991, the US population was 70 percent larger. Russia's population was 149 million and the United States 253 million. The 20th-century loss of Russian lives from unnatural causes and the loss of followers of Eastern Orthodoxy by unnatural deaths or conversions to atheism has been so extraordinary the global imprint of both populations has been lessened. This has affected the composition of diversity on the planet and is a very powerful aftermath of the Russian and Soviet empires.

An era of nation-states didn't arrive in the regions of the Soviet sphere until 1991. When it did, some new empire-aftermaths surfaced that were an outcome of Soviet-defined borders that merged diverse people for administrative reasons, and policies on atheism and internationalization that demanded bonhomie among diverse religious and ethnolinguistic groups. Without being forced to get along, ethnic and religious discrimination rose, with some groups calling for independence. Outcomes from these aftermaths must be added to the older ones from long histories of discrimination against Jews and Muslims that began in the Russian Empire and continued in the Soviet Union.

European empires—Intra-European empires

Before the Islamic conquest of much of Iberia in the 8th century, Europe was white and predominantly Christian, but it had a flourishing Jewish population. After the conquest, Muslims (dark- and light-skinned) were added to the mix in Iberia. During the Spanish Inquisition (1478–1834) policies were implemented to restore blood purity to Iberia. The goal was to convert or cleanse Muslims and Jews from Iberia. Many converted,[19] many were killed, and about 460,000 Muslims and Jews[xxxvii] migrated to different locations, including the Polish Lithuanian Commonwealth and the Ottoman Empire.[20] The Commonwealth had been accepting persecuted Jews from all over Europe and became recognized as "heaven for the Jews." The Ottoman Empire had earned a reputation for valuing the contributions Jewish immigrants (as a subjugated population) could make to the empire. The Spanish Inquisition was an early example in this era of altering and reversing diversity. It was not the last example of erasing religious diversity in Europe.

After the Ottoman loss in the Great Turkish War (1683–1699) Muslims transported into Hungary during Ottoman rule (1541–1699) were encouraged to leave. In the 19th and 20th centuries, newly independent Balkan nations encouraged Muslims to emigrate to Turkey or a predominantly Muslim nation on the Balkan Peninsula, like Albania.[21]

European states were no different from most states in the world. They preferred populations to be homogenous. It was in Europe where the notion of a sovereign nation-state having a homogenous population was born,[22] and homogeneity implied ethnic, racial, and religious uniformity.

With the rise of Protestant faiths, it became clear that the desire for religious homogeneity was also intra-faith. The 16th and 17th centuries were plagued by wars ostensibly based in religion. It was the Roman Catholics vs. the Protestants.[23] At wars end there was a sign of acceptance of religious diversity between states, but not within them. National leaders could now select Roman Catholicism or designated branches of Protestantism as the official religion. Residents followed the official faith or faced discrimination. To avoid discrimination, many fled to the Thirteen Colonies.

The history of the Atlantic slave trade in Europe illustrates Europe's preference for racial homogeneity. Most of the key players (buyers, transporters, and sellers) were European, but slaves from this trade affected diversity in Europe only marginally. Very few black slaves were sold here. Early on the Portuguese sold slaves mainly on the Iberian Peninsula and in Italy. In the early 16th century, Italy, Portugal, and Spain had cities where black slaves made up 5–10 percent of the populations.[xxxviii] An emphasis on blood purity brought slave imports into Europe to a virtual end,[xxxix] and black populations began decreasing.

Within Europe, blacks that were free or unfree faced discrimination.[xl] This became worse in the 19th century when the field of scientific racism was gaining supporters in Europe, and in the United States. Scientific racism saw races as inherently inferior or superior, and supported the subjugation of Negroid Africans and yellow Mongoloids to white Caucasoids.[xli]

The preference for homogenous populations didn't mesh with the activities of empires where diverse populations were divided or annexed in the treaties ending wars, new populations were transported in to meet needs for labor or security, and discrimination instigated mass migrations to other empires. Discrimination against Jews in the Russian Empire ended up triggering a significant 19th-century diversity event in Europe. Seeking support from existing Jewish communities, hundreds of thousands moved to countries in Central and Western Europe where life was about to get worse.

Reversing diversity became a European theme in the 20th century. In and around WWII Europe underwent multiple genocidal, and ethnic cleansing campaigns. The Germans prosecuted the single largest recorded eradication of targeted populations on a mission to create an ethnolinguistically homogenous state. Their primary targets were populations viewed as sub-human: Jews, ethnic Slavs, Roma (also called Gypsies), and people of color.[24]

Hitler assigned death quotas of 50 to 85 percent to the Slavic Polish, Ukrainian, Czech, and Belarusian populations. For the Slavic Soviets, his plan called for 30 million to die from starvation. He was stopped but not before making serious quota inroads including 2.6 million Soviet POWs dying from hunger,[xlii] and killing 17 percent of the Polish population.

For Jews and Roma, the goal was complete elimination. Before the Nazis surrendered as many as 70–80 percent of Europe's Roma were murdered, and an estimated 5–6 million Jews were exterminated, or 2/3rds of Europe's population. Jewish populations in Poland, Latvia, Lithuania, Hungary, Germany, Austria, Slovakia, Greece, the Netherlands, and Yugoslavia were reduced by 70–90 percent. Researchers at the Holocaust Memorial Museum in Washington, D.C. have estimated that 15–20 million people were exterminated in Nazi concentration camps.[25]

Croatia, then a region of Yugoslavia was aligned with Nazi Germany and engaged in genocide on a mission to create a homogenous population. The Croatian Ustaše targeted Roma, Jews, and Serbs.[26] Many Serbian Eastern Orthodox had the option of converting to Roman Catholicism, the religion of most Croats, or transport to a concentration camp. The number of Serbians murdered has been estimated at between 300,000 and 500,000, or about ten times the number of Jews or Roma, which had much smaller populations.[xliii] The brutality of the Ustaše, such as displaying the body parts of victims in storefront windows, has been compared to the savagery of the Nazis.[xliv]

Diversity was also diminished in and around WWII by voluntary emigration, evacuations, people taking flight, and expulsions. Between 1943 and 1947, 12–14 million Germans were expelled or fled to Germany. The Nazis evacuated some in an attempt to save them from the approaching Red Army, and some evacuations were authorized under the Potsdam Agreement, although the orderly methods prescribed often turned chaotic and changing that was not a priority. The Nazis had executed a reign of terror that left few sympathetic to Germans—Nazi or not.

The most significant exodus of Germans was from Poland and Czechoslovakia. Many Germans living in Poland had been relocated there during the war to take the place of murdered Polish Slavs and Jews. In the Sudetenland region of Czechoslovakia, an estimated three million Germans were expelled or felt compelled to leave.[27] During the cleansing of Germans from Central and Eastern Europe, an estimated 500,000 to one million died in conditions generally described as inhumane.[xlv,xlvi]

Highly skilled Germans and German Jews of all skill levels voluntarily exited Germany in droves. European interest in German immigrants was poor. Most went to the United States. Some skilled Germans were war criminals attempting to evade capture and imprisonment. Foreign receptivity to these folks might seem non-existent, but national leaders in South America, like Argentina's President Juan Peron (1946–1955) leaned toward fascism, possibly influenced by fascist policies in the old mother country, Spain.[28] Nations in South America became a refuge for an estimated 9,000 German war criminals, including Josef Mengele, the Angel of Death, and Adolf Eichmann, one of the masterminds of the Final Solution.[xlvii,29]

There were Allied Powers that saw the usefulness of German scientists, for varied reasons including gaining intelligence on German developments in weapons of mass destruction, like Sarin nerve gas. In the United States eighty-eight highly skilled Nazi scientists captured near the end of the war, and another 1,000–1,500 scientists and technicians were brought to the United States ostensibly "under temporary, military custody" in Operation Paperclip. Their resumes deleted any involvement in the concentration camps. Several became instrumental in developing Cold War technologies and advancing the space program.[xlviii]

In Operation Osoaviakhim (1946) the Soviet Union forcibly brought an estimated 2,200 German and Austrian scientists and technicians in addition to their families to the Soviet Union. Many had been Nazis, and some had participated in the Final Solution. They helped to develop the Soviet space program and technologies used in the Cold War.[xlix]

A fairly large population of non-German Europeans emigrated from Europe because their lives were endangered. Right after WWII, there was a policy to repatriate enslaved or imprisoned people. Exceptions were possible when a return implied danger. For example, the Soviets viewed Nazi-imprisoned comrades with suspicion. If they returned to the Soviet Union, they would experience a life of hard labor. About 1 million imperiled people were relocated to Australia, Canada, the United States, and Sweden.

People that couldn't find safety and security in Old World Europe were again coming to the New World. Old World Europe's preference for ethnic and religious homogeneity, insufficient economic opportunities, incessant wars driven by imperial ambitions, desires to eliminate troublesome populations, like prisoners, generated diversity in the New World from the beginning to the end of the Era of Empire.

In the 18th century, one-third of Portugal's population immigrated to Brazil. Half the population of Ireland immigrated to the United States in the 19th century. In 1945 the United States had more than 50 percent of the global Jewish population. Most came from Europe.[30] At the end of the Era of Empire people of European blood were a majority in almost all forty-nine New World nations.

European empires played an outsized role in transforming the New World Americas into the world's most racially and ethnically diverse regions. Meanwhile, after WWII Europe had nearly restored homogeneity. Yugoslavia remained a very diverse country even after the genocidal deviance of the Croatian Ustaše. The Soviet Union, which had a European population majority, also had an ethnolinguistically diverse population. That was it for diversely populated countries in Europe. "Thanks to war, occupations, boundary adjustments, expulsions and genocides"[1] Europe had all but erased diversity in the first half of the 20th century. Discrimination, however, stayed alive and well. Expulsions, genocides, occupations, and wars created new sources for discrimination within Europe's ethnolinguistic groups. For example, Germans faced widespread discrimination following the world wars.

It seemed like a *non sequitur* when European nations began importing diverse populations to facilitate rebuilding a region razed by war. But they did. For some nations, doing this helped lessen the guilt from the genocides of WWII and the histories of conquering and subjugating the so-called uncivilized colonial populations. Germany, among others, began guest worker programs. In Germany, most guest workers were Turkish Muslims. In the motherlands of the French, Dutch, Portuguese, and British empires, immigrants and guest workers were a mix of diverse non-white ethnicities and non-Christian religions that came from current and former colonies.

This new receptivity to diverse populations was by no means a complete break with the past. Most countries implemented multicultural policies that separated like immigrants and guest workers from nationals.[31,32] Separation encouraged newcomers to maintain their home-country cultures and languages. It was a formula for keeping differences that perpetuate discrimination. In a region with a long and sordid history of racial and ethnic discrimination, it seemed like an ill-conceived practice.

European overseas empires in the Old World

Europeans prized homogeneity at home, but they had no qualms about increasing diversity in their colonies. Colonies existed to deliver economic benefits for the motherlands of empires. When unskilled labor was needed, it was secured from cost-effective sources wherever.

Old-World colonies almost always had adequate indigenous unskilled labor. British Malaya (SEA) was unusual in having plantations and needing additional unskilled labor. With slavery in the process of being abolished in Europe's empires, free labor and indentured servants from China and India filled these needs.

Indentured servants and free labor from China and India worked in many Old-World European colonies. Chinese free laborers gained a reputation in Southeast Asia for being industrious, inexpensive workers. This made them popular with profit-minded colonial administrators, but less popular with indigenous populations that preferred homogeneity and a captive audience for their services. Whether they were very industrious or average workers, the Chinese and Indians faced discrimination everywhere they went to work.

While most Old-World colonies had sufficient unskilled labor, they had insufficient skilled labor. Expats from the motherlands of empires filled these positions. White Europeans were holding the choicest jobs in Africa and Asia and managing or more likely discriminatorily mismanaging the unskilled indigenous populations. In some colonies, like Myanmar and Aden (later incorporated into Yemen) skilled Indian administrators from British India represented the British Empire.

There wasn't a need for unskilled labor in the Middle East, but the Arab slave trade continued delivering slaves here into the Era of Nation-States. It was embarrassing to the British that protectorates and mandates in MENA were still using slave labor even after WWII ended.[li] After all, one of the primary responsibilities of mandate oversight was to guarantee the rights of racial minorities. It was probably unreasonable to allocate this responsibility to a nation that had subjugated more than any other.

The decades and in some cases centuries of white Europeans discriminatorily mismanaging indigenous populations and ruling as superiors over inferiors remains a powerfully enduring aftermath of Europe's empires.

New-World European overseas empires

In the sparsely populated New World, diversity came from immigration and lots of it. There were three continents of lucrative economic opportunities, and grossly insufficient labor to capitalize on them. Over the centuries, immigrants came from every Old-World continent to fill these labor needs. Skilled labor came from Europe, and unskilled labor came from the most cost-effective sources at the time. Every new labor source faced discrimination, and for anyone that was not of European blood it took on a feel of permanence.

The first overseas colonies were in the Americas. In the 16th, 17th, 18th, and early 19th centuries labor needs were met by prisoners from the motherlands, indigenous populations, slave labor primarily from Africa, indentured servants that were often treated like slaves from Asia and Europe, and immigrants from Europe. The New World Americas became diverse composites of indigenous people and populations from Old World Africa, Asia, and Europe. As views and laws on human rights evolved, skill requirements changed, and the size of some minority populations became a cause for concern, cost was no longer the primary determinant when selecting labor. Now there was a marked shift toward recruiting workers from Europe.

Latam

The very first European settlers to Latam were the men staffing the discovery voyages. These men, and they were all men, were hardy risk takers. They traveled long journeys on ships with crude technology and few comforts over treacherous seas to who knows where. Most were prisoners with nothing to lose.

Later tales of gold and silver brought scores of settlers and immigrants from the Iberian Peninsula and smaller populations from other European countries. They came to get rich and initially did it on the backs of the indigenous people, collectively called the Amerindians. If the backbreaking labor didn't kill them, diseases of the white man did because they had no natural immunities to the imported diseases of smallpox, diphtheria, typhus, and influenza. Estimates for the Amerindian population in 1500 vary, with 50 million as a middle estimate.[33] One hundred years later the Amerindian population was up to 95 percent smaller.[lii] People of European blood were the new majority.

The opportunities to mine gold and silver, and grow sugar, indigo, and cocoa required additional labor. The Portuguese had a solution. They had trading posts in their west African colonies that were already selling slaves to Europe. In 1526 the Atlantic slave trade began. In time other European empires participated as buyers, transporters, and sellers fulfilling the "noble" mission of increasing the wealth of the motherland.[34]

Latam buyers purchased about 95 percent of the estimated 10–13 million Africans (blacks) sold in the Atlantic slave trade. About half worked the plantations on islands in the Caribbean.[35] These islands were so-called slave economies with black to white ratios ranging from 4:1 to 10:1.

Brazil acquired more slaves and slavery existed here longer than any other European colony. After the Atlantic slave trade ended in 1859, Brazilians bought slaves from Arab slave traders and the owners of emancipated US slaves.[36] New US citizens became enslaved Brazilians. In 1888 Brazil became the last New World nation to abolish slavery. When it did, it had a majority population that was black and mulatto.

Most Latam colonies became independent in the early 19th century. On the practice of slavery, independent Latam was very different from colonial Latam. Decisions to abolish slavery took shape during preparations for the wars for independence. Slaves and free blacks agreed to fight for the side that offered the greatest freedoms. Blacks would be key to the Colonials winning independence.

Abolishing slavery created the need for a new labor source. Hundreds of thousands of indentured servants from Asia made the long journey to the New World. The British recruited from the Indian sub-continent, the Dutch from Indonesia, and Spain from the Philippines. Some were also kidnapped. In today's parlance, they were victims of human trafficking. Victims commonly came from China and Japan where desperate economic conditions left millions vulnerable. Indentured servants brought ethnic but also religious diversity to Latam because most followed Hinduism, Islam, or eastern religions.[37,liii] After their contracts expired many remained.

When the wars for independence ended, there were vast amounts of uncultivated land, either because owners lost their slaves or the land belonged to the Spanish Crown. In the latter case, the land now belonged to new governments without the capability to manage it. In either case, it was easy for blacks to become squatters without pushback—at least for a while.

Being a squatter was popular because it gave blacks a feeling of freedom—they had their own land. It was a godsend because the jobs blacks were skilled for were the same ones with the same masters they had as slaves.

Blacks enjoyed a period of heightened social status as free vote-wielding citizens. Elections brought many black and mulatto politicians into office. Mexico's president, Vincente Guerrero (April 1829 to December 1829) was of mixed Amerindian and African descent. Armed with national power he issued a decree to expel all Spaniards from Mexico. Less than a year after assuming office, a firing squad killed him. Guerrero was not the only elected black or mixed-race national leader who mistakenly thought he had the power to marginalize or eliminate the white population.

Guerrero was like many people with African ancestry, he was angry about slavery, and he wanted revenge. For whites, blacks seeking revenge conjured up images of the Haitian Massacre (1804). Whites continued to enjoy economic power, and they used that to regain political control. Marginalization returned to black and mixed-race populations. Blacks lost the land they were squatting on, and new legislation restricted voting to men with certain levels of education, and land ownership. It wasn't long before the *casta* system, the system of social hierarchy that stratified populations by the purity of their white blood, was reimplemented with tweaks.[38] Discriminatory practices in independent Latam were looking a lot like those from the ruling periods of the Spanish and Portuguese empires.

Whites in nations that had lost their majority, and others concerned with losing it, took measures to solidify a white majority. Latam went through a whitening period. In the first 100 years of independence 6–11 million mostly southern Europeans migrated to different Latam countries. But more were wanted. Several nations including Argentina, Brazil, Chile, Uruguay, and Costa Rica secured white majorities, but many that wanted them did not.[39,liv]

While an obsession with whiteness engulfed South and Central America, Haiti's obsession was blackness—to a degree. The first leader of independent Haiti ordered the killing of all European-born French. An estimated 20,000 were slaughtered in the 1804 Haitian Massacre.[lv,40] Haiti's population was now virtually all black and mulatto. At independence in 1804, there was a belief that anyone with black ancestry would have the same social status, but this was mistaken. In colonial Haiti, some mulattoes were permitted to buy or inherit the land of their white fathers. At independence, mulattoes had economic power, but the blacks did not. They also had lighter skin, which continued to infer superiority. Mulattoes became a superior class; at least until a black became the leader of Haiti. Rotating discrimination between blacks and mulattoes tied to the national leader's ancestry became a staple of Haitian society and a real deterrent to nation building.[lvi]

Slavery, indentured servitude, immigration, indigenous populations, and miscegenation turned Latam into the world's most racially and ethnically diverse region. "Managing" diversity were discriminatory practices that had origins in empire rule but were perpetuated by the leaders of Latam's independent nations. Many remain as potent aftermaths of the centuries of empire rule and the misguided national leaders that followed. The perpetuation of discriminatory practices remains a salient problem in Latam.

ESNA

The colonization of ESNA trailed Latam by about a century. The land that would comprise the future United States had an indigenous population, called Native Americans, of about 3–10 million, most however lived west of the Thirteen Colonies. The indigenous people in Canada, called Aboriginals, was believed to be about 10 percent of this amount.[41] Like Latam, these populations were decimated in the ensuing decades and mostly from white man's diseases.

The Thirteen Colonies needed far more labor than the Native Americans could provide if they were amenable to the arrangements, and often they were not. Labor needs were primarily satisfied from indentured servants, black slaves,[42] European settlers and immigrants, and offspring of all the above.

The first indentured servants were European. Many were fleeing religious persecution and poverty, and most came from the British Isles. An estimated 50–70 percent of the *settlers* to the Thirteen Colonies (about 300,000–375,000) couldn't afford their passage so they exchanged servitude for passage. The average age was between fourteen and sixteen,[43] and most were under nineteen.[lvii] Some were kidnapped,[44] and others legally sent by their parents or the state. Sending children to the colonies was a solution to pauper children on the streets of Britain.[lviii] Indentured servants served 4–20-year contracts,[45] and many died before reaching adulthood or before the end of their contracts. Survivors received freedom and plots of land that were often 10 hectares (25 acres) or more.[lix]

Many non-black children born in the Thirteen Colonies became indentured servants. (Black children were slaves, not indentured servants.) Some were orphans, some bastards, and others voluntarily placed into servitude by their parents. It was not uncommon for parents to believe that they had obligations to raise children who would be productive members of society. At the age of ten children often carried out adult labor, and "many, if not most, did not remain in the custody of either parent until adulthood." A mulatto child with a white mother was technically an indentured servant until the age of thirty or thirty-one. In one colony the indenture was for life. These children were said to be treated more harshly than slaves because miscegenation was severely frowned upon particularly when the woman was white.[lx]

British prisoners represented about 10 percent (about 60–70,000) of the European settlers to the Thirteen Colonies.[lxi] Many were political prisoners and commonly Irish Catholics; most others committed what today would be considered misdemeanors, such as stealing food. This is one reason it has been said, with great exaggeration, that a bunch of chicken thieves settled America. Chicken thieves were a minority of the country's settlers.

When demands for labor increased further, European indentured servants were seen as too pricey. This view was especially applicable to the Irish Catholics despised for their religion and ignorance. Slavery became a preferred labor source. Very early on blacks were indentured servants with defined terms, much like their white counterparts. Soon they became chattel slaves. They and their offspring became the permanent property of their masters with little chance of manumission. Between the arrival of the first slaves in 1681 and the end of the trade in 1865[46] an estimated 388,000 black slaves landed in the United States.[lxii]

Canada did not have needs for labor like its southern neighbor. Plantations were the grandest driver of slavery, and Canada lacked the right climate. ESNA's tropical island colonies, on the other hand, were filled with plantations. These colonies qualified as slave economies with black to white ratios ranging from 4:1 to 10:1.

At independence in 1776, the population of the United States was 2.5 million. The majority had English blood, with significant Irish, Scottish, and German minorities. Blacks were about 17 percent of the population, and most were slaves (92 percent).[47] (There was no survey for Native Americans at this time, but most lived outside US boundaries.)

The population of free blacks increased after independence. By 1804 all northern states had abolished slavery, although some called for long processes to freedom. But, being free and being equal were two very different concepts. Discrimination against blacks, free or unfree, was ordinary.

The plantation rich American south was not keen on emancipation. They leveraged the Haitian Massacre of 1804 as proof of the extreme danger they would face if they freed the slaves. Some southern slaves were freed, and some, albeit not many, ran plantations with significant slave populations.[lxiii,lxiv]

The importance and even acceptability of slave labor in the United States had been declining for some time. At independence five of thirteen former colonies prohibited slavery. When the civil war commenced in 1861, slavery was forbidden in most states.

Labor needs continued to grow from the expansion of the United States landmass. It had more than doubled since independence. Filling these labor needs were Europeans. By 1870 the US population was 15 times larger than in 1776. About one-third of the newest immigrants were German. One third came from northern Europe excluding the Irish, who independently represented a third.

A letter to the London Times from an Irish immigrant in 1850 illustrated why immigrants were flocking to the United States. "I am exceedingly well pleased at coming to this land of plenty. On arrival I purchased 120 acres of land at $5 an acre. You must bear in mind that I have purchased the land out, and it is to me and mine an 'estate forever,' without a landlord, an agent or tax-gatherer to trouble me. I would advise all my friends to quit Ireland—the country most dear to me; as long as they remain in it they will be in bondage and misery."[lxv]

Amazing about this sentiment in 1850 is that discrimination against the Irish was pervasive. "In the popular press, the Irish were depicted as sub-human. They were carriers of disease. They were drawn as lazy, clannish, unclean, drunken brawlers who wallowed in crime and bred like rats. The Roman Catholic Irish were viewed with suspicion because it was said their devotion to the pope made their allegiance to the United States suspect ... In 1849 the secret Order of the Star Spangled Banner was founded in New York to resist Catholic immigration. The Protestants wanted to stop the growth of the Irish minority."[lxvi]

In 1863 the Emancipation Proclamation freed all of America's slaves. In 1866 the 14th Amendment to the US Constitution gave citizenship and the vote to black males, and male Native Americans that paid taxes. In some southern states, blacks outnumbered white voters. In 1868 the United States had its first black majority legislature in South Carolina. The notion of free slaves ruling whites set off alarms.

Measures were enacted in southern states to prevent blacks (and Native Americans) from voting. Some were legal, and others illegal. Laws defining eligibility requirements for voting could include educational levels, land ownership, or both. Laws were written to be colorblind and consistent with the US constitution, but they clearly targeted blacks. Relative to voting, most black men were in nearly the same bind as women that were black, white, Native American, and Asian. They couldn't vote.

Opportunities in the United States continued to outpace the labor force. Western territories knee deep in the California gold rush found indentured laborers, most coming from China as a solution. The Chinese quickly earned a reputation as very hard workers. In a nation that prized hard work that should have been a good thing, but they were rebranded as job stealers, and people that forced Americans to work for lower wages. In 1882 the United States passed the Chinese Exclusion Act, an immigration law that placed an ethnic/racial bias on immigrants. White Americans preferred white immigrants—but not all whites.

One hundred years after independence the US population was 98–99 percent immigrant or descendants of immigrants. Most were Europeans with a heavy weighting from the United Kingdom (Ireland was part of the UK between 1801 and 1922), and Germany. Ten percent were of African descent.

The industrial revolution created additional needs for labor that was easily met by the millions of Europeans from the south and center of Europe seeking safety and work. In the Russian Empire, there were Jewish pogroms and the Russian Civil War (1917–1922). Several European countries were experiencing hyperinflation, and WWI was inflicting mass carnage across Europe, the Ottoman Empire, and the Russian Empire. In total nearly 25 million immigrants arrived mostly from Italy, Greece, Hungary, Poland, and Russia including 2–4 million Jews from the Russian Empire (mainly from Poland and Ukraine). There were fewer immigrants from the Ottoman Empire, but the first wave of Turkish- and Arabic-speaking immigrants came at this time.

This massive influx of non-northern European immigrants was unsettling. The Immigration Act of 1924 banned immigrants from many Asian countries and curtailed immigration from everywhere but northern Europe and Latam, although immigrants from the latter were negligible. While this law limited what were apparently the less-desirable immigrants, it was powerless to halt discrimination against the same ethnicities already living in the United States. But this was nothing new. Discrimination faced every new immigrant group to the United States until they fitted the mold of the American nationality. At this time this meant English speaking, Christian, a hard work ethic, individualism, belief in the rule of law, and the duty to create heaven on earth.[lxvii]

Discrimination was not supposed to be part of American policies or society. Americans expressed their desire to be different from the motherland on this point and countless others. America's Declaration of Independence (1776) said, "we hold these truths to be self-evident that all men are created equal." In 1945 it was still not evident. Over 3.5 centuries the population of the United States had become quite diverse, but any equality was limited to male, white, Christians descended from countries in north-western Europe, excluding the Irish Catholics.

The final chapter of the Era of Empire, WWII, sounded a wake-up call on America's discriminatory practices that created receptivity to civil rights movements. In the 1960s laws were passed to strengthen the commitment to equality for all people regardless of "race, color, religion, sex, or national origin." In the coming years, four things became evident: old habits die hard, there were workarounds, discriminatory acts can be subtle and operate at an unconscious level, and the majority can reject minority anti-bias measures as unfair. The United States is an example of how complicated it is to eradicate discriminatory behaviors that began in the Era of Empire as ordinary and were seamlessly perpetuated in the Era of Nation-States in a nation constitutionally committtted to equality.

Oceania

Europeans began settling Oceania 2.5 centuries after Latam, and slavery was no longer an option for labor. Immigrants from the British Isles were the primary labor source and most went to Australia, the giant of Oceania. Australia soon took on the look of a British Isles mini-me, right down to discrimination against the Irish Catholics.

In time diversity increased and so did discrimination. In 1901 Australia became virtually independent, and in the same year, implemented the "White Australia" immigration policy. It effectively banned immigrants from Asia and the Pacific islands, called for the deportation of existing non-white contract laborers, and denied citizenship to Asians, Africans, and the indigenous Aboriginals. It also effectively banned whites from the south and east of Europe. A more appropriate nickname for this policy would have been Australia's Northern White European immigration policy, or even Diversity Reversal. New Zealand's immigration policy, which restricted Asian immigrants, was comparatively liberal.

In 1945 Australia's population was again homogenous—definitely white, predominantly Christian, English-speaking and of northern European blood.

There remained a small population of dark-skinned Aboriginals that faced severe discrimination. New Zealand was different in having a sizeable indigenous Maori population that was mostly Christian and English speaking. The smaller island nations in Oceania had indigenous majorities. Fiji was exceptional in having an Indo-Fijian plurality descended from indentured servants that came from India to work on Fiji's plantations. Being a significant minority did not lessen discrimination.

Oceania's experiences with diversity and discrimination is in some ways similar to other New World regions. These were all lands that attracted diverse people. For many, they became too diverse, and there were whitening periods and policies, although the "White Australia" policy was the most extreme. There was irony in colonials detesting discrimination in the mother country and then perpetuating it in their independent nations. This was an irony that would also take place in many Old-World colonies when they became independent.

In 1975 and 1993 Australia and New Zealand respectively passed laws to protect people from racial discrimination. Since this time these nations have been discovering how complicated it is to undo centuries of discriminatory practices once viewed as ordinary. In the Australian Government's Health Performance Framework 2014 Report, they indicated that discrimination against Aboriginals is still considered by many as ordinary.

It is promising that some nations are taking concrete steps to address discrimination because it remains an enduring muted topic in many nations in the Era of Nation-States with many future consequences. Unaddressed aftermaths of discriminatory practices don't fade over time.

*****

One of the most potent aftermaths of the Era of Empire was changing the world from relatively homogenous indigenous societies to a heterogeneous mix of indigenous and foreign populations. Ironically, the rulers of the empires preferred homogeneous societies at home. They are unquestionably easier to govern. These preferences really became clear in the cleansing initiatives that took place in the motherlands of the Ottoman and Russian empires and some European states when the Era of Empire was winding down, and it was no longer considered ordinary to use discriminatory practices like formal social hierarchies, and forced emigration. The Chinese didn't need to cleanse away diversity because they made a point of keeping the "inferior" foreigners out.

What was bequeathed to future independent nations was not homogenous populations. There were combinations of diverse religious and ethnolinguistic groups, that had histories of discriminatory practices. Per the UN Charter, these fledgling nations were to do something that had never been done before: manage diverse populations fairly. It was exactly what was needed, but it had utopia written all over it. Instead, it was more likely for new nations to carry on discriminatory traditions but modified to meet the ideas or goals new national leaders had for ordering populations, which sometimes included retribution for the historical practices of the empires.

Notes

1. Government instigated movements were often a pretense for isolating untrusted or undesirable people.
2. Beginning in the BC period, there were states that abolished slavery before reinstating it. In the middle of the 2nd millennium, some states selectively banned slavery; for example, Muslims in the Russian Empire couldn't own Russian slaves. Later in the 2nd millennium, states began permanently abolishing slavery and serfdom. In the empires, this process only began in earnest following the French Revolution (1799).
3. Some is used because figures for changing residences and status as free and unfree could not be found, not even as estimates.
4. Some Christians were trusted, including Christians in the harems, those serving as administrators in the government, and members of the Janissary Corp., an elite infantry unit that served the sultan. The latter two groups had to convert to Islam. Sex slaves, such as those in the harem could not be Muslim.
5. The first known massacre by the Ottomans that is unrelated to war occurred in the 16th century. This was a massacre of Shias from the Alevis branch.
6. Turkey does not consider the cleansing of these populations as genocides.
7. The Yazidis are Kurdish people that practice a unique syncretic blend of Christianity, Islam, and Zoroastrianism.
8. Buddhism is not a polytheistic faith because it has no gods, but because there is a belief in many devas which some describe as god-like, it is sometimes inaccurately categorized as polytheistic.
9. Hindus endured the greatest violence, but they were the majority population. Depending on the Mughal ruler violence was also perpetrated against Buddhists, Jains, Sikhs, and Shiite and Sufi Muslims.
10. The destruction of shrines and temples occurred because the interpretation of diverse iconography was that Buddhists were practicing idolatry and polytheism. Both are forbidden in Islam. Buddhists are however nontheistic.
11. This includes the children of female slaves automatically killed at birth.
12. Castration was much more common for black slaves because white slaves had greater protections, like Christian polities prohibiting castration.

13. Christian polities prohibited castration giving white slaves a far greater chance of making it to the slave markets and fetching higher prices. This made the numbers for enslaved and sold much closer for whites than blacks.

14. Some Christian slave traders in Venice and Genoa sold Christian slaves in the Ottoman Empire.

15. Economic arguments prevailed and permitted slavery to continue in the colonies of the British and French empires after abolition.

16. Traders in the Arab slave trade involved not only Arabs and Africans but also Persians, Turkish and Indians. Trading in people was considered just another way for people to make money and a particularly lucrative one.

17. Overseas Chinese is a term invented in China to refer to people that do not live in China but were born in China or have Chinese descendants. Living in China, carrying a Chinese passport, or even visiting China are not pre-requisites to being labeled as Overseas Chinese.

18. It was a non-standard practice in the Russian Empire to incorporate conquered lands and people. But these polities in the Caucasus were incorporated.

19. Many said they converted for political reasons, but behind the scenes, they maintained Jewish or Islamic beliefs. These were the crypto-converts and it was important to keep this a secret.

20. A historian of Catholicism, Professor Agostino Borromeo, of Sapienza University in Rome has estimated that the number killed through the Spanish Inquisition, which excludes unofficial tribunals, was about 12,500. The total number killed, including unofficial tribunals, has been variously estimated to be between 30,000 and 300,000.

21. Some classify the expulsion of Albanians from Serbia during the Serbian-Ottoman War (1876–1878) as ethnic cleansing.

22. Some International Relations' writers attribute the origin of the nation-state to the Peace of Westphalia (1648), while others vigorously contest this. Generally, it is accepted that the term did originate and develop in Europe. It was in Europe in the 19th century that widespread movements to be independent nation-states emerged. Nation-states were viewed as having homogenous populations, but it was accepted that homogeneity had to be developed. After independence institutions were built, like schools where language and history could be taught to support a common identity. Then came movements to develop a common nationality. Developing homogenous populations was a two-part strategy and a primary motive was to defend against foreign conquest.

23. It was not really the Roman Catholics versus the Protestants. It was the Roman Catholic Habsburgs, versus anyone supporting the fall of the Habsburgs.

24. Jews, Slavs, and people of color had all been pawns of empires before becoming its ultimate victims.

25. The term holocaust is generally only used to describe the genocide of 5–6 million Jews.

26. The conflict between Serbs and Croats had been brewing since the creation of the Kingdom of Serbs, Croats and Slovenes in 1919. But this outcome was not inevitable; it was instead the product of a radical political group—the Ustaše.

27. Germans had lived in this area for centuries before its inclusion in the borders of the new nation of Czechoslovakia in 1918.

28. Argentina's support for the Nazis during WWII was globally controversial during the process of admission as a UN member state. Initially, being aligned with the Allied Powers

was required for UN membership. Argentina only announced support for the Allied Powers in March 1945 when their victory was evident.

29. The involvement of the Catholic Church in securing passage for Nazis is controversial and disputed. Many Vatican-related documents have been archived and remain inaccessible. However, Pope Pius XII (1939–1958) was known to be too silent on Holocaust-related initiatives.

30. Many Jewish immigrants were from the Russian Empire but within present-day Poland.

31. The rationale for keeping guest workers separate was that they were temporary workers who were initially expected to return to their home country. The rationale for keeping immigrants separate was to honor their cultures in contrast to assimilation policies, like those used in the United States.

32. Multiculturalism has the appearance of a modified millet system.

33. Estimates range from 10–100 million.

34. The United States also participated, but this was for its own account and not the motherland.

35. Some smaller colonies in the Caribbean became part of ESNA when the Spanish Empire lost them to the British Empire.

36. At emancipation, there was no compensation paid to US slaveholders; some illegally sold their "former assets" in Brazil.

37. Indentured servants commonly worked plantations in Brazil, Guyana, Peru, and Suriname.

38. Tweaks were needed because it had become difficult to identify who was mixed with black, white, or indigenous blood, and by how much.

39. Latam was competing for immigrants with the United States, but it was just not as attractive, and people in Europe knew it. Most European immigrants to Latam had been landless peasants anxious to escape poverty and continuous wars in Europe. Reports to relatives back home described fewer wars, but also few opportunities to secure land or become rich.

40. This was a fraction of the blacks and mulattoes executed between 1802 and 1804 under Napoleon's orders to kill all blacks over the age of twelve.

41. When first settled, according to Canada's Commission on Aboriginal Health the indigenous population of the land that would define independent Canada's borders was about 500,000.

42. Early on several thousand Native Americans were enslaved. In 1750 the practice of Native American-chattel slavery officially ended, but forced labor persisted.

43. Canada, Australia, and South Africa were also recipients of many child-indentured servants from the British Isles.

44. Some adults were also kidnapped and sold in the colonies to work as forced labor.

45. According to emmigationinfo.com about 300,000 indentured servants were Irish, and their contracts were for periods of 7–20 years. The contract for British indentured servants was 4–7 years.

46. Purchasing slaves became illegal in 1808. However, discussions about ending the slave trade and later lax enforcement of the law prohibiting the sale of slaves ignited sales. More than 25 percent of all slaves purchased in the United States took place between 1801 and 1825. Slavery was illegal throughout the US in 1865.

47. In 1776 less than 150,000 slaves had arrived in the Thirteen Colonies. A population of 400,000 reflects procreation.

References

i. "The Growing Sunni-Alevi Divide in Turkey." *NewME*, University of Oslo, 2014.

ii. Serfes, Nektarios. "In Memory of The 50 Million Victims of The Orthodox Christian Holocaust." *Serfes.Org*, October 1999.

iii. Hassanpour, Amir. "The Kurdish Experience." *Middle East Report*, July/August 1994.

iv. Durant, Will. "Our Oriental Heritage." First Communications, 1997.

v. Elst, Koenraad. *Negationism in India, Concealing the Record in India*. Voice of India, Delhi India, 2014.

vi. McHugo, John. *A Concise History of Sunnis & Shi'is*. Saqi Books, 2018.

vii. Crooke, Alastair. "You Can't Understand ISIS if you don't Understand the History of Wahhabism in Saudi Arabia." *The Huffington Post*, August 27, 2014.

viii. "African Slaves in the Arab World." *Assyrian International News Agency*, October 3, 2006.

ix. Segal, Ronald. *Islam's Black Slaves: The Other Black Diaspora*. Farrar, Straus, and Giroux, 2001.

x. *Appleton's Annual Cyclopaedia 1891 and Register of Important Events*. New York: D. Appleton, 1892.

xi. "The Arab Muslim Slave Trade of Africa, The Untold Story." *Originalpeople.org*, November 15, 2012.

xii. "'Horrible Traffic in Circassian Women—Infanticide in Turkey.' *New York Daily Times*, August 6, 1856." Lostmuseum.cuny.edu.

xiii. Bostom, A. G. "The Legacy of Jihad: Islamic Holy War and the Fate of Non-Muslims." Prometheus Books, 2005.

xiv. Davis, Robert C. *Christian Slaves, Muslim Masters: White Slavery in the Mediterranean, the Barbary Coast and Italy, 1500–1800*. Palgrave Macmillan, 2003.

xv. Clarence-Smith, W. G. (Ed.). *The Economics of the Indian Ocean Slave Trade in the Nineteenth Century*. Routledge, 1989.

xvi. "The East African Slave Trade." *BBC.co.uk*. Retrieved April 17, 2018.

xvii. Thornton, John. *Africa and Africans in the Making of the Atlantic World, 1400–1800*. Cambridge University Press, 1998.

xviii. "The Upper Han." *The Economist*, November 19–25, 2016.

xix. Potichny, Peter. "The Struggle of the Crimean Tatars." *Canadian Slavonic Papers / Revue Canadienne Des Slavistes* 17, no. (2–3) (1975): 302–19.

xx. Hosking, Geoffrey. *Russia, People and Empire*. Harvard University Press, 1997.

xxi. Lowe, Heinz-Dietrich. "Russian Nationalism and Tsarist Nationalities Policies in Semi-Constitutional Russia, 1905–1914." *The University of Heidelberg*. Retrieved December 20, 2018.

xxii. Forbes, Ethan, Suzanne Lauer, Kathleen Koonz, and Pam Sweeney. "A Resource Guide for Teachers: Russian Jewish Immigration 1880–1920." *FitchburgState.edu*. Retrieved December 20, 2018.

xxiii. Applebaum, Anne. Applebaum, Gulag: A History, p. xvii. Random House, 2003.

xxiv. Allworth, Edward, A. *Central Asia*. Duke University Press, 1995.

xxv. Snyder, Timothy. *Bloodlands: Europe Between Hitler and Stalin.* Vintage, 2010.

xxvi. Magocsi, Paul R. *A History of Ukraine: The Land and its Peoples.* University of Toronto Press, 1996.

xxvii. "Holodomor 1932–1933." *Holodomorct.org.* Retrieved December 20, 2018.

xxviii. Sinner, Samuel D. *The Open Wound: The Genocide of German Ethnic Minorities in Russia and the Soviet Union, 1915–1949 and Beyond.* North Dakota State University, 2000.

xxix. "Population and Migration: Migration since WWI." *The YIVO Encyclopedia of Jews in Eastern Europe.* Retrieved December 20, 2018.

xxx. Ghosh, Palash. "How Many People Did Joseph Stalin Kill? *International Business Times,* March 5, 2013.

xxxi. Courtois, Stephane, Nicolas Werth, Jean-Louis Panné, Andrzej Paczkowski, Karel Bartosek, Jean-Louis Margolin, and Mark Kramer. *The Black Book of Communism.* Harvard University Press, 1999.

xxxii. Davies, Norman. *Europe: A History.* Harper Perennial, 1998.

xxxiii. Lustiger, Arno. "How Stalin 'The Breaker of Nations,' Hated, Murdered Jews." *The Washington Times,* August 16, 2003.

xxxiv. Bullock, David. *The Russian Civil War 1918–1922.* Osprey Publishing, 2008.

xxxv. "World War I Casualties." *Center-Robert-Schuman.com.* Retrieved December 20, 2018.

xxxvi. Andreev, Evgeny M., Leonid E. Darsky, and Tatiana L. Kharkova. "Population Dynamics: Consequences of Regular and Irregular Changes." In *Demographic Trends and Patterns in the Soviet Union Before 1991,* edited by Wolfgang Lutz, Sergei Scherbov, and Andrei Volkov, 423–440. Routledge, September 11, 2002.

xxxvii. Ryan, Edward. "Spanish Inquisition." *Encyclopedia Britannica.* Retrieved April 6, 2018.

xxxviii. Wheat, David. "Iberian Roots of the Transatlantic Slave Trade, 1440–1640." *The Gilder Lehrman Institute of American History.* Retrieved October 15, 2017.

xxxix. Carreira. A. *The African Slave Trade from the Fifteenth to the Nineteenth Century.* UNESCO, 1978.

xl. Earle, Thomas F., and Lowe, K. J. P. Eds. *Black Africans in Renaissance Europe.* Cambridge: Cambridge University Press, 2005.

xli. Gould, Stephen Jay. *The Mismeasure of Man.* W. W. Norton, 1996.

xlii. Snyder, Timothy. "The Reich's Forgotten Atrocity." *The Guardian,* October 21, 2010.

xliii. "Axis Invasion of Yugoslavia." *The United States Holocaust Museum,* 2016.

xliv. Tapon, Francis. *Hidden Europe: What Eastern Europeans Can Teach Us.* Wanderlearn, 2012.

xlv. Douglas, R. M. *Orderly and Humane: The Expulsion of the Germans after the Second World War.* Yale University Press, 2012.

xlvi. Reinhardt, Kurt. *Germany 2000 Years: Volume 3.* Continuum, 1992.

xlvii. Hall, Allan. "Secret Files Reveal 9,000 Nazi War Criminals Fled to South America after WWII." *Daily Mail,* March 19, 2012.

xlviii. Jacobsen, Annie. *Operation Paperclip: The Secret Intelligence Program to Bring Nazi Scientists to America.* New York: Little, Brown, 2014.

xlix. "Operation 'Osoaviakhim.'" *Russianspaceweb.com.* Retrieved October 31, 2018.

l. Judt, Tony. *Postwar: A History of Europe since 1945.* New York: The Penguin Press, 2005.

li. Miers, Suzanne. "Twentieth Century Solutions to the Abolition of Slavery." *Yale.edu.* Retrieved May 1, 2018.

lii. "The Story of ... Smallpox—and other Deadly Eurasian Germs." *PBS.* Retrieved August 10, 2017.

liii. Meagher, Arnold. *The Coolie Trade.* Xlibris, 2008.

liv. Andrew, George Reed. *Afro-Latin America.* Oxford University Press, 2004.

lv. The Post-Revolutionary Period: 1804–1820. Retrieved May 5, 2017.

lvi. Nicholls, David. *From Dessalines to Duvalier: Race, Colour and National Independence in Haiti.* Rutgers University Press, 1979.

lvii. Mason, Mary Ann. "Masters and Servants: The American Colonial Model of Child Custody and Control." *The International Journal of Children's Rights* 2 (1994): 317–321.

lviii. Jones, Lori. "Not Here by Choice: Canada's Importation of Child Labourers." University of Ottawa, Canada, September 2011.

lix. "Indentured Servants in the U.S." *Pbs.org.* Retrieved November 16, 2016.

lx. Mason, "Masters and servants: the American colonial model of child custody and control."

lxi. Tomlins, Christopher. "Reconsidering Indentured Servitude: European Migration and the Early American Labor Force, 1600–1775. Journal of Labor History 42, no.1 (2001): 5–43.

lxii. Gates, Henry Louis. "How Many Slaves Landed in the U.S.?" *Pbs.org.* Retrieved November 16, 2016.

lxiii. Gates, Henry Lewis. "Did Black People Own Slaves." *The Root,* 2013.

lxiv. Seybert, Tony. "Slavery and Native Americans in British North America and the United States." *SlaveryinAmerica.org.* Retrieved August 4, 2014.

lxv. "German and Irish Immigration." *Ushistory.org.* Retrieved May 3, 2015.

lxvi. Kierdorf, Douglas. "Getting to know the Know-Nothings. *The Boston Globe,* January 10, 2016.

lxvii. Huntington, Samuel P. "The Hispanic Challenge." *Foreign Policy,* October 28, 2009.

· 1 0 ·

BORDERS—INCREASING DIVERSITY

Aftermaths of Empire

Before the Era of Empire, there were thousands of relatively small polities with homogenous populations living within borders as permanent as their ability to defend them. Colonies were different. They were created during a competition for global supremacy when it was indispensable to have a landmass and population that was large enough to provide a defense against conquest. It was also highly desirable to have economically self-sustaining colonies, and this too meant broad areas. The empires commonly achieved size by defining borders that contained diverse ethnolinguistic groups.

Borders for the sub-Saharan colonies of European empires often encircled very diverse populations. Nigeria's borders enclosed more than 240 distinct ethnic groups. Borders for several sub-Saharan nations, including Nigeria had a Muslim-majority population in the north and mostly Christian and indigenous religious populations in the south. For more than a thousand years Muslims had been enslaving non-Muslims in this region, and now they lived as fellow colonials.

When the British partitioned British India into India and Pakistan (1947) they were trying to reduce the deep-seated potential for conflict between Hindus and Muslims. India would be a Hindu-majority secular nation that protected religious freedoms for its diverse religious populations. Created as a nation for Muslims, Pakistan was also to be secular.

The announcement of the partition triggered a cross-border migration of millions of Hindus and Muslims, that seemingly took most by surprise.[i] Naturally they were woefully unprepared for the mayhem of mass murder and rape. Afterward, cross-religious discrimination and conflict escalated.

The British oversaw the creation of the final borders for Iraq. Joined together was a majority Arabic-speaking Shiite population and a minority Sunni population that was either Kurdish- or Arabic-speaking. In the closing century of the Ottoman Empire, these three groups lived in separate administrative divisions, but there was no question that Arabic-speaking Sunnis were socially superior to the Shias and Kurdish-speaking Sunnis. Now they lived in the same nation with a common government and an Arabic-speaking Sunni king. Iraq was a new nation built on a diverse and delicate foundation.

Following WWI instead of the victorious empires annexing the territory of losing powers, some populations were permitted to create independent states. Carved from the Ottoman and Austria-Hungary empires in 1918 were the borders for the Kingdom of Yugoslavia.[1] The population of this nation was not remotely homogenous, but creating a defensible nation required size and many ethnolinguistic groups in this area were small.

Yugoslavia's position was not unique. Many European nations, also seeking size, had combined diverse ethnolinguistic groups. But afterward, they created homogeneity from diversity by building a common nationality. Doing this is never simple. In this case, it was really complicated. There were large populations of Roman Catholics and Eastern Orthodox that were ethnically Serbian, Croat, and Macedonian, in addition to Sunni, Shiite, and Sufi Muslims that were Bosnian and Albanian.

Thirty-three years after independence Yugoslavia experienced a brutal ethnicity-based civil war amid WWII. At wars end, it was again united under one government that had the extra challenge of managing the civil war's deep-seated scars.

Czechoslovakia was carved from the Austria-Hungary Empire. The borders merged Czech and Slovak ethnolinguistic groups, in addition to Ukrainian, and German-speaking Bohemians (called Sudeten Germans). The latter accounted for nearly a quarter of the nation's population. Hitler seized the Sudetenland in 1938. After WWII "wild expulsions" took place, and most Germans vacated Czechoslovakia.[ii]

Carved from former Ottoman lands was the future nation of Israel. Rationalizing this location for a Jewish homeland was easy. Under the Ottomans, Jews had a favorable existence compared to the discrimination they had faced

in Europe, Persia, and Russia. They had a separate millet and city-state. Persecuted Jews from Europe and Russia were welcomed and sometimes encouraged to immigrate to the Ottoman Empire. By 1880 Jerusalem had a Jewish
majority.[iii] Palestine was also the Jewish Holy Land. It was the historic land of
Israel referenced in the Hebrew Bible. Theodore Hertzl, called "the author of
the vision of the Jewish State," wrote in the Israeli constitution, "Palestine is
our ever-memorable historic home."[iv] The Jews had lost this home on multiple
occasions. The last loss was to the Ottomans in the 16th century. There were
multiple options under consideration for a Jewish state, but for all the reasons
above, Palestine seemed best.

Support for creating the Mandate for Palestine, the mandate allocating
land for the future nation of Israel, was also expressed by Emir Faisal, the Arab
spokesperson during the post-WWI Paris Peace Conferences. Some believe
Faisal was exchanging his support for British support for a territorially defined
independent Arab caliphate. Some have said Faisal conditionally supported a
Jewish state within the Arab caliphate.[2,3] At the Syrian Conference in Damascus led by Faisal in 1919, his updated views, which may have been influenced
by news that there would be no Arab caliphate or empire,[4] were evident in a
unanimous resolution opposing a Jewish state in southern Syria.[v]

After WWI what support the future state of Israel had in MENA
began dwindling. There was no promised Arab caliphate or empire, and
the region was under control of the French and British empires. Religious
intolerance against Christians and Jews began rising. When anti-Semitism
began building in Europe in and around WWII, it found a receptive audience in MENA.

A Jewish homeland in MENA became symbolic of the loss of Islamic
power, and it was. In all likelihood, the allocation of land for a Zionist state in
MENA would not have occurred if the Ottoman Empire had been an Allied
Power, rather than a Central Power, during WWI. If an Islamic power had
been a primary Allied Power during WWII, it would have obtained a permanent seat on the UN Security Council, and quite possibly vetoed Israel's
recognition as a sovereign. Most nations in MENA did not want a Zionist
state in their midst.

Israel's borders like those for Czechoslovakia, Iraq and other nations in
the Middle East, India, Pakistan, nations in sub-Saharan Africa, some former
Soviet republics, Yugoslavia and other former colonies with suboptimal borders are additional outcomes of the competition for global supremacy left to
the successor states of empires to manage or mismanage. Consequences have

included cross-border wars, civil wars, ethnic cleansings, genocides, and other forms of discrimination.

Notes

1. In 1918 the name was the Kingdom of Serbs, Croats and Slovenes.
2. In the 1919 Faisal-Weitzman agreement, Emir Faisal conditionally accepted the Balfour Declaration, a statement by the British government supporting a home for the Jewish people. Faisal's support for a Zionist nation was also documented in a letter from Faisal that is dated March 3, 1919, to the US representative to the Paris Peace conferences, Felix Frankfurter. The letter was, however, written by T. E. Lawrence.
3. It was not preposterous that Arab Muslims would support a Jewish state. Muslims and Jews had a long history as allies, partners, and mutual targets of Christian aggression that dated to the 7th century. During the First Crusade, the Spanish Inquisition, and the Russian Empire Jews and Muslims were threatened by Christians. (Note: Pope Urban II did not target Jews, but he condoned the actions of crusaders.)
4. The McMahon-Hussein Correspondence (July 1915–March 1916) is used to demonstrate that the United Kingdom agreed to support an Arab caliphate of specific geographic dimensions in exchange for the Arab Revolt. The legitimacy of the letters as a treaty is disputed. The duplicity of the UK is not. The Sykes-Picot agreement (May 1916) agreed to allocate some lands promised for the Arab caliphate to Britain, France, and Russia. The Balfour Declaration (1917) allocated some lands promised for the caliphate to a future Jewish nation.

References

i. "How the Partition of India Happened–And Why Its Effects are Still Felt Today." *The Conversation.com*, August 10, 2017.
ii. Jenkins, Jolyon. "The Sudeten Germans Forgotten Fate." *BBC.co.uk*, February 7, 2004.
iii. "Pre-State Israel: Under Ottoman Rule (1517–1917)." *Jewishvirtuallibrary.org*, Retrieved August 4, 2017.
iv. Herzl, Theodore, Jacob de Haas, Binyamin Ze'ev Herz, and Sylvie d'Avigdor. *A Jewish State: An Attempt at a Modern Solution to the Jewish Question*. The Maccabean Publishing, 1904.
v. Hurewitz, J. C. *Diplomacy in the Near and Middle East*. Van Nostrand, 1958.

· 11 ·

SOCIAL HIERARCHIES—
INSTITUTIONALIZING DISCRIMINATION

Aftermaths of Empire

Monarchs didn't fret about ruling increasingly diverse populations because they were hierarchically ordered. Everyone knew their place, and there was little tolerance for those that forgot it. In the Islamic empires Christians, Jews, and Hindus accepted their subordination to Muslims. In Europe's colonial empires, Africans and Asians accepted the superior position of Europeans. In the Russian Empire, Muslims and Jews knew they had lower social positions than the Eastern Orthodox. None of them liked it; subjugation is not like ice cream.

Heredity was a primary determinant of a person's level on a social hierarchy.[1] Rulers bred rulers. All rulers of the Ottoman Empire came from the House of Osman. Nobles also bred nobles. Some empires permitted some self-made men to enter the nobility, but generally, social immobility was established at birth. The rulers and nobles formed an inherited privileged oligarchy, and the masses were their inherited unprivileged subordinates. Women were a special category because they inherited a subordinated status to men at every level in every empire.[2]

When empires conquered lands, they turned hierarchies' upside down. A wealthy conquered hereditary "noble" could be converted to a penniless landless peasant. A peasant- or prisoner-conqueror could become noble-like with extensive land holdings. The alteration of social hierarchies following conquest was one reason wars of conquest could be so bloody. There was plenty to lose, like freedoms, privilege—a cornerstone of wealth, and being forced to pay higher taxes. But, once the conquest was complete, accepting a new designated station in life was the least bad option.

With the introduction of new populations, hierarchies underwent additional adjustments. For some this was negative, but not all. For example, when slave labor was introduced, slaves regardless of their former social status, descended to the very bottom of a social hierarchy. This contrasted sharply with the situation for free peasant immigrants following the official religion from the mother country. They had the ethnicity and religion that brought status and privilege.

Social hierarchies designated privilege for select people and populations, and they also restricted who could accumulate wealth. They baked privilege and discrimination into societal foundations. At this time, however, it was not called discrimination; it was called social ordering. Like everything, there were variations by empire, but the order could also vary by time period and ruler. Below are some general characteristics of social hierarchies by empire, and also for select colonies.

European empires—Intra-European empires

Religion figured prominently in many hierarchies. Early on the pope sat at the top of Europe's uber hierarchy, or he shared it with Europe's secular monarchs. When separation was placed between church and state, the pope was on top of Rome's hierarchy, and monarchs were on top of their polities.

After the hereditary monarch came the hereditary nobles, who often functioned as government bureaucrats administering state functions. Everyone at the top was a landowner. Until industrial revolutions, land was the primary source of wealth, and the monarch, other political elites, and the church owned most of it. In some cases, it was possible for a non-elite to acquire an estate and become an elite, but this was not common. Elites didn't care for non-elites and barriers were generally insurmountable.

The poor, unprivileged masses were at the bottom often with sub-stratification. For example, laborers following the official religion could have a higher social position than those following a non-official religion. To get an indication of the importance of following the official religion, those following a non-official religion could be grouped with drifters, criminals, prisoners, and slaves.

Somewhat perversely free people in the lower strata paid the highest taxes. Rulers never wanted to jeopardize the support of their wealthy supporters with fees. Napoleon Bonaparte knew full well that the overtaxed French masses were not impotent; they could incite revolutions. This is why Napoleon took the opportunity to introduce ethnolinguistic discrimination (ordering). Subjugated to the French were the non-French masses who also paid the highest taxes. The Dutch masses paid 4X the taxes of the French masses. The Prussians were forced to hand over 1/3rd of their annual GDP as a tribute to the French.[i]

In the Revolutions of 1848, it became evident that the masses were no longer feigning acceptance of their discriminatory positions in society. Generally deemed failures, these revolutions had many positive impacts. Political elites were on notice that the masses rejected hereditary rule, divine right rule, immobile stratified societies,[3] and unfair taxes.[ii,iii]

It wasn't long before democratic elections and the accumulation of wealth made possible by industrialization and capitalism were additional determinants of social position. Social mobility was inching its way into Europe.

Europe's New World colonial empires

Latam

The obsession with blood purity that enveloped Iberia traveled across the Atlantic to colonies in Latam. Social hierarchies in Latam were called the casta, and they were based on blood purity.

People born in Spain or Portugal, (actually any Christian born in Europe) that was 100 percent white, and was not a crypto-Catholic,[4] was deemed to have the purest blood. Called the *Peninsulares*, they sat at the top of the casta. Next up were criollos or creoles, the Peninsulares Latam-born children. Peninsulares and creoles were the largest landholders, and they controlled the governments and economies. Amerindians were supposed to be considered one of the pure races. Reality told a story of blood purity being white blood.

Maintaining blood purity was essential to retain a position at the top of the hierarchy. It might seem simple to do this at a time when miscegenation was either illegal or socially taboo throughout the world. But in Latam white males outnumbered white females and miscegenation was condoned. It was common for black and Amerindian females to voluntarily or forcibly become companions. There was a significant benefit to having a child that was mulatto or mestizo. These were the brown people, and they formed the next level in the hierarchy.[5] Below this were people who had not a trace of white blood. First came free blacks and zambos, a black and Amerindian mix.[6] At the very bottom of the casta were slaves. Most were black, but some were Amerindian.[7,iv]

Common to all social hierarchies in this era, and in this case the casta, a person's social level determined economic opportunities and tax rates. Free people at the bottom had the fewest opportunities and the highest tax rates.

The independent nations of Latam had the opportunity to alter their social hierarchies when they became independent. Initially, there were changes, but these were reversed, and hierarchies began looking a lot like empire; whites maintained and controlled access to power, privilege, and wealth.

The United States

The primary determinant of social class in the Thirteen Colonies was wealth, and land was the primary component. Unlike the British Empire's mother-land, there were many opportunities to acquire property and improve one's social standing.

Principally based on wealth, there was an inherent gender, racial and religious component because the best economic opportunities were available to male Protestants with northern European blood. This meant male and female Catholics, Native Americans, and free blacks had little chance of experiencing life near the top of society. Anyone unfree had no chance. Their position was fixed at the bottom. With a foundation based on the notion of equality of opportunity, an independent United States was meant to be different.

Social position was established by individual economic achievement or having the luck of inheritance. The latter created an inherited upper social class, but the members of the upper class or any class were not static. In America's democratic, capitalist systems anyone could theoretically rise to the top or plunge to the bottom. The United States had a flexible hierarchy that delivered social disorder rather than order. But this was a price for social mobility.

In spite of America's commitment to equality of opportunity social mobility has never been universally accessible. For more than a century after independence, access was harder for anyone not male, Protestant, and of northern European blood. This meant the lower levels of the hierarchy were fairly fixed and filled with Native Americans, blacks, Catholics, and non-northern

Europeans. The primacy of some people created the problem of wealth, and all that it can buy, perpetuating a discriminatory ordering of society, and mimicking a quasi-fixed immobile hierarchy.

Early on social mobility in the United States was uniquely producing thousands of rags to riches stories, and almost as many riches to rags stories for male, Protestants, of northern European blood. In time more males and females of diverse ethnicities and religions have been scaling and descending a flexible social hierarchy. The commitment to equality of opportunity has continued a slow pace of progress.

Europe's Old-World colonies

Social hierarchy in colonies in the Old World generally followed a simple structure: Europeans were on the top and the indigenous populations were stratified below them. The process of social restructuring after conquest generally followed a pattern that can be seen by way of example. When Ottoman Algeria became a French colony in 1830, the hierarchy turned topsy turvy. The newly arrived European administrators (Christians) were at the top of society. Below them were other European "settlers."[8] Then came two levels of indigenous Muslim populations: public sector workers then private sector workers,[9] followed by slaves who were generally black and non-Muslims.

Europeans were leaders when it came to abolishing slavery. This should have terminated the bottom stratum, but abolition never ended cleanly. In French Algeria, slavery was abolished in 1848, but it would take until the early 20th century to seriously enforce abolition. Similar scenarios were common throughout Africa.[v]

Social stratification in British India was as unique as the circumstances. This was the only Hindu-majority colony colonized by an Islamic empire before colonization by a European empire. Religion was of paramount importance to social hierarchy in Islamic empires, but not in the British Empire, at least not from the government's perspective.

When the British Empire replaced the Mughal Empire in 1858, Britain's Christian administrators replaced the Mughal's Muslim administrators at the top of the hierarchy. At the next level were indigenous administrators that could be Hindu or Muslim. There were proportionally fewer Muslim administrators in these influential positions because many Muslims refused to complete a secular education, and this was a requirement.

Below the administrators were the masses, both Hindus and Muslims. To Muslims, equality with Hindu polytheists, and having national laws prioritized over sharia law was an insult to Islam and a giant social plunge. Some dissatisfied Muslims developed Islamic revival movements and called for jihad by the sword.[10,vi] For Hindus, the Muslim rejection of equality heightened tensions that had been brewing from the unconscionable levels of discrimination Hindus were subjected to under Muslim rule. Hindus and Muslims might be legally equal, but socially the Muslim minority faced something quite common—discrimination by the majority that ensured social inequality.

Not all Hindus had the same social level, but this was not something the British established. The Hindu caste system stratifies followers at birth into five social levels, including four castes for people of different professions, in addition to the Dalit or untouchables.[11] The British were disinclined to address the blatant inequality embedded in the Hindu caste system. They knew that trying to alter religious practices in a colony was playing with fire. If a caste system was going to be addressed, it would be done by independent nations.

Islamic empires

The Islamic empires based social stratification on some combination of heredity, profession, religion and wealth; however, religion was of paramount importance to social position. All religious populations were fitted into the empire's social order, which gave preference and privilege to people following the official religion. Sometimes the official religion had an ethnolinguistic component, and sometimes converts to the official religion were placed in a lower stratum.

In the Ottoman Empire, there were large populations of Muslims, Christians, and Jews. Among the masses, Muslims were on top, but not all Muslims, just Sunnis—but not all Sunnis, only those that were born as Muslims and spoke Turkish, Ottoman/Turkish, or Arabic.[12,13] Kurdish-, Iranian-, or Persian-speaking Sunni Muslims and converts fell below this group and sometimes far below.

At the next level were the *dhimmis*. Dhimmis were select groups, mostly Christians and Jews, that enjoyed a protected status and were permitted to practice their religion. This status did not confer social equality. Dhimmis were a subordinated class, and they were easily identifiable by prescribed clothing and markings on their homes.[14] Below the dhimmis were: Muslims categorized as heretics, such as Shias; members of some syncretic Islamic faiths, which could include Sufis;[15] and slaves.

In the final century of the Ottoman Empire, there were changes to the hierarchy. In an attempt to curry favor with the British, French, and Russian empires the Ottomans decided to eliminate the second-class status of the dhimmis. The measure failed when it was rejected by Muslims who saw the notion of equality with Christians as tantamount to lowering their social status to that of an infidel.

American law professor Mark Movsesian has tied the Muslim massacre of Armenians between 1894–1896 and the Armenian genocide in 1915 to the rejection of Christian equality. He said, "Law that does not reflect the values of a society is bound to fail." Further, "if the conflict between the law and values is great, and touches a society's core beliefs, significant disorder, including violence against vulnerable communities, can easily occur."[vii]

The Young Turks (1908–1914) implemented another change. They deprecated the social position of Arabic-speaking Sunni Muslims. Something that resulted in overt discrimination,[viii] and became a motivator for the Arab Revolt.

The Chinese Empire

Social stratification in the Chinese Empire could vary by dynasty, but a general driver was Confucian practices that called for a nested hierarchy that contemplated profession, age, wealth, and gender. There was also an unofficial level for deviants. It was unofficial because including them in the Confucian order would have conferred legitimacy.

The Son of Heaven had the top profession. Below the Son were bureaucrats also called mandarins, followed by farmers, landlords, and artisans. Situated just above the deviants and last in the official order were the merchants. The deviants were at the very bottom in what was called the "half-human, half-chattel" category. This included slaves, the penetrated member of a gay union, prostitutes, and soldiers. Soldiers engaged in violence, which was a discouraged act of moral inferiority.

Confucianism also had a hierarchy for families that was ordered by gender and age. The father was at the top, sons next, and daughters at the bottom. A mother was superior to her sons, reflecting the importance of filial piety.

Russian Empire

Social hierarchy in the Russian Empire (1721–1917) is generally depicted with two levels and described as the service nobility on top, and the tax paying serfs, or the masses,[16] on the bottom.[17]

Russian nobility was quite diverse. Nobles could be non-Russian and non-Christian, including non-Orthodox Germans or Armenians, Muslim Tatars, and Polish, Russian, and Ukrainian Jews. Many Romanov emperors were also non-Russian. Within the masses, some non-Russian peasants also had a position of privilege. At least as far as tax rates were concerned. Non-Russian peasants generally lived on the periphery, which could be thousands of miles away from Moscow. Tax burdens were minimized to reduce the risk of rebellions on the edge of the empire.

When Russian conquests reached lands populated by Muslims and Jews, the simple two-level social hierarchy became more complex. In the 18th and 19th centuries, a significant Jewish population was added to the empire from the conquered Polish-Lithuanian Commonwealth, and large Muslim populations were added with the colonization of Central Asia, and the annexation of Crimea and areas in the Caucasus. Discrimination including transportation under inhumane conditions, pogroms, and special laws illustrated a lower social status for Jews and Muslims than the Eastern Orthodox masses.

The Soviet Union

The communist Soviet Union was supposed to be a classless society, but it was not. There were two social levels: Communist Party members and the masses. Just like non-communist societies, political elites held power, and this enabled the accumulation of wealth and privilege that created two very different classes. In a so-called classless society, this was a source of enormous discontent. The masses were anyway unhappy with their flat hierarchy because social equality implied being poor with no opportunity for change.

*****

Across the empires, hierarchies were similar from the perspective of being hierarchies of discrimination that perpetuated power, wealth, and privilege for select people. The criteria for being elite was, however different. Hierarchies in Europe's overseas empires would be called racist today. In the Islamic and Russian empires, religious intolerance would spring to mind. The Chinese Empire's social ordering by profession conjures up arrogance. Every empire qualifies as sexist. All provoke revulsion today. History is like that; it never measures up to the modern standards that come from change.

In time, popular revolutions brought change. When the Era of Nation-States came around, there was democracy, capitalism, socialism, communism, and Islamism. All promised to end the revulsion by putting the kibosh on immobile social hierarchies. But many leaders continue to be charmed by ordered populations and the perpetuation of power, wealth and privilege for select people. It's another empire aftermath.

Notes

1. Inherited social status demotivated everyone. Inherited rulers had fewer incentives to improve the life of their subjects, and the masses lacked motivations to work hard to reach a higher social level.
2. Women were the original motivation for social hierarchies because they were the first slaves. Upon conquest, women were enslaved, and men were killed.
3. Serfdom began ending in earnest after the French Revolution (1799). Masses that were now free were unhappy with social immobility.
4. Crypto-Catholics were Muslims or Jews that converted to Catholicism during the Spanish Inquisition but continued to hold the beliefs of Islam or Judaism respectively.
5. In Brazil brown people are called *pardos*.
6. There were many more categories of mixed persons.
7. Amerindians that converted to Christianity were supposed to be protected subjects. To discourage Amerindian enslavement by deviant whites, in the 16th century the Catholic Church forbade the mistreatment or unjust enslavement of Amerindians. It was not very effective. Neither was the Spanish Crown's bans on the slavery of Amerindians in 1493 and 1530.
8. The first immigrants from empire motherlands to Old-World colonies were called settlers even though these lands were settled centuries ago.
9. Algeria's Jewish minority became French citizens in 1870. Algeria's Muslims were offered citizenship too, but they had to forego sharia, and few did. With citizenship, Jews were socially elevated above the non-citizens in the Muslim-majority.
10. Jihad, which literally means struggling can pertain to internal, external, and personal struggles. Jihad by the sword means a struggle carried out with arms.
11. Although the caste system is a Hindu belief, most religious groups in South Asia adopted something similar, including a Dalit-like class. Caste systems are present in many tribal-ethnic groups in remote areas of the world.
12. This population was also stratified by profession.

13. In the Shiite empires, Shias were on top.
14. The humiliating practice of forcing people to display identifiable marks was not limited to the Ottomans. In the Era of Empire, for example, Jews and Muslims in the Spanish Inquisition and Jews in Nazi Germany were required to do something similar.
15. Sufis can be Shia or Sunni
16. The masses were all peasants, but not all peasants were serfs. Serfs were about half.
17. The noble class functioning as service providers for the government was common in Europe in the Middle Ages (5th-15th centuries) and in some places beyond.

References

i. Lieven, Dominic. *Empire: The Russian Empire and its Rivals*. New Haven, CT: Yale University Press, 2000.

ii. Hobsbawm, Eric. *The Age of Capital (1848–1875)*. Barnes & Noble, 1975.

iii. Hill, Jonathan Richard. "The Revolutions of 1848 in Germany, Italy and France," 2005, *Senior Honors Theses*. Https://commons.emich.edu/honors/45.

iv. "Las Castas-Spanish Racial Classifications." *Nativeheritageproject.com*, June 15, 2013.

v. Brower, Benjamin Claude. "Rethinking Abolition in Algeria. Slavery and the 'Indigenous Question.'" *Cahiers, d'Etudes Africaines*, 195, no. 3 (2009): 805–828.

vi. Qureshi, H. M. Z. *Muslim Revivalism in 19th Century India*. Oxford: St. Cross College, 2015.

vii. Movsesian, Mark L. *Elusive Equality: The Armenian Genocide and the Failure of Ottoman Legal Reform*. St John's. Law Scholarship Repository, 2010.

viii. "The Great Arab Revolt." *Kinghussein.gov.jo*. Retrieved June 15, 2018.

· 1 2 ·

GENDER DISCRIMINATION

Aftermaths of Empire

Gender discrimination against women is not an Era-of-Empire aftermath; it existed long before 1453. Indeed, the world has forever been a collection of patriarchal societies. The "history of man" has been a history of women subordinated to men: wife to husband, sister to brother, nun to priest, male manager to female worker, male voter to female non-voter, etc. It is the history of men leading government, religion, the economy, and the family. However, the empires perpetuated discrimination against women.

With the spread of organized religion, the empires expanded the legitimacy of subordination and may have provided additional applications for it. Verse 4:34 in the Quran says: "Men have authority over women because God has made the one superior to the other, and because they spend their wealth to maintain them. Good women are obedient. They guard their unseen parts because God has guarded them. As for those whom you fear disobedience, admonish them and send them to beds apart and beat them. Then if they obey you, take no further action against them." In the Bible (Colossians 3:18) it is written: "Wives, submit yourselves to your husbands, as is fitting in the Lord."

Late into the Era of Empire gender discrimination got its first break. In the 19th century, some western nations[1] were advancing industrialization, and democratic forms of government separated church from state. Separating church wasn't much of a break for women because men were still controlling the government, religion, the economy, and the family. Absent sacred texts that legitimized gender subordination, men used their powers in government to create laws to do the same thing, in some cases mimicking laws in the bible. When women got married, for example, their property, including their bodies became their husband's.

Placing separation between church and state in combination with industrialization did offer an opening through increased access to secular education. This was initially limited to upper- and middle-class girls, but by the early 20th century the number of public primary and secondary schools for girls was increasing.

Other aspects of industrialization were not good news for all women because opportunities for work shifted from within the home to outside the home. Being able to work outside the home was liberating and offered a steady income, but mothers had fewer paid-work options. The prospects to change this with legal solutions or social change were virtually non-existent. Democratic forms of government gave the right to vote, and the right to run for office to men,[i] and the notion of a woman's place at home was sacrosanct.

The world wars were a catalyst for addressing gender discrimination. In WWI and WWII, men went to fight, and women had to *man* the economy and the household too. After WWI, women in many western nations were emboldened and successfully organized to secure the right to vote. These women now had a powerful tool to chip away at patriarchy. At least the portion enshrined in laws.

Women in western nations were emboldened again after manning the economy and managing the family in WWII. This time progress was better because many western governments were examining discriminatory laws, views, and practices. Women were not top of mind, but they became so when they took their cues from civil rights movements, organized and made their subjugated status a vote-defining political issue. Discriminatory laws were repealed and others passed to support gender equality, but this was not a silver bullet. Cultures of patriarchy impeded enforcement and perpetuated unregulated forms of female gender discrimination, for example, women maintaining responsibility for the home and family.

The women in western nations were a small fraction of all women. Women living in European colonies, or successor states of the Islamic, Chinese, and Russian empires with long histories of autocratic and non-secular rule, and strongly patriarchal societies faced many more challenges for lessening discrimination. Without a vote, and men overwhelmingly dominating government and any positions of influence, most challenges were effectively unassailable.

Like other forms of discrimination, gender discrimination was meant to end in the Era of Nation-States. Nations signing the UN Charter committed to the equal application of fundamental freedoms. But commitments weren't taken seriously. This did not mean that the issue of gender inequality in the Era of Nation-States was universally unaddressed. Where women had the freedom to speak, assemble, and vote, they were not letting the issue of inequality die. There would be considerable variations in the pace of progress around the world, with direct ties to aftermaths from the Chinese, European, Islamic and Russian/Soviet empires.

Note

1. Western nations include nations in Western Europe, Australia, Canada, Israel, New Zealand, and the United States.

Reference

i. Hobsbawm, Eric. *The Age of Empire: 1875–1914*. Weidenfeld and Nicolson, 1987.

· 1 3 ·

LANGUAGE

Aftermaths of Empire

Before the Era of Empire, a tower of babel was alive and well. Afterward, there were nine languages collectively connecting most nations, minimally at the official level.

With the English language, the British Empire connected most people from England, Ireland, Scotland, Wales, eleven of Oceania's twelve nations,[1] and the twelve nations of ESNA. The connectivity provided by English in the region of ESNA geographically stops at the Mexican border. But, language connectivity with Spanish resumes south of the border.

In Latam, eighteen out of twenty-three countries use the language of the Spanish Empire's motherland as a national language. Similar to Spanish, Portuguese, the official language of the Portuguese Empire is spoken in the region's most populous country Brazil. The only countries in Latam not connected by language are the handful colonized by Britain, France, or the Netherlands where the national languages are English, French, and Dutch respectively.

With minor exceptions, empires in Europe did not mandate the use of their languages,[2] and there are almost as many national languages as nations. When nations were economically isolated, this did not create communication challenges. When trade began increasing, coincident with industrial revolutions, polities in Europe started mandating or encouraging students to learn multiple languages in school. In the 19th century, for example, the Netherlands made Dutch, English, French, and German compulsory languages in secondary school.[i]

In the New World, languages of the empire motherlands became national languages.[3] This occurred because most early immigrants came from the homelands of empires. In Europe's Old-World colonies empire-motherland languages became official languages. It would have been impossible to govern without a standard vehicle for official communications across the multiple ethnolinguistic groups in a colony. It wasn't that challenging to do this. Many government administrators were from the motherlands of empire, and it was easy to find local people willing to learn a new language when the reward was a government position carrying a higher social status. Others learned official languages as students in schools run by missionaries attempting to convert local populations to Christianity.

Islamic empires introduced Arabic throughout MENA. It was the language of the Prophet Muhammad, the Quran, and religious discourse. However, use beyond men of religion and some in the government was uncommon. In the Ottoman Empire, the official language was Ottoman Turkish, a composite of Turkish, Arabic and Persian. Ottoman decline and the rising influence of the British and the French in the late 19th and early 20th centuries spurred movements in MENA to reject foreign influence and develop distinct state cultures (nationalities). The use of Arabic as an official language became common. In time, Arabic became the official and national language of nations in MENA except for Iran, Turkey, and Israel.[4]

The spread of Mandarin began during the Han Dynasty (206BC to 220AD). It was the official language of the Ming and Qing dynasties. In a written form it was also a lingua franca among the East Asian intelligentsia. Beyond this, languages spoken in the Chinese Empire were as different as ethnicities. This changed in the Republic of China (1912–1949) when a Sinicization campaign made Mandarin the national language of China and the most commonly spoken first language in the world.[5]

Russian was the official language of the Russian Empire, but there were many ethnolinguistic groups in the empire. In the late 19th century, there was a minimally successful campaign to create a Russian nationality, which included speaking Russian. In the 20th century, a Sovietization campaign that included the Russian language was more successful because there were now public schools throughout the Soviet Union that could teach Russian. Many learned Russian in school, but it was not a compulsory language in all republics. About half the Soviet population would speak Russian as a primary or secondary language.[ii]

*****

In the Era of Nation-States, some nations changed their official languages, in part to dispense with the lingering memory of their subjugators, but it was more common for official languages to remain because they enabled communications among a nation's ethnolinguistically diverse populations and also the larger communities of like speakers that shared a history of empire. For example, English-speaking Nigerians from different ethnolinguistic groups could freely communicate with each other and readily communicate with people in ESNA, Oceania, and the British Isles, in addition to many in nearby Ghana, and other former British colonies in sub-Saharan Africa.

Notes

1. Tok Pisin, also called pigeon-English, is the most commonly spoken language in Papua New Guinea.
2. In the 18th and 19th centuries, French was voluntarily adopted as the lingua franca of diplomacy between the European, Russian, and Ottoman empires in addition to Europe's intelligentsia. (Some powerful French kings forced the use of French for diplomacy.) It fell from favor in the Russian and Ottoman empires when France militarily advanced on their lands, enforced capitulations, and/or managed debts.
3. National languages are those most widely spoken, or officially designated as such. Official languages are those chosen for government affairs.
4. Arabic is an official language of Israel.
5. Within Mainland China some regions speak Cantonese, but Simplified Chinese connects Mandarin and Cantonese speakers. It is a mutually intelligible script.

References

i. "Foreign Language Teaching in Schools in Europe." *European Commission*, 2001.
ii. Schiffman, H. "Language Policy in the Former Soviet Union." *Upenn.edu*. Retrieved November 2, 2018.

· 1 4 ·

THE RISE OF INTER-GOVERNMENTAL ORGANIZATIONS

Aftermaths of Empire

The empires conquered and ruled thousands of tribal-ethnic groups, commonly combining multiple groups into administrative districts. Into these population mixtures could be added other diverse populations to meet labor needs and others geographically shifted for security reasons, for example, untrusted ethnic or religious communities. Upon independence, colonial borders became national borders, and diverse people became nationals[1] in fledgling nations.

In 1814 a leading statesman in Europe, Count Metternich said that Italy was not a nation like England or France where people shared a common language, religion, and history. It was instead a geographical expression. In 1947 Chief Obafemi Awolowo called Nigeria, with its more than 240 ethnic groups, a mere geographical expression. After 1945, many new nations were resembling geographical expressions.

Governing diverse nationals lacking a common language, history, culture, or religion was a problem added to the to-do lists of national leaders that already included protecting fundamental freedoms for all and building nations with adequate infrastructure and institutions to deliver political and economic security. Colonies weren't usually completely bereft of infrastructure and institutions, but the empires were not preparing colonies for independence. After 1945, even if empires wanted to help with nation-building, offers could be rejected by national leaders that gained support by bashing imperial powers: the very same leaders woefully unprepared for nation-building.

The leaders of new nations were not without sources for assistance to address their to-do lists. The Era of Empire provided plenty of examples of what can happen to weak states, and these had to be avoided. Support for nation building, facilitating fundamental freedoms for all, and maintaining a stable, peaceful world became responsibilities of new intergovernmental organizations (IGOs) created with direction from WWII's Allied Powers.[2,3]

In 1944, forty-four states convened at the Bretton Woods Conference to hammer out details for the International Monetary Fund (IMF), and the World Bank.[4] Both began operating in 1946 as IGO banking institutions within the umbrella of the UN.[5]

The original objective of the World Bank was to facilitate the reconstruction of WWII's war-torn economies. It was soon apparent that new nations needed help building nations because they too could pose a risk to global stability. The World Bank's charter was expanded accordingly.

The IMF's charter was to facilitate global financial stability and economic growth, an imperative re-emphasized between WWI and WWII. Austria, China, Germany, Greece, Hungary, Poland, Romania, and Russia had episodes of hyperinflation[i] that created enormous instability that was a contributing factor to WWII.

Also, under the UN umbrella was the International Court of Justice, the UN's principal judicial arm responsible for amicably resolving inter-sovereign disputes. There had to be a way for nations to solve their differences peacefully; invading another sovereign, let alone conquest were no longer options.

The United Nations

The UN was the lynchpin of the IGOs created to facilitate the transition to nation-states. The final provisions were hammered out[6] at conferences of fifty states aligned with the Allied Powers[7] in San Francisco between April 25, 1945, and June 26, 1945. The duration of the conferences and continual attendance by high-ranking politicians and diplomats was a testament to the importance of this new organization, and this was not misplaced. The empires had viewed the world's land and people as pawns in a game for global supremacy; a game played out with centuries of debilitating wars of conquest, followed by discriminatory practices, and punctuated with the grand finales of WWI and WWII. The game had to end.

Among the most influential participants, the Soviet Union's support was tepid. At one-point Soviet attendance at the conferences was questioned. This possibility seemed almost unbelievable. Soviet Premier Stalin had told US President Roosevelt that he supported the UN and its fundamental premises so much "he would grant freedom of religion, private ownership, and greater democracy in the Soviet Union."[ii] In exchange FDR agreed to concessions for Soviet influence in Central Europe. Perhaps the Soviet's waning support was an outcome of the death of FDR, or maybe support was always halfhearted, and Stalin was a skilled politician pandering to a receptive American president.

By the end of the conferences, there was agreement on the responsibilities of the UN, including its associated organizations. They were to oversee peace during the decades of dismantling reluctant empires and beyond, guide the construction of national institutions committed to equal freedoms for diverse people, resolve inter-nation disputes, and deliver help to build economically viable nations.

The UN Charter was aligned with democratic principles, but it did not explicitly require members to commit to democracy. The desire for Soviet support may have influenced any specific reference to democracy. The Soviet's viewed their constitution as the most democratic in the world.[iii] But they called their system communism and defined democracy differently.[8] There were also others participating in the conferences that would have objected to committing to democracy, like dictators in Latam and Saudi Arabia.

Political persuasions of participants notwithstanding, there were democratic principles in the UN Charter, and it was imperative to peace that all UN members honor their commitments. Particularly important were honoring the sovereignty of member nations, "the principle of equal rights," and "promoting and encouraging respect for human rights and for fundamental freedoms for all without distinction as to race, sex, language, or religion." Should a member fail to honor their commitments, this created a problem. As an IGO, the UN had no direct authority over its sovereign members, and the UN Charter specifically prohibited the UN from interfering in intra-sovereign matters: "nothing should authorize intervention in matters essentially within the domestic jurisdiction of any state."

How could the participants leave out a means to rein in a recalcitrant member? The UN Charter is based on the principle of "sovereign equality of all of its Members." But, powerful members, like the United States or the Soviet Union didn't really see themselves as equal to other nations, and they certainly would not have accepted being forced to forego sovereignty by another nation or group of nations. The same was true of less powerful members, but they weren't delusional about their sovereign equality. A May 6, 1945, NY Times article covering the San Francisco conferences said many participants "had reluctantly accepted the idea of virtual world dictatorship by the great powers."[iv] A virtual dictatorship was apparently preferable to the return of direct empire dictatorships.

The UN was not completely powerless faced with a recalcitrant national leader unless that leader was also on the permanent Security Council. The four major Allied Powers of WWII: China, the Soviet Union, the United Kingdom, and the United States, in addition to France became the five permanent members of the powerful UN Security Council.[9]

These five members looked a lot like the greatest powers of the Era of Empire, with two notable exceptions. The United States was the new kid of global powers, and an Islamic power was missing. The latter occurred because the Allied Powers did not include an Islamic military power.[10] The same was true for Latam.[11] Being a major Allied Power was a requirement to be a permanent Security Council member.

Serendipity played a role in China, France, the Soviet Union, the United Kingdom, and the United States becoming allies during WWII.[12] Now, history's sometime allies and other times adversaries were all on the same permanent Security Council team charged with keeping the peace. But what if they were not aligned on keeping the peace? Armed with the right to veto UN actions, these five held a potent weapon that could be misused to reinvigorate and perpetuate global power including supporting empire-like behaviors, like wars.

There were vigorous debates about giving the permanent Security Council members the right to veto "substantive" UN resolutions. A veto would put these members in a catbird seat that could effectively negate elements of the Charter and empower them to effect resolutions with global implications. Opponents of the veto did not prevail. Permanent Security Council members were supposed to be responsible for deploying their military forces to stop a nation infringing on another's sovereignty. None would have agreed to this without a means to control the deployment of their militaries.[13]

It had to be assumed that the five permanent members would fulfill their obligations to support the Charter and ensure peace. However, skepticism was warranted. Alignment on the same side during WWII was based on defeating the common enemy of fascism.[v] These five had different views on political and economic systems and imperialism. The Soviet Union was an autocratic communist entity. China was fighting a civil war for and against communism. France, the United Kingdom, and the United States were champions for democracy and capitalist-weighted systems.

Views on imperialism were equally at odds. The United Kingdom was the world's greatest imperial power. France was an imperial power that was reluctant to let go. Until very recently China had thousands of years of history as an imperial power. The United States was a stalwart anti-imperialist. The Soviet Union's behaviors reflected a re-emerging imperial power. Before WWII ended, it was preparing Central Europe for control by Moscow. In the case of Poland, it was actively pursuing political control in contravention to Stalin's agreement among the Big Three in Yalta to permit free elections.[vi] The British were so concerned about the Soviet Union they created two plans called Operation Unthinkable to halt Soviet aggression.[14] The seeds of incompatibility among the five permanent members of the Security Council were everywhere.

There were obvious concerns about the potential effectiveness of the UN and in particular the Security Council, but there was no question that the UN Charter represented a far superior roadmap for the world than the alternative. This was a continuation of the increasingly ruinous competition for global supremacy. The UN Charter was signed and ratified by its original members in 1945.

GATT

Operating independently from the United Nations, the General Agreement on Tariffs and Trade (GATT) was created to facilitate international trade.[15]

In the Era of Empire, trade was conducted on a win-lose basis: the empires won, and the colonies lost. Colonies supplied raw materials to empire motherlands for processing, and they were captive markets for goods from the motherlands. Being on the losing side of trade was a source of colonial angst and a motivator for independence. However, having national leaders in charge of trading relationships was no guarantee that trade would generate positive results.

Trade decisions made by national leaders facilitated the Great Depression (1929–1940).[16] In response to rising unemployment, protectionist policies were implemented that stymied global trade. Because people now paid more for domestic goods, this reduced purchasing power and increased unemployment. It was the worst of outcomes—everyone lost.[17]

The perpetuation of protectionist policies would put a real damper on nation-building for dozens of new nations, keeping them weak and vulnerable. Free flowing trade was a vehicle for nations to obtain advanced goods that could fast track economic development and stability. Without this, nations would be reinventing the wheel over and over again. Ending protectionist trade policies was an essential role for GATT. It came into effect in 1948.

*****

The world at large was in agreement that the mayhem of battling empires, punctuated by the death, destruction, and depravity of WWII had to end and the transition to nation-states was vital to achieving this. But, shifting from colonial dependents to self-sustaining nations was a daunting process, which was made less so by the creation of several IGOs with essential responsibilities for facilitating the transition from empires to nation-states. There was one crucial component where sovereigns were on their own. It was imperative that their national leaders honor their commitments to the UN Charter and focus on building stable and secure nations that delivered a higher quality of life for their people. Alas, national leaders are human with a natural desire for power that can trump all.[vii]

Notes

1. Being categorized as a national commonly implies citizenship, which was not always the case. New national laws denied some classes of people citizenship, leaving some as residents.
2. Axis Power nations did not participate in the development of these plans.
3. From 1942–1945 forty-seven nations signed a treaty, the Declaration of the United Nations, pledging support for the Allied Powers and their opposition to the Axis Powers. These nations were called the United Nations.
4. The World Bank was originally called the International Bank for Reconstruction and Development.
5. The IMF and World Bank do not dispense foreign aid. Both institutions loan money to their members. There are times, however, when low-income countries have been victims of corrupt or incompetent administrations, and their loan amounts are reduced to permit a fresh start for a subsequent administration.
6. Many details were defined during the creation of the League of Nations after WWI. The start of WWII was a good indicator that the League offered some excellent learning experiences for the design of the UN.
7. Some states (nations and colonies) only became Allied Powers in 1945 when victory was at hand. It was a pre-condition to participating in the San Francisco conferences. Axis

Power nations including Germany, Italy, and Japan, and fascist Portugal and Spain were not allowed to participate. Neutral nations, like Switzerland, also did not attend.

8. The Soviets saw democracy in terms of equal rights for all regardless of ethnicity, religion, income, gender or age. But there were no rights to fundamental freedoms like freedom from unlawful detainment or freedom of religion. Also, there was no rule of law or multi-party elections.

9. Had it been the League of Nations rather than the United Nations that had become the global organization for peace, permanent members of its Security Council (called the Executive Council) would have been Britain, France, Italy, and Japan. The United States was supposed to be a member too, but the US Congress failed to ratify participation.

10. Iran was officially neutral during WWII, but its ruler Reza Shah was pro-Axis. Turkey was neutral until 1945 when the Allied victory seemed assured. Saudi Arabia was formally neutral but supported the Allied Powers, although they did not send troops. The Egyptian military played a token role supporting the Allied Powers, but it was mistrusted due to some high-ranking support for the Axis Powers. Iraq and the Grand Mufti of the Mandate for Palestine chose alignment with the Axis Powers.

11. US President Franklin Delano Roosevelt suggested that Brazil should be a member of the permanent Security Council, but this was rejected because it was not a global power or a global military power. It did send about 25,000 troops to fight for the Allied Powers. Troop participation by Britain, China, the Soviet Union, and the United States is counted using millions.

12. China had close relations with Germany and Italy in the interwar years. Still, there was no commitment to either side until the United States entered the war in 1941 and the national leader of the Republic of China (1912–1949), Chiang Kai-shek, thought the Allied Powers were assured victory. If not for Hitler's duplicity, the Soviet Union would not have been an Allied Power. Stalin had entered into an anti-aggression pact with Hitler, and a neutrality pact with Japan because he wanted the western powers entangled in wars. He wanted the Soviet Union to be the only major power that was unentangled in war and free to expand the Soviet empire.

13. This role of the permanent Security Council members never materialized as envisioned, but the veto remained.

14. These were secret plans devised in 1945 and 1946 to invade the Soviet Union or defend against a Soviet invasion.

15. The original vision was for the International Trade Organization (ITO) to be part of the UN. When the US Congress failed to ratify the ITO's charter it didn't progress. A different independent organization, GATT, went into effect in 1948.

16. Years for the Great Depression varied in different parts of the world.

17. Cascading impacts from the Great Depression had an impact on the rise of Nazi Germany.

References

i. Taylor, Bryan. "The Century of Inflation." *Global Financial Data*. Retrieved October 27, 2017.

ii. Kern, Gary. "How Uncle Joe Bugged FDR: The Lessons of History." *CIA.gov*. Retrieved December 27, 2018.

iii. Vishniak, Mark. "Lenin's Democracy and Stalin's." *Foreign Affairs*, July 1946.

iv. "Memorandum of Conversation. Stettinus and Molotov, 8:00 PM, May 3, 1945. Edward Stettinus Papers. The University of Virginia.

v. Hobsbawm, Eric. *The Age of Extremes: A History of the World 1914–1991*. Vintage Books, 1994.

vi. Schlesinger, Stephen C. *Act of Creation: The Founding of the United Nations*. Westview Press, 2003.

vii. Russell, Bertrand. *Power a New Social Analysis*. Allen and Unwin, 1938.

· 1 5 ·

WARS WINNERS AND LOSERS

Aftermaths of Empire

The competition for empire was a period of wars and more wars—500 years of empires winning and losing wars as they vied for global supremacy. In one way, the extension of influence, the European empires won. Their influence reached every region, completely dominating four: Western Europe and the three New World regions. The New World became near-Western European mini-mes right down to having European-blood majorities. In comparison, the Chinese, Islamic and Russian empires each influentially dominated one region in the Old World.

Really, there was no outright winner because the competition took everyone out. The Chinese, Islamic and Russian empires had been dissolved before the end of the Era of Empire, and so were most European empires. The British Empire was the only empire standing tall when the competition ended, although British colonies occupied during WWII would take issue with this. The British had succeeded in extending their rule over the largest expanse of land in history. But like every empire still standing, according to the UN Charter, they had to forego their colonies on request. So, if the British won, it wasn't much of a win, particularly when merged with the guilt that all empires felt, or should have felt, for centuries of aggressive and immoral behaviors.

If winners are defined as those best positioned to succeed in the Era of Nation States, the list includes some that weren't even competitors. During the competition, it was normal to create some colonies with expansive borders, and for nations to expand their permanent boundaries. In the Era of Nation-States, there is no unclaimed land, borders are no longer fluid, and annexing sovereign land is against international law. The window for nations to expand their borders has closed.

While the window was open Brazil, Canada, China, France, Germany, Iran, Italy, Japan, Russia, Saudi Arabia, Spain, Turkey, the United Kingdom, and the United States expanded their borders. Some colonies in Africa, Asia, Latam and Oceania like South Africa, India,[1] Indonesia, Argentina, and Australia were bequeathed expansive borders, and like the others noted above this included fertile land and access to the sea. These created enormous advantages in the Era of Nation-States.

Even greater advantages accrued to Iran, Spain, Turkey, China, France, Russia, and the United Kingdom. These were empire motherlands that spread their religion, language, values, and systems and embed common histories throughout their empires. This offered a foundation to rebuild a sphere of influence in the Era of Nation-States. The latter four also had the advantage of permanent Security Council seats. As a military and economic superpower and the holder of a permanent Security Council seat, it's fair to add the United States to this list. It had not created a foundation from which to build a sphere of influence, but its religion, language, values, and systems had origins in Europe, offering Americans the possibility of leveraging the foundations of Europe's empires.[2]

Among China, France, Iran, Russia, Turkey, and the United Kingdom it cannot be overlooked that the Chinese, Islamic and Russian empires lost the uber competition for global supremacy. Or maybe it was just round one. Each produced powerful successor states and the agony of defeat rarely fades into oblivion.

There were losers aplenty. In every war, one or more states and ethno-linguistic groups lost. Among the biggest losers were conquered indigenous populations everywhere. Their religions were impugned, social positions destroyed, rights removed, and resources commandeered. Some conquered people were raped, tortured, imprisoned, enslaved and uprooted. Millions died from forced labor, castration, inhumane conditions of living or transport, imported diseases, famines, ethnic cleansing, and fatalities from wars of conquest and independence.

The Spanish Empire counts among the greatest commanders of natural resources. Between 1521 and 1660 16,632,648.20 kg of registered pure silver and 181,234.95 kg of registered pure gold was shipped to Spain.[i] This pillaging took a toll on Amerindians and black slaves that worked the mines and transported cargo. The estimated life span of a "human mule" was two months.[ii] Long after the pillaging occurred its history remains as a reminder of the world's greatest heist, and the depraved rapacity of imperial powers.

Wars of conquest were bloody. In the Mahdist War (1881–1899), the British Empire and Egypt fought together for control of the Sudan. An estimated 5–6 million Sudanese died, leaving Sudan with a population of 2–3 million.[iii] In Mexico's War for Independence (1810–1821), estimated war deaths are 300,000 or 5 percent of the population.[iv] In the Algerian War for Independence (1954–1962) fought against France, the estimates for war dead range from 350,000 to 1.5 million. According to French governmental records, about 26,500 were French soldiers.[v]

Indigenous populations often gave their all to prevent conquest, but battling a goliath power was futile. Without question the conquered, subjugated people lost and lost big, and many of their descendants still carry painful memories of empire subjugation.

Understanding aspects of the winners and losers of the competition for global supremacy offers insights into present and prospective geopolitical behaviors, and challenges for global geniality among diverse people. They vary by empire.

Islamic empires

Early on Islamic empires dominated the competition for global supremacy, but later the Mughal and Ottoman empires disbanded after suffering defeats at the hands of the Christian European and Russian empires.

The Ottoman Empire was Islam's most powerful and enduring empire. It existed from 1299 to 1922 and reached into Africa, Asia, and Europe. It played key roles in maintaining a balance of power among the European, Islamic, and Russian empires in Eurasia, preserving the Islamic caliphate and protecting the Middle East from European conquests.

At a time when the Russian Empire was building a contiguous land empire in Eurasia, a weakening Ottoman Empire was in Russia's path. The Russians and Ottomans were at war twelve or more times between the 16th and 19th centuries. The Ottomans secured one decisive victory. Each Russian victory chipped away at Ottoman lands in Central Asia and Eastern Europe and placed conquered Muslims in harm's way as possible victims of transport or cleansing campaigns.

A declining Ottoman Empire also made a tempting target for industrializing European empires. In the 19th and 20th centuries, European empires successfully conquered Ottomans lands in North Africa and subjugated the Muslim populations. It was also in the 19th century when the British Empire overpowered the Mughal Empire.

The Ottomans also endured intra-Islam indignity. The Ottoman and Persian Shiite empires engaged in nearly a dozen wars between the 16th and 19th centuries. The Ottomans won most, but the Shias captured extensive lands in the Middle East and central Asia, engaged in the voluntary or forced conversion of Sunni Muslims, and cleansed Sunni religious leaders from their lands.

The Ottoman Empire was contracting, but it had not thrown in the towel. In the 20th century, rulers saw an opportunity to rebuild power. They made a double or nothing bet in WWI and lost. Islam's mightiest empire was gone. Ottoman lands in MENA were colonized, occupied or protected by the British, French, and Italians, with a portion set aside for a Jewish homeland. Being on the wrong side of WWI was a costly mistake.

During WWI there was the embarrassment of the Ottoman caliph's failure to inspire jihad against the Allied Powers. Just as badly, Arab-Ottoman Muslims in the Arab Revolt fought against the Ottoman Empire. According to Bernard Lewis. Princeton University Professor of Near Eastern Studies: "The moral significance of an Arab army fighting the Turks and, still more, of the ruler of the holy places denouncing the Ottoman Sultan and his so-called jihad against the British, French, and Italian empires with their significant colonial Muslim populations was immense."[vi,3]

The loss of the Ottoman Empire affected the global Muslim community in another way. In 1924, a decision was made by the Turkish government to end the caliphate. Muslims from all over the world convened a Caliphate Council to select a successor, but they were not successful.[vii] It was the first time in Islam's history that there would be no widely recognized religious successor to the Prophet Muhammad serving as the leader of the Muslim community.[4]

There were losses everywhere in the Islamic world. At the beginning of the Era of Empire Muslims knew only victory. In the end, Christian empires were ruling or "overseeing" Muslim lands everywhere. Then came one final loss. Muslim nations during WWII either chose neutrality or alignment with the Axis Powers;[5] once again choosing to be on the wrong side of history. Muslim nations ended up as minor players during the preparations for a newly unfolding global order.

In defeat, the Islamic empires left behind some significant victories. Second to the achievement of the Christian empires, Islamic empires set the stage for forty-nine future Muslim majority nations. The Arabic language became an official language in twenty-five nations; the third highest after English and French. Persian Shiite empires established Shiite Islam as an organized branch of Islam, and expanded followers to 10–20 percent of Muslims and nearly 50 percent of Muslims in the Middle East. In South Asia, the Mughal Empire facilitated creating the largest regional population of Muslims. Islamic empires created a foundation for Islam as a major enduring force in the world.

Chinese Empire

For centuries China was globally admired as an advanced civilization. Then came the Century of Humiliation. This was when the Chinese ceded Hong Kong,[6] and "negotiated" the so-called unequal treaties where the Chinese forewent sovereignty to barbarian powers and the Russian Empire permanently acquired about 1.5 million km^2 of land (in Outer Manchuria), a landmass larger than 173 of today's nations.

Toward the end of the humiliating century, the Chinese Empire's relatively small neighbor Japan inflicted some mortifying losses. In the First Sino-Japanese War (1894–1895) China lost Taiwan and the Liaodong Peninsula. In the Second Sino-Japanese War (1937–1945) 10–20 million Chinese citizens died from unnatural causes.[viii] The Chinese were victorious in this war, but it was the United States that compelled the Japanese to surrender, leaving the Chinese with a score to settle, maybe two.

Losses notwithstanding, the Chinese succeeded in creating one of the world's largest nations by landmass and population, expanding its influence throughout eastern Asia, and obtaining one of the five permanent Security Council seats. They created an enduring foundation for reinvigorating and perpetuating global power.

Russian/Soviet Empire

The final sixty-four years of empire for a proud military juggernaut were demoralizing. The Russians had a third more soldiers, but they lost the Crimean War (1853–1856) to a coalition that included the French, British, and Ottoman empires. In 1905 they lost the Russo-Japanese war to the comparative pipsqueak Japan. More mortification was around the corner. In 1917 the Russian Empire withdrew from WWI. They were only present for part of the war, but they lost 3–4 million soldiers and civilians, more than any other belligerent.[ix]

No longer a party to WWI, the new Russian leader, Vladimir Lenin, entered into the shameful Treaty of Brest-Litovsk to minimize the chance of a German assault. The terms were harsh and humiliating. Some said Lenin, who was vocal in his hatred for the European imperial powers, wanted to hand the Central Powers victory, but they lost, and Russia piled on more shame.

It looked like Russia (this time as the Soviet Union) was trying again to stack the deck for a German victory when it entered into the Molotov-Ribbentrop non-aggression pact with Germany two days before the official start of WWII. In further support for the Axis Powers, in April 1941 the Soviets signed a neutrality pact with Japan. But in June 1941 Germany and other Axis Power nations, but not Japan, invaded the Soviet Union. Now, the Soviets joined the Allied Powers. From the perspective of global power in the Era of Nation-States, Germany did the Soviet Union a favor.

On a mission to expand power further, the Soviets began building an empire of communist states. This ended-up instigating the Cold War. More than forty years of propaganda touting communist superiority and deprecating the first-world democracies, Russia was humiliated again.

The Russians succeeded in creating the largest nation by landmass, and expanding their influence throughout Eastern Europe and Central Asia. The Soviet Union controversially and temporarily extended influence throughout Central Europe. The Russians did not, however, succeed in creating a reliable foundation for expansion through language, common history, and religious aftermaths. But, Russia is a militarily powerful, veto-wielding Security Council member that has won a spot among global powers. For some, inclusion in the Russian sphere offers an alternative to the influence of western democracies, communist China, or Islamist states.

European empires

Europe's history is filled with wars and more wars. Every nation and empire suffered losses. The Polish-Lithuanian Commonwealth and the Swedish Empire lost all or most of their empires to the Russian Empire. Wars of conquest and independence decimated the Spanish Empire.

The French were serial losers. They lost most of their New World-empire in the late 18th century to the British. In the early 19th century the First French Empire was defeated by a European and Russian coalition.[7] The French were defeated again in the mid-19th century by a coalition of German-speaking states. WWI gave France a chance to settle a score with Germany. The Germans reciprocated in WWII when France was partially occupied, and operated, in part as a client state of Nazi Germany.

The Germans and Austrians were also serial losers. Over time the Habsburg Monarchy, also called the Austrian Monarchy, lost all its polities to coalitions of European powers and the Ottoman and Russian empires.[8] WWI's Allied Powers put the final nail in the Habsburg coffin and also killed the German Empire. The Germans and Austrians were soon angling for a comeback in WWII. The German-speaking duo lost again, this time to a coalition that included the British Empire, the Soviet Union, and the United States.

Victors and vanquished in WWI and WWII notwithstanding, there were no winners in Europe's carnage and physical destruction. And no winners in the competition for global supremacy; all of Europe's empires were dismantled. But Europe's empires left behind four continents dominated by European-blood majorities and Christianity, in addition to large populations of European language-speakers on every continent. This created a strong foundation for perpetuating influence in the Era of Nation-States. They also left behind six continents of history as the world's most successful conquerors and subjugators, which has been influential in tempering influence in the Era of Nation-States.

The United States

The United States made the short list of former colonies that became winners by expanding their landmass during the Era of Empire. It stands alone in rising from colony to superpower during this era.

Being absent from the constant wars of empires gave it increased possibilities for developing its economy, so much so it was loaning money to Allied Powers in WWI, and its participation in WWI was solicited and conditionally accepted. Victory gave it an opportunity to limit the expansion of empires. In WWII it played a more expansive role in victory, assuring its position atop the world stage. It used its presence to facilitate the creation of the United Nations, an organization committed to transitioning the world from empires to nation-states. The United States parlayed its wins to play a decisive role in ending the Era of Empire.

After WWII the United States was one of two economic and military superpowers. It had eclipsed the economic and military power of its former colonizer and everyone else in the world. While much of the world lay in shambles, the United States was intact and healthy; its economy had been growing 11-12 percent per year during the war.[x] Its industrial capacity at wars end dwarfed the capacity of any other nation. The United States only entered the global competition for supremacy on the tail end, but in 1945 all appearances indicated that it had been the greatest winner of the competition for global supremacy. This was incorrect.

The most valuable takeaway for any competitor was the creation of a foundation to build and perpetuate power in the Era of Nation-States. The United States might have been able to benefit from the foundations laid by Europe's empires, but they lacked historical ties with Europe's former colonies and experience building cross-nation relationships. Paradoxically, as the most powerful progenitor of Europe's dismantled empires, it was partially bequeathed the history of Europe's empires as conquerors and subjugators. This was not your normal thrill-of-victory spoil of war. This tempered American influence, but this global-power ingenue would soon create its own sources for modulating and rejecting its influence.

Notes

1. India's situation is a little different. The borders for independent India (1947) enclosed hundreds of previously self-governing princely states in addition to Portuguese India (1505–1961).
2. Argentina, Australia, and Saudi Arabia could be added to this list. All are regional dominants that share the religion, language, values, and systems of the motherlands of empire. They could piggyback off this to build a sphere of influence. But, like the United States, they lack historical colonial ties, and the history and experience as a competitor for global supremacy.
3. Turkish schools teach that the Arabs and the Arab Revolt is responsible for the loss of the Ottoman Empire. Some Arab schools teach students if the Turks had not discriminated against them, they would not have revolted.
4. There was no widely recognized caliph between 1258 and 1261 when the Mongols sacked the Abbasid Caliphate.
5. A few states officially aligned with the Allied Powers when victory was assured.
6. In 1984 the British agreed to return Hong Kong to China in 1997.

7. During the Napoleonic Wars (1803–1815) the Persian, Ottoman, and Russian empires all participated as allies and adversaries of Napoleon. In the final battle, it was the Europeans and Russians that defeated Napoleon.
8. The United States was part of the WWI Allied Power coalition.

References

i. Hamilton, Earl J. "Imports of Gold and Silver into Spain, 1503–1660." *The Quarterly Journal of Economics* 43, no. 3 (May 1929): 436–472.
ii. Andrews, G. R. *Afro-Latin America, 1800–2000*. Oxford: Oxford University Press, 2004.
iii. Henderson, K. D. *Survey of the Anglo-Egyptian Sudan (1898–1944)*. London: Longmans, Green, 1946.
iv. Krauze, Enrique. "In Mexico, a War Every Century." *New York Times*, September 14, 2014.
v. Evans, Martin. *Algeria: France's Undeclared War*. New York: Oxford University Press, 2012.
vi. Lewis, Bernard. *The Middle East: A Brief History of the last 2,000 years*. Scribner, 1995.
vii. Ekinci, Ekrem Bugra. "The Rise and Fall of the Islamic Caliphate in History." *The Daily Sabah*, March 3, 2017.
viii. "Sino-Japanese War." *History.co.uk*. Retrieved May 16, 2018.
ix. "World War I Casualties." *Centre-Robert-Schuman.org*. Retrieved December 28, 2018.
x. Goodwin, Doris. "The Way We Won: America's Economic Breakthrough During World War II." *The American Prospect*, Fall, 1992.

· 1 6 ·

POSTSCRIPTS

Aftermaths of Empire

For more than five hundred years, the prevailing wisdom was that global powers had colonial empires. This wisdom was dead. After 1945 no one was to maintain or increase power by subjugating people without their consent or forcibly commandeering land. It didn't work out perfectly. Some empires had postscripts—they weren't letting go.

There were no postscripts for WWII's losing empires; these empires were dissolving. But, outside WWII conquests, these empires were small. It was the winning Allied Powers that added the postscripts, but not the United Kingdom or the United States. Postscripts from Islamic empire successor states came later.

British leaders knew their colonies were not ready for independence, but most rejected offers of help. They wanted immediate independence and received it when requested. Some British leaders may have liked to maintain the power and glory that accompanied ruling an empire where the sun never set, but they had to accept that their day in the sun had ended. Should they waver, reminders were everywhere. The public was demonstrably unsupportive of empire. Colonies had been justified as a means to help—to civilize—the less fortunate while being suitable investments for economic growth. In reality, most British colonies consumed cash and after WWII British subjects[1] in Britain wanted investments to focus on rebuilding the United Kingdom. The

British people had also come to see the civilization objective as farcical when correspondents, like Winston Churchill, reported the British massacring Africans resisting colonization using the newly invented Maxim machine guns. Then came the 1956 reality of their former protectorate, Egypt, defeating Britain (and France) and taking control of the Suez Canal.

It was the Netherlands, Portugal,[2] China, France, and the Soviet Union that added empire postscripts. The French and Portuguese did end runs around the UN Charter. France created a constitution that made colonies, an integral part of the French Union and Portugal relabeled their colonies provinces of Portugal. They said it was for the benefit of their colonies and it may have been; most colonies were not prepared for independence. How could they be? It was standard practice for the empires to staff central colonial governments with expatriates from home. These bureaucrats were not directed to prepare colonies for independence.

Being unprepared was not the only reason to confiscate self-determination decisions. Little Portugal had gained a presence on the world stage through its empire. Relinquishing its empire would make it a globally insignificant nation. France relied on its empire to project power too. After being occupied by Germany for most of WWII (1940–1944), it was not feeling particularly muscular. Losing its colonies would make this worse.

The insecurities of France and Portugal notwithstanding, their re-labeled colonies wanted independence. The Portuguese provinces of Angola, Guinea Bissau, and Mozambique in sub-Saharan Africa fought long and brutal wars for independence. From the French Union, Algeria in sub-Saharan Africa, and Cambodia, Laos, and Vietnam from Southeast Asia fought extended wars for independence. Indonesia, a colony of the Netherlands, also had to fight for independence.

China also worked around the Charter. Mao Zedong, leader of the new People's Republic of China (PRC) "restored" lands from one of the Chinese Empire's most expansive dynasties, the Qing (1644–1911).[3] Mao, the leader of backward China, offered the hackneyed rationale of civilizing backward feudal societies. Buddhist-majority Tibet and Muslim-majority Xinjiang were re-annexed into the officially atheist PRC.

The grandest end run was by Soviet Premier Stalin. He manipulated and negotiated self-determination decisions to expand the perimeter of the Soviet sphere into the heart of Europe and northern China. Central European countries occupied by the Soviets at the end of WWII were virtually or in reality annexed into the Soviet sphere. The Soviets insisted that these nations had self-determined their governments, but in Poland, Czechoslovakia, East Germany, and Hungary the self-determination process included: mysterious deaths, forced resignations of non-communist leaders, politicians appointed by the Soviets rather than elected, election ballots filled with pre-screened communist candidates, and the destruction of non-communist parties. In Mongolia, the Soviets made sure there would be no opposition to communist rule. Once communism was "self-determined" it was abundantly clear that none of these nations were sovereigns; they were under the thumb of Moscow.

The disposition of Poland to the Soviet sphere[4] was unique and tragic. Poland had fielded the fourth largest Allied Power military force and lost 17 percent of its population. It was not fighting to be returned to Russian rule. But the Soviet Union was occupying Poland at wars end, and Stalin wanted Poland. The Baltic countries didn't even get a faux self-determination process. Their interwar period of independence following the dissolution of the Russian Empire was usurped by annexation into the Soviet Union.[5]

Because Yugoslavia and Albania had not been occupied, or "liberated" by the Soviet Union during WWII, they had greater freedom to maneuver. They really did self-determine communism, and they voluntarily became members of Cominform, the official forum for communist parties under Soviet control. Membership was temporary. In 1948 Yugoslavia was ejected. In 1961 Albania exited the Soviet sphere and entered the Chinese sphere.

Any doubts that Central Europe, excluding Albania and Yugoslavia, were in the Soviet sphere were soon erased. In 1956 when Hungarians revolted against Soviet policies, it was brutally suppressed. In 1968 the Soviets responded to Czechoslovakian political reforms with an invasion and forced a change of government.

The Soviet Union's postscripts had extraordinary repercussions and not just for the nations denied self-determination decisions. Its affront to the unfolding era of nation-states per the UN Charter instigated the Cold War. The Cold War became the mother of all postscripts.

There were no Islamic empires to make an end-run around the Charter; the last was disbanded after WWI. This did not negate the presence of aspiring leaders with eyes on the revival of a Muslim empire or caliphate. In time national leaders in Egypt, Libya, Iran, and Iraq would give it an unsuccessful go. There were also religious leaders like, Hassan al-Banna founder of the Muslim Brotherhood, and Iran's Ayatollah Khomeini that saw nation-states as antithetical to their aims to restore a global Islamic community. Al-Banna influenced Islamic militants, such as those in ISIS that trampled on the sovereignty of nations in the early 21st century in the manner of an invading vengeful empire pursuing a caliphate by restoring the lands ruled by Islamic empires, but "taken from them" by European and Russian empires.

The reaction to Khomeini's desire to create a united Islamic community spawned a postscript, not unlike the Cold War. The conflict and competition for Islamic supremacy between Shias and Sunnis wasn't settled in the Era of Empire. Now it was being reignited. Just like first- and second-world nations in the Cold War, battles would be fought as proxy wars. In this case the Iran-Saudi proxy wars.

Just like the Era of Empire, people that wanted nothing more than to be left alone were caught up in competitions between global powers, but the Era of Nation-States was supposed to be different.

*****

There was a long list of vanquished in the Era of Empire, but to think that they were subdued forever was foolhardy. Losers rarely accept defeat. The French rose from the ashes on multiple occasions. The German Empire was neutered after WWI, only to return stronger as the Third Reich. An observer in 1453 might have believed that the Islamic and Chinese empires were so far advanced that the Europeans and Russians were hopeless. Then came the Europeans first mover advantage in industrialization and it looked like the Chinese, Islamic and Russian empires were so far behind it was hopeless. Wrong again.

*****

No period in history has had a grander impact on the world we live in than the Era of Empire. This was when many foundational components of the world were established. When the competition began in 1453 there were three inhabited continents; when it ended, there were three more. These became the Old World and the New World respectively.

When the Era of Empire began, organized religions were present on 2¼ continents. When it ended, they were majority religions on the six inhabited continents. Christians dominated 4.5 continents. Islam dominated a quarter of all nations. In 1453 the world was a tower of babel. In 1945 nine languages propagated by expanding empires were connecting nations all over the world. The aftermaths of religion and language have made the world less complicated and easier to navigate. They have also created immense populations with conflicting religious beliefs and disconnected by language.

By importing and exporting diverse populations to fill needs for labor or satisfy objectives for security, the empires changed the world from homogenous to heterogeneous societies. "Managing" these diverse populations was accomplished with discriminatory practices, like social hierarchies, enslavement, and massacres. Diversifying and socially stratifying the world created enormous challenges for the leaders of new and old nations alike. It was utopian to think that national leaders could commit to equality and these challenges would fade into oblivion

The competition for empire created victors and vanquished. In the end, the Europeans were on top although surveying the European continent in 1945 would have drawn a different conclusion. It was only apparent by observing the global footprints of descendants, languages, and religions, the designation of three western permanent UN Security Council members, and the rules enshrined in the UN Charter to guide an era of nation-states.

A re-run of the Era of Empire's conquering empires competing for global supremacy is unlikely, but a world united behind the ways of European and other western powers is out of the question. It was starry-eyed to believe the western-influenced plans for the Era of Nation-States finalized at the San Francisco conferences while WWII was winding down after five globally terrifying years, would be dutifully carried out after the competitors for global supremacy had time to rebuild and reassess their strategies.

Notes

1. Until 1983 all citizens of the British Commonwealth were called subjects.
2. Portugal was not a member of WWII's Allied Powers.
3. China used this same rationale in the early 21st century when it usurped small islands/atolls claimed by other nations in the South China Sea.
4. The Soviet sphere included nations from the regions of Eastern Europe, Central Asia, and Central Europe, except Yugoslavia and Albania.
5. In the Molotov-Ribbentrop Pact, Stalin and Hitler agreed that the Baltic countries would be part of the Soviet Union. Even though Hitler violated the pact and a Nazi signature was worthless after WWII, Stalin demanded that this "secret pact" be honored.

· 1 7 ·

UNDOING EMPIRE

The transition from an era of empires to an era of nation-states was monumental and unprecedented. In the Era of Empire conquering armies and militias overpowered indigenous populations to extend political power across continents. Autocratic, repressive rule controlled economic resources and presided over hierarchies of discrimination. The characteristics of the Era of Nation-States were to be completely different. There would be dozens of relatively small independent nations with internationally recognized borders, and each would be committed to encouraging human rights and fundamental freedoms, refraining from the use of armed forces except in the "common interest," acquiring power through economic growth, and respecting the sovereignty of every nation.

When the transition began in 1945 about a quarter of today's nations were independent sovereigns. Most of these became independent in two waves between 1776 and 1945. Starting in 1945 there were four more waves.

Wave one took place between 1776 and 1829. When it began, there were already several independent nations, many of which also ruled empires, including China, Denmark, France, Great Britain, the Netherlands, Portugal, Russia, Spain, and Sweden. To secure independence in wave one you had to fight for it. Nineteen New World colonies in the Americas successfully waged wars for independence from the British, French, Spanish, and Portuguese empires. One, the United States was part of ESNA; the rest were from Latam. When this wave ended, most independent nations were in the New World Americas and Western Europe.

The second wave (1830–1944) brought independence to several new nations in Western Europe and the Middle East. Many were successor states of the defeated Austria-Hungary, German and Ottoman empires of WWI. A handful secured independence in the melee of the revolutions ending the Chinese and Russian empires. Excluding the Middle East, for all but two nations created after WWI, independence was as temporary as the lapse between the end of the Russian Empire and an expanding Soviet Union. [1,2] Finland escaped the Soviet clutch. When it did, it attached itself to Western Europe. Yugoslavia was a communist nation but escaped rule by Moscow.

Waves three through six took place between 1945 and 1991 and yielded 136 new nations; on average that was three new nations per year. Wave three (1945–1959) was the Asian wave. Twenty-five percent of today's countries secured independence from European empires, nearly doubling the tally of sovereign nations. Except for Central Asia, which had been incorporated into the Soviet Union, this wave brought independence to colonies in all other Asian regions. With few exceptions, [3] the nations of Eastern Asia, South Asia, Southeastern Asia, and Western Asia (the Middle East) were now independent.

The fourth wave took place in the 1960s and 1970s and yielded independence for another quarter of today's countries. This wave was centered in sub-Saharan Africa. The fifth wave took place in the 1970s and 1980s. This was when most smaller island nations from ESNA and Oceania became independent from European empires.

The sixth wave was a rogue wave. Unexpectedly, the Soviet sphere dissolved (1989–1991) and Central Europe, Eastern Europe, and Central Asia became regions of nation-states.

*****

The year 1945 marked the end of the competition for global supremacy and the start of the transition to nation states. National leaders were completely unprepared for the challenges of nation building which were complicated again by empire aftermaths and postscripts. Independence was though contagious, and the regional rollout of nations was rapid and unstoppable. Predictably it was also calamitous.

Notes

1. Turkey became independent in 1923. Saudi Arabia and Iraq became independent in the 1930s. Lebanon became independent in 1942.

2. Independence for most of these nations would not have occurred without US President Woodrow Wilson making participation in WWI contingent on the provision of self-determination for territories in the losing empires. That it turned out to be temporary for most was an indication that the world had not yet accepted the idea of self-determination.

3. Some nations chose to remain tied to Britain a little longer, including Brunei (SEA), and MENA's Bahrain, Kuwait, Oman, Qatar, and the UAE. Independence for Cambodia, Laos, and Vietnam was clouded by the Second Indochina War (1955–1975).

· 1 8 ·

EPILOGUE

Shifting the world from a configuration of empires to nation states is the most ambitious endeavor ever undertaken by humans. Before this, the most ambitious was a 500-year competition for global supremacy between the Chinese, European, Islamic and European empires. Grasping the essentials of these two truly unprecedented ventures is key to securing context that can simplify understanding the world where we live.

For hundreds of years the Chinese, European, Islamic, and Russian empires dictated the directions of the world. They controlled commerce and the factors of production, shifted and ordered populations like pawns on a chessboard, and applied aggression without sufficient forethought to the consequences. Repression, discrimination, and persecution were pervasive. This draconian era in history came to a close in 1945. The agreed upon plan for replacing it spelled motherhood and apple pie. Execution relied on UN members, and very importantly the five permanent members of the Security Council, adhering to commitments in the UN Charter. Most did not.

Before the Charter's unanimous approval in 1945 there were blatant signs that the Soviet Union had no intention of abandoning empire. The Molotov-Ribbentrop Pact negotiated on behalf of Stalin and Hitler may have contained a secret land agreement, but the Soviet's overt meddling in Central Europe while an Allied Power was not a secret. Lands were being prepared for annexation. Radio stations were commandeered to broadcast Soviet propaganda, and trained secret police were installed.[i] The confiscation of assets was reminiscent of colonial rule.

During different WWII conferences, the Big Three (the Soviet Union, the United Kingdom, and the United States) were negotiating aspects of the impending global configuration of nation states. At Yalta (1945) FDR wanted the UN, Churchill wanted democratic elections in Central and Eastern Europe, and Stalin wanted Central and Eastern Europe in the Soviet sphere. Stalin was broadcasting and rebroadcasting an empire comeback. High-level Soviet participation at the San Francisco conferences had been in limbo but ostensibly occurred as an insurance policy. If the UN succeeded where the League of Nations failed the Soviets wanted to make sure they would not be denied a promised permanent Security Council seat with its unique power to veto transgressions, like those from the Soviet Union. Stalin was right to be paranoid, after all, he wasn't honoring his Big Three commitments.[ii,iii]

Stalin gave a war-weary world reasonable doubt of his imperial ambitions by overseeing faux free elections in Central Europe where every nation selected communist governments.[1] By 1950 the Soviet Union had forcibly taken control of Central Europe and vetoed forty-one UN initiatives; no one else had vetoed any. Among the many vetoes were the admission of new UN members that would strengthen the first-world alliance,[2] a measure calling on the Soviet Union to end its blockade of Berlin in 1948, and measures to address an unfolding Korean War.[iv]

It was becoming obvious that the needed alignment among the five permanent members of the Security Council was missing. They lacked agreement on: the meanings of self-determination, fundamental freedoms for all, and a global configuration of nation-states; what it meant to infringe on sovereign rights; and what their roles were in a world of nation-states, including overseeing peace.

The Soviet Union and China were aligned on a mission of global communism.[3] This mission was the antithesis of the UN Charter. It called for very controlling, repressive, expansive states, like empires. This, however, is not how they saw it.[v] They painted themselves like Robin Hoods stealing from the rich and giving to the poor. They were offering the global masses a superior alternative to the flawed, discriminatory system of capitalism.

The Russians and Chinese were strange bedfellows. During the competition for empire, no one had taken more land from the Chinese than the Russians. The Russians also tangled in Xinjiang province in violation of a non-aggression pact and provided support for Mongolian independence from China.

Fearing the worst, Winston Churchill said, "if the Western democracies stand together in strict adherence to the principle of the United Nations Charter, their influence for furthering those principles will be immense and no one is likely to molest them." The problem with this was that the western democracies were not supposed to do this. The plan called for nations united.

Churchill was anyway asking a lot from the western democracies, many of which had only recently recommitted to democracy. Democracy in Europe was nearly destroyed in the interwar years. Most nations dissolved their legislatures, some adopted fascism, and communism gained adherents. Capitalism had a rough ride too, made rockier by its ugly outcomes during the Great Depression. To the surprise of many, after WWII, democracy and capitalism were adapted and revived in Western Europe, while fascism and Stalinism, a Stalin-styled communism, found tepid support outside Iberia. The western democracies did end up united; however, it was not without molestation.

The Cold War commenced. From a permanent Security Council perspective, the United States, France, and the United Kingdom from the First World, stood in opposition to the Soviet Union and China from the Second World. Actually, until 1971, it was only the Soviet Union because Taiwan held China's Security Council seat and Taiwan's alignment was with the First World.[4]

Early into the Cold War (1948) all permanent Security Council members agreed that Israel should become a sovereign nation. It wasn't long before the Soviet Union was having second thoughts about supporting anything that France, the United Kingdom, and the United States supported, even though the Russians had played a conspicuous role in the emergence of the Jewish Question. The Soviet Union became a supporter of Arab nations that were committed to the elimination of Israel, a UN recognized sovereign.

The Soviet Union's deceptive support for the UN Charter gave a green light to others to welsh on their UN commitments. France, a western democracy had already done this. In 1946 France altered its constitution to make colonies part of the French Union. Colonists were now French citizens with equal rights. Who would want independence when they could be French citizens? Quite a few, minimally the ones that weren't granted equal rights because citizenship was not available to everyone.

If France could camouflage imperial actions so could others. China, France, the Netherlands, Portugal, and the Soviet Union all thwarted colonial independence.[5] None provoked a UN resolution to intervene.[6] Perhaps it was due to the veto power afforded to the permanent members of the Security Council, or because there was a preoccupation with self-preservation. The Soviet plan called for a Europe of communist nations in 20–30 years.[vi] For others there was the paranoia of secret Soviet plans.

With the Soviet Union threatening world peace and the UN Security Council neutered as a peacekeeper, nations had to develop strategies to defend their sovereignty. Nations on opposite sides during the world wars were joining forces. On April 4, 1949, France, Germany, Turkey, the United Kingdom, Portugal, Canada, the United States and others in Western Europe became part of the North Atlantic Treaty Organization (NATO).

On February 15, 1950, the Soviet Union signed a mutual defense treaty with the People's Republic of China (PRC). Later in 1950, the Korean War began. This was the first major Cold War conflict.[7] The Soviet Union and China supported communist North Korea, while a UN-supported military coalition with the United States in the lead defended anti-communist South Korea.

The Soviets could have vetoed UN Resolution 83 providing for UN-sanctioned military assistance to South Korea,[8] but they chose not to vote on the resolution. After the fact, Stalin rationalized the non-vote in a letter to the president of Czechoslovakia. It was portrayed as the work of a brilliant strategist distracting the United States and painting the Americans as warmongers. He thought this would give the Soviet Union an unfettered opportunity to turn Europe into a collection of communist nations. Omitted from the letter was making it clear that their so-called Chinese ally would bear the burden and also be distracted in the war,[9] giving the Soviet Union a second opportunity for expansion. While China was distracted, Russia could leverage unrest in Eastern Asia to promote the safety of Soviet communism.[vii]

Stalin's letter was proof positive that the permanent Security Council members as a guarantor of peace was a farce. Duplicitous permanent Security Council members in combination with the Sino-Soviet alliance conjured up some of the worst possibilities discussed at the San Francisco conferences. Like the fear a permanent Security Council member would force the adoption of communism, and the UN would be powerless to stop it. This motivated more military alliances. Between 1951 and 1960, the Philippines, Thailand, South Korea, and Japan signed collective defense treaties with the United States. In the Rio Treaty (1947) nineteen Latam nations aligned with the United States for protection.[10] In 1955 the Warsaw Pact was created between the Soviet Union and seven satellites in Central Europe.[11]

The problem with the creation of powerful militaries and alliances was that war was not the answer and could not be the answer. By 1964 all five permanent members of the Security Council could detonate nuclear bombs. War between the nuclear-armed First and Second Worlds was a formula for mutually assured destruction. This was the WWIII that the end of the competition for global supremacy and the creation of the UN were supposed to prevent.

A worse turn of events for the Era of Nation-States was scarcely imaginable. The plans devised in San Francisco in 1945 to facilitate the transition from empires to nation-states were words on a page. Brand new nations embarking on a foundational decision—their choice of government became pawns in a superpower global chess game for and against communism. The world was embarking on an unprecedented transition without foresight, plan, or neutral overseer.

Another essential part of that transition, per the UN Charter, was the construction of nations committed to equal freedoms for all, and the protection of fundamental human rights. From the beginning of the Era of Nation-States, success on this front was similarly challenged.

Communism had no use for freedom from fear, freedom of thought, conscience, or arbitrary detention. Freedom of religion was replaced with the freedom to be an atheist. Holding religion dear could cost people their lives. Fundamental human rights were not an issue; there were none. Reports on the implementation of communism in the Soviet Union, China, Cambodia, Ethiopia, and Vietnam told of: the imprisonment and mass slaughter of landowners, intellectuals, clergy, and others perceived to oppose communism; the wholesale destruction of houses of worship; widespread censorship; massive expropriations; and widespread famines triggered by collectivized agriculture. Tens of millions were murdered and tortured, and hundreds of millions repressed.[12] Meanwhile, the UN was powerless to intervene in anything intra-nation.

To the first-world's western democracies, communism didn't just threaten freedoms and human rights it threatened the totality of their political and economic systems, religion, society and life itself. China's Mao said if the mass casualties from nuclear strikes against the western world could enable global communism, he was willing to have the Chinese pay this price. Global communism was the mission espoused by Mao, Marx, and Lenin. Each knew that everyone had to be communist for it to work. There could be no opponents.

Western democracies may have lived in fear of the Red Scare of communism stealing their freedoms and rights, but they were crummy overseers for the freedoms and rights of people in some of their "allied" nations. At one-point US President Jimmy Carter (1977–1981) stepped up to the plate and supported policies that tied foreign aid to human rights. Allies in Central America rejected the policy, and gave the Soviet Union an opportunity to build alliances in America's backyard.[viii] Converting a national leader from the First to the Second World and vice versa was easy. Allegiance, such as it was, was sold to the highest bidder.

Some first-world democracies with the motivational backdrop of WWII's genocides and other crimes against humanity implemented initiatives to limit overt discrimination. But this was in their nations. Many of these same nations condoned the despotic, discriminatory behaviors of allied anti-communist dictators ruling third-world nations. There was, however, plenty of blame to go around for the failures to address discriminatory practices. The UN prohibition on interfering in intra-nation matters made it completely reliant on national leaders to honor their Charter commitments to facilitate fundamental freedoms for all, and a universal respect for human rights. Those honoring these Charter commitments were in short supply.

Heaped upon empire aftermaths, like diverse and discriminated populations, were the normal daunting challenges of nation-building, in addition to the abnormal challenges related to the Cold War. Tackling this myriad of challenges would have tested qualified leaders, but most leaders were not qualified. Underskilled, inexperienced and misguided national leaders were everywhere. The success of most countries was riding on a wing and a prayer. Underqualified leaders neglected their nation-building responsibilities, like facilitating fundamental freedoms for all, and they introduced countless intra-nation problems by engaging in despotism, divide and rule practices, instigating civil wars, and participating in and presiding over serious levels of corruption.

One UN recourse was to supply resources, like loans from the World Bank. These were readily accepted but getting national leaders to honor the terms less so. Instead of national leaders investing in education or infrastructure that could support nation building, money was often squandered, or landed in the pockets of political elites and their cronies.

It's common to frame Cold War-related conflicts as proxy wars between the Soviet Union on a mission of spreading global communism, and the United States as the chief missionary for democracy. But this was only part of the story. The Cold War was a hellish period in history where many national leaders and wannabes settled scores and abused their power. A leader just had to be seen as a valuable ally to a permanent member of the Security Council, and they could operate with virtual impunity.

Some Cold War-related conflicts had nothing to do with political and economic ideology. Some national leaders professed to be anti-communist (not democratic, just anti-communist) or communist as a ruse to secure financial and military aid from first- or second-world nations. They could be anti-communist one minute and communist the next. Allegiance was sold to the highest bidder. Some national leaders didn't even pretend to be communist or anti-communist; they simply exchanged allegiance for foreign aid. Any leader, including despots like the Democratic Republic of the Congo's (DR-Congo) Sese Seko, Noriega in Panama, or the Duvaliers in Haiti could use the specter of communism to get the undivided attention of the United States. The United States alone dispensed more than $300 billion in foreign aid during the Cold War.[ix] The second-world nations dispensed aid too. Anyone professing a desire to lead a communist nation could entice the Soviet Union or China, including despotic Mengistu in Ethiopia, Ho Chi Minh in North Vietnam, Pol Pot in Cambodia, and Kim il-Sung in North Korea.

The Cold War became a cover for national leaders angling for global power or to engage in retribution for events with ties, often loose ties, to the Era of Empire. Libyan leader Muammar Qaddafi was neither communist nor democrat. He supported both communist and non-communist insurrections in Latam, Northern Ireland, and sub-Saharan Africa. He was a vocal anti-imperialist[13] that ironically aspired to empire. Cuba's communist leader Fidel Castro was unabashed in his hatred for the United States and sent revolutionaries to support communist insurrections in Latam and sub-Saharan Africa. Fidel Castro, like Mao, hated the United States so intensely he was prepared to sacrifice his people. He proposed the "launching of a nuclear strike on the United States." He said, "the Cuban people are prepared to sacrifice themselves for the cause of the destruction of imperialism and the victory of world revolution."[x]

China and Russia may have begun the Cold War as communist comrades, but this didn't last. They had been competitors in the Era of Empire, and they were competitors for communist leadership. The Sino-Soviet split began in 1960. Tensions became so intense, nuclear war seemed probable. Harvard Professor Jeremy Friedman characterized the intense conflict between the Soviet Union and China as a shadow Cold War.[xi]

Between 1945 and 1991 there were more than one hundred Cold War-related conflicts where a total of 20 million died. All but 200,000 were from new nations.xii One extremely destructive aftermath of the reality of, or the specter of, Cold War conflicts was that first-, second- and third- world nations, many of which had been previously unarmed with modern weapons, were now filled with them. Armed conflicts during the Cold War set nation building backward all over the world. Additional armed conflicts in the post-Cold War period made possible by weapons proliferation promised more of the same. There were other destructive Cold War spillover effects. First- and second-world nations supporting leaders that feigned ideological alignment left many corrupt and repressive despots in power for decades. Acquiring power and lives of luxury, not nation building was their priority.

It was the hellish period of the Cold War that neutered the aspiration of a world configured by equal independent sovereigns that was so prominent at the San Francisco conferences. Into the void of UN directions and reneged member commitments came the influence of familiar faces. Russia, returning as the Soviet Union was more powerful than it had ever been. The projection of power by Mao put China back on the world stage. The United States was a fresh face and quite capable.

France and the United Kingdom were not the powers they had been in the Era of Empire, and this was not their goal. A compelling presence on the world stage would come through a collective presence. After WWII, the nations in Western Europe decided they would collectively and peacefully acquire power primarily with a regional alliance that later became the European Union (EU). Military strength for the union came through NATO. Additional power on the world stage came through their two permanent Security Council members, the United Kingdom, and France.

World powers looked a lot like they had in the Era of Empire with one big exception; there was no Islamic power. There had been chances for Arab Muslim states and other Muslim states to create a coalition, like the EU that would keep them present on the world's stage. During WWI Emir Faisal was an heir apparent to a potential Arab empire or coalition, but he knew the challenges were significant. "The Turks departed from our lands and we are now as children. We have no government, no army, and no educational system." "The Arabs are diverse peoples living in different regions. The Aleppan is not the same as the Hijazi, nor is the Damascene the same as the Yemeni. That is why my father [the Sharif of Mecca] has made the Arab lands each follow their own special laws that are in accordance with their own circumstances and people."xiii,14

There were also newer challenges with creating a coalition of Muslim nations. Europe had been influencing this region for more than a century, and the European notions of sovereign nations and nationalism were attractive. Throughout the Ottoman Empire, diverse Arab tribal and ethnic groups lived in relative isolation with a fair amount of responsibility for governing. Separate cultures and histories developed. After WWI many groups weren't yearning for an Ottoman replacement and definitely not a European replacement; they were aspiring to be independent nations. Discoveries of oil further minimized interest in a union of Muslim states from those that were resource endowed. MENA would take the path of a collection of small and mid-sized Sunni- and Shiite-majority nations, one unwanted Jewish state, and no member on the permanent Security Council.

The unwanted Jewish state motivated successive Arab-Israeli wars. Because the Soviets supported the Arabs and the United States supported Israel, the UN was powerless to stop them. At least, the Shias and Sunnis appeared to have buried the hatchet and were more or less co-existing in peace, but this changed. The Iranian Revolution took place in 1979 triggering a major earthquake in Shiite-Sunni relations. Iran's Ayatollah Khomeini, the Supreme Leader of a Shiite nation, tried to unite Islam under his rule. This challenged the Sunni leader of Shiite-majority Iraq, Saddam Hussein, instigating the 20th century's longest war—the Iran-Iraq War (1980–1988). And it challenged the rulers of Saudi Arabia, the leaders of the Muslim world's most influential nation. Now the most powerful Sunni and Shiite nations were competing for religious and political influence.

The Iranian Revolution ended up elevating the presence of two Islamist nations, Iran and Saudi Arabia, on to the world stage. Their place among China, the EU, Russia, and the United States was different. These were relatively middling powers, and they lacked a permanent seat on the Security Council. Where they were similar was that they were building spheres of influence in geographic areas ruled by predecessor empires, in this case, Islamic empires.

When the Cold War ended, there was hope that the ideals of the United Nations would get a restart and nations of the world would honor Charter commitments; in particular aspects of democracy like free and fair elections and protecting fundamental freedoms for all. Stanford University professor Francis Fukuyama suggested this was "The End of History." He wrote, "What we may be witnessing is not just the end of the Cold War, or the passing of a particular period of post-war history, but the end of history as such: that is, the end point of mankind's ideological evolution and the universalization of Western liberal democracy as the final form of human government."[xiv]

The UN became an overt supporter of democracy. "World leaders pledged in the Millennium Declaration to spare no effort to promote democracy and strengthen the rule of law, as well as respect for human rights and fundamental freedoms."[xv]

There was more good news for democracy when the internet surfaced. It was perceived as a force for good broadcasting previously censored information about life in the freedom rich, first-world nations. Repressed people would demand democratic freedoms. Branding the internet as a force for good was naive. It was just as easy to publish propaganda that made it a force for evil, and to brand democracy as unjust.

It was similarly naive to think that the world had agreed that liberal democracy would have the last say on government. The Cold War exposed communism's weaknesses relative to democracy and capitalism, but it was not democracy that won; it was the First World, and one look at the anti-communist despots on their payroll would cast doubt on a shared goal of implanting democracy. The real mission was to defeat communism. If they succeeded in getting converts to democracy, so much the better. It was a mission similar to the anti-fascist common enemy that bound WWII's Allied Powers.

It was equally naive to think that the UN's overt support for democracy would motivate an autocrat to convert. A post-Cold War conference to re-commit to the UN Charter was out of the question. The UN may have become an overt supporter of the principles of democracy, but support was not unanimous. Noticeably absent were autocratic China, Iran, Russia, and Saudi Arabia. Across the world the desire for an IGO committed to nation-building, peace and fundamental freedoms for all had waned. In 1945 the world was filled with subjugated colonials, and free people living in fear of conquering empires and WWIII. Now, colonies had gained their independence, and the threat of conquering empires had diminished.

Many nations chastised the UN Charter as a document filled with western ideals and a vehicle for western imperialists and other permanent Security Council members to control the world. Some refused to honor the terms of IMF and World Bank loans because conditions were too western and not customized for developing and non-western nations.[xvi] If there had ever been universal agreement on humanistic principles, and the meaning of self-determination; this was no longer the case.[xvii,xviii] The Cold War put a forty-four-year curse on the Era of Nation-States that permanently eviscerated the UN and the motherhood and apple pie ideals that drove its creation, like fundamental freedoms for all.

Still, there was a glimmer of hope that the permanent Security Council members would be united in upholding peace and security. On August 2, 1990 Iraq, invaded Kuwait and shortly afterward declared Kuwait its 19th province.[15] The Security Council supported a military response. China, Sunni and Shiite Muslim nations, Russia, and the western world condemned Iraq's actions. The US-led military coalition in the Gulf War (1990–1991) included thirty-two nations.

Following 9/11 the Security Council unanimously adopted a resolution calling on all member nations to facilitate justice. For the first time in history, Article 5 of NATO was invoked, which calls for a joint response when a NATO member is attacked. But it was not just NATO members that responded. Fifty-nine nations participated in Operation Enduring Freedom, including China, Iran, and Russia. The UN Security Council appeared to be working again.

These united responses turned out to be rare. The world was still ideologically divided. Nations were autocracies or democracies, capitalist-weighted or socialist-weighted, Muslim or non-Muslim, western or non-western, fiercely protecting religious freedoms or religiously intolerant. Security Council members continued exercising their vetoes to protect their interests and the interests of those in their present or prospective sphere of influence.

Russia vetoed resolutions that would have negated its illegal annexation of Crimea in Ukraine, and that would have provided for UN peacekeeping in Georgia following the Russo-Georgian war. China and Russia vetoed actions condemning human rights abuses or unfree and unfair elections in Myanmar, Syria, and Zimbabwe that were supported by France, the United Kingdom, and the United States. The United States vetoed actions against Israel.

Islamic powers didn't have a veto, but they had a collective voice. The Organization of Islamic Cooperation (OIC) became the largest voting bloc in the UN, and they were using their combined heft to advance and alter UN initiatives. In 1990 OIC members adopted the Cairo Declaration of Human Rights, a sharia-inspired non-universal version of the UN's Universal Declaration of Human Rights. Among differences, the Cairo Declaration does not support freedom of religion or equal freedoms for women.[xix]

In the post-Cold War period the global stage continued to be occupied by China, the EU as a successor to the European empires, Iran and Saudi Arabia as successors to Islamic empires, Russia, and the United States. The power quotients were however changing. Russia was a single nation not a union of fifteen republics with virtual control over the Central European region. This didn't alter Russian power as much as might be expected. Former Soviet republics aspiring to shift to the EU sphere, like Estonia, Latvia, and Lithuania had already done, were put on notice that there would be no more defections. Russia let the entire world know that former Soviet republics were part of its near abroad—its sphere of influence. The Russian military supported these positions.

In 2009, four months after the UN attempted to extend its mission in Georgia following the Russo-Georgian war, Russia passed a law giving it the "right" to invade sovereign nations if people of Russian blood were in danger. In the Russian Empire and the Soviet Union, the transportation of "trusted" Russians into territories or republics had been part of Russia's security program. Now, these Russians became a lawful reason to compromise the territory of a sovereign nation. In February 2014, a coup in Ukraine ousted the president, an ally of Russian President, Vladimir Putin. In March Russia exercised a "legal right" in violation of international law to invade Ukraine and then annexed the Ukrainian region of Crimea with its majority ethnic Russian population.[16]

When voices all over the world protested this violation of international law, Putin dismissed the protests by saying "In people's hearts and minds, Crimea has always been an integral part of Russia."[xx] This was Russian propaganda at its best. There are few populations in the history of the Russian Empire more persecuted than the indigenous Muslim Tatars of Crimea. By 1945 the Tatars had experienced five episodes of expulsions or forced emigration.[17]

After this, an enormous re-militarization campaign on the Crimean Peninsula took place. Russia was letting nations in the former Soviet sphere know that their old master was nearby. The military juggernaut had once again commanded a position on the world stage in spite of its relatively weak economic performance. In 2014 Russia had the 10th largest GDP, which was 10–20 percent of the GDPs of China, the EU, or the United States.[18]

During the Cold War, China's presence on the world stage was minor compared to the Soviet Union or the United States. Economic performance was one reason. In 1978, the Soviet Union's GDP was 5.5 times larger than China's. In 1978, China implemented economic reforms. By 1992, the GDPs in China and Russia were relatively similar, and the Chinese economy was no longer hindering the power of its presence on the world stage.

In 1995 the World Trade Organization (WTO) superseded GATT, removing many trade restrictions that had existed between first- and second-world nations. China became a WTO member in 2001. In 2017 China's GDP was eight times larger than Russia's. Russia's military power was greater, but China was catching up.

The objective to be a military superpower was something new in the Chinese playbook, and this was a necessary change for a re-emerged Chinese global power. The Chinese Empire had been a relative military weakling that cost it dearly during the Century of Humiliation. This time, China's presence on the world stage would be felt economically and militarily.

China's global influence was already soaring through trade and its expanding military, when it became a generous contributor of foreign aid and an enormous supplier of loans to support its Belt and Road initiative, a strategy to physically and electronically connect China to Asia, Europe, and Africa by leveraging Chinese loans, goods, and services. Some saw China as a neo-colonial power using Chinese debt to finance initiatives to keep nations tied to its sphere of influence,[xxi] and others saw China working to recreate its tributary empire.[xxii] Both perceptions were at odds with China's portrayal of a benevolent nation facilitating mutual prosperity.

In the early 21st century China expanded its military capabilities by fortifying some atolls in the South China Sea. China rationalized the takeovers of land and surrounding water claimed by other sovereigns as being part of the territories ruled by the Chinese Empire.[19] The Permanent Court of Arbitration, an IGO located in the Hague, Netherlands, ruled against China's claims in 2016. China ignored the ruling.

Retaking lands under the rationale that they had been part of a predecessor empire brought to the fore the insanity that would ensue if all the major players from the Era of Empire chose to do the same. Britain could contest China's ownership of Hong Kong, Portugal could contest Macau, and Japan, Taiwan and Manchuria. China would though be able to challenge Russia for Vladivostok. Russia could rationalize the acquisition of countries in Eastern Europe and Central Asia, just like Crimea. What would be the fate of the Marshall Islands if the former rulers/overseers of Spain, Germany, Japan, and the United States all claimed these islands? Turkey could claim much of the MENA region, Syria could claim Spain, and the British most of the world. The British, French, Spanish, Dutch, and Russians could claim parts of the United States.

In the post-Cold War period, the power of the EU was increased. The EU came into effect in 1993 with twelve members. In 2013 there were twenty-eight members; eleven were from Central Europe. A loss in Russia's sphere of influence was the EU's gain. Militarily Europe was also strengthened. At the end of the Cold War, NATO had 16 members. All, but Canada and the United States were European. By 2017 there were twenty-nine members. The thirteen newest members were from Central Europe.

In the post-Cold War period, Iran and Saudi Arabia continued expanding their ideological influence through sponsorship of mosques, madrassas, preachers and "aid" for Islamic militants committed to their ideological goals. Saudi Arabia with its much greater financial capabilities has had wider reach. In 2014 Turkey became another competitor for influence in MENA and the broader Muslim world. Turkey's President Erdogan (2014–?) has been increasingly characterized as an aspiring caliph reviving Ottoman greatness.[xxiii] This was a significant turn of events. Turkey has been a member of NATO since 1952 and in some stage of accession to the EU since 1987. In MENA, Turkey's forecasted shift was not wholly welcome. Repositioning away from the west and democratic rule might be welcome but not a new potential competitor for regional power.[xxiv]

The newest member of the global powers was the United States. Before the end of WWII, the United States was hailed as a giant killer for winning independence from the British Empire, and the grandest advocate for ending subjugated empire rule. After WWII it inherited some former colonial angst more appropriately directed at Europe's empires, and it was cast as a neo-imperial power, among other uncomplimentary characterizations. Most damaging to its reputation has been its steadfast, but controversial support for Israel, its hypocritical support for despots during the Cold War, bypassing UN support when launching the Iraq War (2003–2011), and the regular displays of international ignorance so unseemly for a superpower.

After the Cold War, security concerns were diminishing, and many nations wanted to distance themselves from the United States, even their long-time Western European allies. Previously inconceivable, during the Iraq War, France and Germany[20] aligned with Russia against the United States.[xxv] This Euro friendship with Russia began to fade in 2009 when Russia slashed gas supplies to Europe, due to a dispute with Ukraine. The year 2014 saw the relationship really wane. This was when Russia was involved in shooting down a passenger jet filled with Dutch citizens,[xxvi] and in violation of international law annexed Crimea and promoted succession in eastern Ukraine.

Western European nations may have needed a refresher course on the basis and value of the relationship between nations on both sides of the North Atlantic, but five EU members from Central Europe that border or are across the sea from Crimea and Ukraine did not. They saw the United States as key to their defense should Russia invade their nations. All the above, in addition to the increasing frequency of terrorist acts from anti-western Muslim militants, helped to renew the Atlantic Alliance.

Rising Russia, China, Iran, Saudi Arabia, and Turkey, in combination with reckless North Korea, contributed to keeping the United States, uncomplimentary characteristics and all, clearly influential on the world stage. Minimally as an economic titan with a world-beating military that supports its ongoing role as a global cop. From a choice of global powers, the United States has been seen as the least-worst global-cop option.

The return of the motherlands of empire to the world stage was predictable. Great powers don't yield power easily or lose gracefully. In this case, it was even more predictable. The major players in the Era of Empire had embedded their histories, and implanted their languages, religions, political ideologies and even their people all over their empires. They had created a solid foundation to rebuild spheres of influence on the very same lands controlled by their predecessor empires.

Some nations have demonstrated that they want to cut ties and enter another sphere of influence. There can be valid reasons to do this. Seventy-five years after the Era of Nation-States began, national leaders in less than a quarter of the nations in the world have managed to build advanced economies. There are more nations struggling with basics than there are advanced economies.

All advanced nations have adopted democratic and capitalist-weighted systems. All are western nations with historical ties to Europe's empires except a couple of small oil kingdoms on the Arabian Peninsula, and Japan and South Korea. Japan and South Korea have had close ties with the United States since the end of WWII. So, the presence in one sphere of influence rather than another can make a big economic difference.

Of the hundred plus nations struggling, how much blame can reasonably be placed on the empires and their aftermaths and postscripts, and how much on national leaders? The history of and aftereffects of empires definitely matters. But there is no question that the army of misguided and underskilled *sovereign* leaders are a giant chokepoint of under-developed nations across the globe. This is something that will be examined much more closely in the next section, The Era of Nation-States: Becoming Nation-States.

*****

Will there be changes to the global powers influencing the world? In 1453 Muslims were riding roughshod over Christian powers. The United States and the Russian Empire didn't exist. The major Christian empire was the Holy Roman Empire. The Chinese Empire was 1/3rd the size it would become.

After WWI there were no Islamic empires and the Russian and Chinese empires had dissolved. Shortly after WWII the British Empire where the sun never set was setting. History is unambiguous on great powers—they rise and fall, and sometimes rise and fall again and again. Granted this time is different because empires laid a durable foundation of languages, common history, religions, people, and political systems, but foundational components aren't forever. National leaders have the proven ability to destroy foundations, and the people have the proven ability to compel changes in what constitutes a winning foundation, like separating church from state, democracy, capitalism, and industrialization. Given the chance, who knows what future innovations the people will inspire their leaders to adopt and what the impact will be on the roster of global powers.

Notes

1. Czechoslovakia selected a democratic government, but a Soviet-supported coup in 1948 replaced it with a communist government. When the UN tried to initiate an investigation into the coup, the Soviet Union exercised its veto.
2. There are many similar but different definitions for the First World. The reference here is to an alliance of industrial democracies, including Australia, Canada, Israel, Japan, New Zealand, South Korea, Taiwan, the United States, the nations of Western Europe, and Turkey. Western nations are a subset that excludes Japan, South Korea, Taiwan, and Turkey. The Second World was an alliance of communist nations that included the Soviet sphere, China, and other nations that would in time implement communist systems. The Third World was all other nations that were ostensibly unaligned with the First or Second World.
3. Under Stalin, the notion of a global revolution to implant world communism was abandoned, but support for a gradual domino theory remained.
4. In 1971, the PRC assumed China's seat on the Security Council and promptly used its clout to block Taiwan's membership in the UN, delegitimizing Taiwan as a sovereign nation.
5. In 1958 all overseas territories of France could self-determine independence, although Algeria fought a war for independence until 1962. In 1975 all Portuguese colonies were independent. The Dutch colony of Indonesia successfully concluded a war for independence in 1949. The Soviet Union held its territories until 1991, and China incorporated its territories.
6. In 1963 the UN called on Portugal to honor the right of self-determination. Portugal ignored this.
7. The first generally recognized Cold War conflict took place in Iran, but it was not an armed conflict. The Soviet Union occupied Iran during WWII and then refused to leave until compelled to do so by the United States with UN support.
8. This was the only Cold War conflict where the UN Security Council was able to militarily support an initiative against sovereign infringement that involved a permanent Security Council member. It was possible because the Soviets did not vote.

9. According to the Encyclopedia Britannica (2002), China with 600,000 incurred the highest number of military fatalities in the Korean War. Mao championed the Korean War and was determined to win it. The Soviet Union was not a belligerent in the Korean War, but it did play a significant supportive role.

10. During the San Francisco conferences, Latam nations fought vigorously to ensure the Charter would not negate the Monroe Doctrine or any other agreements with the United States to protect Latam. They wanted assurances that the United States would not be prevented from protecting them from encroachment by the Soviet Union. This request was motivated by Soviet leadership telegraphing its unhappiness with the support some Latam nations gave to the Axis Powers, and in particular Argentina.

11. The Warsaw Pact only engaged in one military action. It was an offensive action against one of its members, Czechoslovakia.

12. Early on, one thing that was deeply troubling to the western democracies was the Soviet Union's superior economic outcomes.

13. Being anti-imperialist was good theatre and an excellent cover for Gaddafi to target anyone he didn't like.

14. As if to prove the challenges of Arab diversity, the Sharif of Mecca, a member of the Hashemite Dynasty with lineage from the Prophet Muhammad and steward of Islam's holiest cities, was overthrown by the House of Saud in 1925. The Saud's became the new stewards of Islam's holiest cities.

15. Iraq's leader Saddam Hussein rationalized the acquisition by distorting and abbreviating the administrative history of Kuwait and Iraq in the Ottoman Empire and blaming the British for Kuwait's separation.

16. Sevastopol in Crimea is a warm water port. Throughout history, the Russians have tried to secure better year-round access to the seas. Protecting Russians, according to a new Russian law, was a good, and lawful excuse.

17. An unfavorable history of enslaving and selling over 2 million white Christians, mostly Russian, between the 15th and 18th centuries surrounds the Muslim Tartars of the Crimean Khanate.

18. All GDP and per capita data are from the IMF or World Bank unless specifically noted. The values are nominal, rather than being based on a purchasing power parity formula (PPP).

19. Mainland China expanded and contracted more than any other empire. China never had an overseas *colonial* empire. It was also never focused on being a maritime power with the notable exception of the 15th-century voyage of fleet admiral Zheng He who briefly (1405–1433) expanded China's *tributary* empire.

20. At this time the German chancellor was Gerhard Schroeder. In office, Schroeder became known as an advocate for Russia. Out of office, he profited handsomely from his allegiance to Russia over Europe and the United States.

References

i. Appelbaum, Anne. *The Crushing of Eastern Europe*. Doubleday, 2012.
ii. "The End of WWII and the Division of Europe." *Europe.unc.edu*. Retrieved November 20, 2018.

 iii. Plokhy, S. M. *Yalta: The Price of Peace*. Penguin, 2010.

 iv. "Security Council Veto List." *Research.UN.org*. Retrieved November 22, 2018.

 v. Van Herpen, Marcel. *Putins's Wars: The Rise of Russia's New Imperialism*. Rowman and Littlefield, 2014.

 vi. Appelbaum, Anne. *Iron Curtain: The Crushing of Eastern Europe*. Doubleday, 2012.

 vii. Kim, Donggil, and William Stueck. "Did Stalin Lure the United States into the Korean War? New Evidence on the Origins of the Korean War." *Wilsoncenter.org*, July 7, 2011.

 viii. Wilsman, Adam R. "Human Rights in an Age of Cold War Violence: The Central American Example." *Vanderbilt University*, May 2011.

 ix. Sibley, Katherine. "Foreign Aid." *The Encyclopedia of American Foreign Policy*, 2002.

 x. Burlatsky, Fedor. "Castro Wanted a Nuclear Strike." *The New York Times*, October 23, 1992.

 xi. Friedman, Jeremy. *Shadow Cold War*. The University of North Carolina Press, 2015.

 xii. Painter, David S. *The Cold War: An International History*. New York: Routledge, 2002.

 xiii. Allawi, Ali A. *Faisal I of Iraq*. Yale University Press, 2014.

 xiv. Fukuyama, Francis. *The End of History and the Last Man*. The Free Press, 1992.

 xv. "Democracy." *UN.org*. Retrieved December 29, 2018.

 xvi. Shula, Kampamba. "Critique of IMF Loan Conditionality." *Researchgate.net*, January 2012.

 xvii. Murphy, Cornelius. "Objections to Western Conceptions of Human Rights." *Hofstra Law Review* 9, no. 2 (1981).

 xviii. Kutty, Faisal. "International Human Rights: A Western Construct?" *The Express Tribune*, December 27, 2016.

 xix. Russell, Jonathan. "Human Rights: The Universal Declaration vs. the Cairo Declaration." London School of Economics and Political Science: The Middle East Centre Blog. Retrieved December 30, 2018.

 xx. "Putin: Crimea has always been an Integral Part of Russia." *The Telegraph*, March 18, 2014.

 xxi. "The Perils of China's 'Debt-Trap Diplomacy.'" *The Economist*, September 6, 2018.

 xxii. Mendis, Patrick, and Joey Wang. "Belt and Road, or a Chinese Dream for the Return of Tributary States? Sri Lanka Offers a Cautionary Tale." *South China Morning Post*, 9 January 2018.

 xxiii. El Amraoui, Ahmed, and Faisal Edroos. "Is Turkish Secularism under Threat?" *Aljazeera*, June 3, 2018.

 xxiv. "Erdogan Trying to Build New 'Ottoman Caliphate'—Saudi Crown Prince." *Ahvalnews.com*, March 7, 2018.

 xxv. Kissinger, Henry, Lawrence Summers, and Charles Kupchan. "Renewing the Atlantic Partnership." *The Council on Foreign Relations*, 2004.

 xxvi. Barnes, Tim. "Flight MH17: Netherlands and Australia say Russia is responsible for shooting down of passenger plane." *The Independent*, May 25, 2018.

SECTION II

THE ERA OF NATION-STATES

Becoming Nation-States

Introduction

To subjugated colonials, independence seemed like the panacea. But it was not even a cure for repressive rule, let alone a remedy for the everyday hardships of life. Building a nation would challenge the most competent leaders, but the general profile of new national leaders was inexperienced, underskilled, and misguided. Injudicious greenhorns were in charge of overseeing the complicated tasks of building the infrastructure and institutions to support a foundation for equality, peace, and prosperity. And they had to do this in an environment with some knotty empire aftermaths, like ethnically stratified, religiously diverse populations living within empire-defined borders.

The greenhorns had access to help. After WWII some IGOs were created to facilitate nation-building, including the United Nations, the IMF, the World Bank, and GATT. A combination of poor design, Cold War complications, corrupt and incompetent national leaders, and the inherent limits of IGOs to manage sovereign nations limited their effectiveness. There were other sources of assistance, but these came with extra strings attached. China, the motherlands of Europe's former empires and later the EU, Iran, Russia/Soviet Union, Saudi Arabia, and the United States exchanged foreign aid for influence.

During the Cold War, foreign aid was reasonably abundant from IGOs and first- and second-world sources, but it was often squandered or used for personal purposes. The influence that accrued to nations supplying aid was as transient as the latest tranche of aid. After the Cold War, it became harder to misuse aid, and aid could be cut off if recipients engaged in despotic practices. But misapplying aid was not impossible when multiple global powers were competing for influence. The latest nation trading aid for influence did not care if a new "client" was indebted to another world power or IGO, and some offered aid and turned a blind eye to national leaders engaging in deplorable behaviors, like human rights abuse. Competing global powers were again limiting the impact exterrnal aid could have on nation-building.

In this section, the nations of the world are grouped into twelve geographic regions that share empire histories and aftermaths. (See Appendix A for a list of nations in each region.) For each region, a brief history of empire and the trials and tribulations of independence is summarized along with travails of select nations. (In a subsequent book, The Era of Nation-States, a more extensive review of nations and this era is covered.)

· 1 9 ·

SUB-SAHARAN AFRICA

All empires, except the Russian Empire, influenced the region of sub-Saharan Africa. China's influence was minimal; it had some fleeting tributary relationships. The influence of Islamic empires came from local empires, like the Sokoto Caliphate (1804–1903), or the small empire ruled by Oman (MENA) in Zanzibar, which is today part of Tanzania. Traders from Islamic empires, and later Sufi Brotherhoods were also influential.

Except for Zanzibar, the only foreign empires directly ruling in this region during the Era of Empire were European, and by the late 19th century they virtually ruled the entire region.[1] In the 15th century, Portugal became the first European colonizer. The Dutch, French, and Spanish had colonies by the 18th century, but most colonization took place in the late 19th century during Europe's colonial carve-up of the region. After this the Belgians,[2] British, Germans, and Italians were added to the region's European colonizers.

Africa was the last frontier for Europe's colonial empires. For most, colonial rule was less than eighty years, beginning in the late 19th century and ending in the 1960s and 1970s. However, empire-run slave trades and Christian missionaries added to the impacts of foreign empires on the region. The Arab and Atlantic slave trades began in the 7th and 15th centuries respectively, and Europe's Christian missionaries began converting Africans in the 16th century.

Conversions to Christianity and Islam created some significant aftermaths. In the 19th century, most still followed indigenous religions. By the early 20th century, most followed Christian or Islamic religions,[3] and unusually there were many nations with significant populations of both religions. Europe's empires merged thousands of tribal-ethnic groups, some Muslim, some Christian, and some following indigenous religions into the colonial borders for forty-six future nations. This generated something unique in the world; a host of nations in northern sub-Saharan Arica (SSA) with large populations of geographically separated Muslims and Christians. Muslims live in the north where they border Muslim-majority nations in the North Africa region, and Christians live in the south.

After WWII, independence was supposed to be granted on request, but colonies renamed Portuguese "provinces" and French colonies incorporated into the French Union had to fight for independence. There may have been more and longer wars for independence, but in 1960 the UN passed the Declaration on the Granting of Independence to Colonial Countries and Peoples to try to end empire resistance. This called for the transfer of "all powers to the peoples of those territories without any conditions or reservations." "Inadequacy of political, economic, social, or educational preparedness should never serve as a pretext for delaying independence."

Empires advancing a lack of preparedness was not without merit, but it was no longer accepted as a valid reason to deny independence. That was the good and the bad news. Ready or not, and mostly not, nations in sub-Saharan Africa overwhelmingly became sovereigns. Portuguese provinces, however, had to continue fighting for independence until 1975 when Portugal traded autocracy for democracy and dissolved its empire. Namibia also endured its struggle for independence from South Africa until 1990.[4]

The grandest problem for nation building in SSA was a severe shortage of indigenous people skilled and experienced in nation-building. In some states, the university educated could be counted on one hand. In a region known as French Equatorial Africa, which was soon to be five independent nations, there were five local university graduates in 1960. The shortage of skilled people, however, was not a deterrent to expelling or encouraging the departure of Europeans and Asians trained and experienced in running governments and economies.

The unwieldy borders defined by the Europeans became permanent by agreement of Africa's new national leaders. This minimized the real possibility of border conflicts, but it also implied a tacit acceptance by these leaders that they were in charge of diverse populations. Initially many assumed the role of unifiers, but it didn't take long to find that it was easier to stay in power with divide and rule practices, which had its own set of consequences. The Era of Nation-States has seen more than a hundred civil wars pitting different tribal-ethnic groups. Extrajudicial murders, rape, torture, and arbitrary imprisonment have been government tools applied to opponents. Several national leaders have been charged with war crimes and crimes against humanity, but there are many more with blood on their hands. Instead of building nations, many created divided, despotic states. National leaders fingering the empires for this outcome were deflecting blame.[i]

Nations weren't ready for independence, but in one way the timing was right. Nation building is expensive, and funds were plentifully available. Many nations had the fortune of abundant extractive resources that were in high demand for rebuilding war-torn nations, particularly in Western Europe. The IMF and the World Bank were also offering loans for infrastructure developments. In the 1980s the IMF and World Bank alone provided more than $100 billion to facilitate political and economic stability. In exchange, national leaders had to commit to economic efficiencies, which many loathed to do because they threatened their systems of patronage. Actually, it didn't. The 1980s is called Africa's lost decade. Patronage won over efficiencies and political and economic stability.

The Cold War also offered an opportunity to exchange influence for aid. But this often instigated additional challenges for political stability. Nations in sub-Saharan Africa were officially or unofficially hosting internal competitions for national leadership. One candidate would align with the First World and another the Second World. A likely outcome was deadly and damaging civil wars that doubled as proxy wars between the First and Second Worlds. Once in office, the allegiance of any national leader could be resold to the highest bidder.

Several countries implemented communist systems and received aid from the Soviet Union. Resemblances to Soviet communism were generally limited to governments assuming total control and eliminating the opposition. The state leveraging its power for the benefit of the people, let alone building a classless society were missing. To secure aid, many countries aligned with the First World. Often the only commitment they made was to be anti-communist, and this was an easy commit. National leaders living the lives of kings and queens knew communism would end their glorious reign. During the Cold War national leaders in this region professing to be communist, anti-communist, or democratic were virtually all dictators.[5,ii] The Cold War chapter is called the Big Men of Africa period.

Global powers meanwhile turned a blind eye to despotism, corruption, and violations of human rights for fear of alienating an alleged ideological ally. The UN was near useless. Cold War politics and Charter limitations regarding intra-sovereign affairs eviscerated it.

For the first couple of decades in the post-Cold War period sources of foreign aid were controlled by the first-world democracies and there were strings attached; nations had to commit to implementing multi-party democracies. National leaders lined up but most implemented façades. African leaders became skilled in illustrating aspects of democracy, much as they had pretended to be communist or democratic. Foreign aid was once again lining the pockets of political elites rather than being invested in nation-building.

An expression surfaced from Africans too familiar with popularly elected politicians campaigning on democratic freedoms and an end to corruption, but then delivering repression, discrimination, and more corruption; "We struggle very hard to remove one cockroach from power, and the next rat comes to do the same thing. Haba! Darn!" The first post-Cold War decades have been called a time of Big Man Democracy.

China's arrival in the 21st century as an alternative source for foreign aid with no conditions on governing has been welcomed by some in Africa, but it has been a source of consternation for the first-world democracies that see dictatorial rule as the bête noir of nation-building. Saudi Arabia's aid in northern sub-Saharan Africa for the construction of mosques and madrassas promoting Wahhabist and other Islamist branches is another alternative to western assistance, albeit, with specified purposes. This has also been unhelpful to spreading democracy. Democracy has a better track record for addressing human rights abuses, poverty, and corruption than autocratic political systems of any type.

Autocratic rule and corruption go together like freeways and cars traveling over 100 km/h (65mph). The former enables the latter. Corruption has been at the crux of many problems in sub-Saharan Africa. It has motivated wars, coups, discrimination, despot longevity, and miserable progress on nation-building, including limiting infrastructure investments like those to construct freeways. In any year, Transparency International (TI) classifies about 90 percent of sub-Saharan nations as having a serious corruption problem. How severe is serious?

President/Emperor Jean-Bedel Bokassa of the Central African Republic (CAR) (1966–1979) decided to crown himself emperor in 1977. Created as a replica of Napoleon's coronation, his ceremony cost $22 million, or about $87 million 2016 dollars. At the time CAR had a total of 260 miles of paved roads. Their former colonizer France footed the bill for the ceremony, but this didn't endear Bokassa to France. When French generosity fell short, Bokassa switched his allegiance to the Soviet Union. When the Soviets didn't meet his desires, he tried to curry favor with leaders in MENA by converting to Islam. This failed, so he reconverted to Catholicism and loyalty to France.

For decades it looked like sub-Saharan leaders were competing for the most ultra-luxurious palaces. The palace of Ivory Coast's President Felix Houphouet Boigny (1960–1993) was said to be an African Versailles. DR-Congo's President Mobutu Sese Seko's palace was called Versailles in the Jungle. It had three palaces, a five-star hotel, schools, a hospital, and a 3.2 km (1.8 m.) runway to accommodate the president's choice of transport—the Concorde. President Omar Bongo (1967–2009) of Gabon lived in a palace that cost $500 million and also had a basilica modeled on St. Peters in Rome. Meanwhile, the masses in all these nations lived in poverty. Every one of these countries was mining copious amounts of extractive-resources, and their leaders were creating examples of the resource curse. If these nations didn't have extractive resources, their leaders might have focused on building industries and infrastructure that gave the masses options to escape poverty.

Corruption can be obscene at the highest levels of government, but it can also extend throughout the political system. In Kenya there was a saying under President Daniel arap Moi (1978–2002); why hire a lawyer when you can buy a judge. The going rate to quash a murder conviction was $500; a rape conviction could disappear for $250.[iii]

Some corrupt activities were beyond brazen. In 2013 a UN working group reported that 80 percent of withdrawals made from the *central* banks of Somalia and Eritrea were for private purposes. Companies wanting to secure a government contract in this region had to be prepared to pay a 10 percent royalty to the private accounts of government officials. But the percentage could go higher. It went as high as 50 percent in Nigeria in the 1980s.[6] Equatorial Guinea's President Teodoro Obiang Nguema Mbasogo (1979-?) is known to have maintained a personal royalty of 30 percent.

Endemic corruption is natural when prosecutions are rare. In 2011 Nigeria's head of corruption, Farida Wazin said: "Fighting corruption in our country is like holding the tiger by the tail—if care is not taken the tiger will devour you." In this region, it's not unusual to accept corruption as an unsolvable problem. It then becomes a self-fulfilling prophecy.

There is no other region with so many instances of cronyism, serious levels of corruption, discriminatory practices, national leaders reigning for decades, the resource curse, and substantive accusations of war crimes and crimes against humanity. It cannot be surprising that per capita incomes in sub-Saharan Africa in the 1990s were much the same as the 1960s when they were gaining independence.[iv]

The Big Men of Africa have created another problem. In a region where more than half the countries have healthy Islamic minorities (>10 percent) or Islamic majorities, Islamic militant groups find audiences naively receptive to Islamism as a solution for superior governance. It takes more than receptivity to shift to an Islamist system, but this doesn't mean there won't be quite a bit of militant mayhem in the process. The Era of Nation-States for sub-Saharan Africa has thus far been a disaster.

Below are short stories of the early decades of nationhood for Liberia, Ethiopia, Nigeria, and DR Congo. Aftermaths from the Era of Empire have created extra challenges but misguided and underskilled national leaders' shoulder most of the responsibility for the region's woeful progress.

Liberia

Liberia's history is unique. In 1820 a private US corporation created Liberia as a home for freed American slaves.[7] Twenty-seven years later (1847) the entire political elite of newly independent Liberia were former US slaves and their descendants, and they were enslaving populations of indigenous people.[8]

Américo-Liberians ruled until 1980 when a military coup led by Samuel Doe annihilated the leading members of the government. Master Sargent Doe led a military junta for five years before being elected president. With the bought-and-paid-for-support of his Krahn ethnic group, he held onto power for a total of ten years. His preferential treatment of the Krahns was also his undoing when it led to civil war, and his gruesome murder. The latter was filmed for all the world to see.

Doe was a severely corrupt, anti-communist despot that was also on the US payroll. Liberia received $500 million in aid before the United States abandoned Doe near the start of the First Liberian Civil War (1989–1996) and the end of the Cold War.

Without Doe, Liberia went out of the frying pan and into the fire. In 1997 warlord Charles Taylor, was elected president with a campaign slogan, "he killed my ma, he killed my pa, but I will vote for him." Two years later opposition to his rule resulted in the Second Liberian Civil War (1999–2003).

Taylor's rule ended in 2003 with an indictment for war crimes and crimes against humanity committed in Sierra Leone—not Liberia. Taylor was convicted of aiding rebels in Sierra Leone, often child soldiers, who committed atrocities, like mutilations, amputations, and sexual slavery. "Blood" diamonds were used to compensate Taylor.

In 2018 Forbes listed Charles Taylor's net worth at $58 million. Meanwhile, Liberians are among the poorest people in the world. Per capita incomes in 2017 were $729.

Ethiopia

Ethiopia counts among the rare nations that successfully fended off foreign empires.[9] After WWII, Ethiopia's Emperor Haile Selassie (1930–1972) enjoyed a presence on the world stage generally reserved for national leaders of leading economies. This recognition came in handy when Eritrea (then part of Italian East Africa) demanded independence. The UN was presiding over the request. Selassie, ruling landlocked Ethiopia was lobbying the United States for control of Eritrea with its coast on the Red Sea. It was fortuitous for Selassie that there was speculation, based on conjecture, that Eritrea was vulnerable to communism. The possibility of communism was a red flag for the United States. US Secretary of State, John Foster Dulles said: "From the point of view of justice, the opinions of the Eritrean people must receive consideration. Nevertheless, the strategic interests of the United States in the Red Sea basin and considerations of security and world peace make it necessary that the country has to be linked with our ally, Ethiopia." In 1950 the UN General Assembly adopted resolution 390 A (V), and Eritrea became an autonomous province of Ethiopia.[v]

In 1962 Selassie independently and in contravention to UN Resolution 390 A (V) annexed Eritrea for which a price was by paid by Selassie and all Ethiopians. Eritreans battled Ethiopia for thirty years (1961–1991) before finally gaining independence.[10] Selassie was overthrown in 1975, and this war was a contributing factor.

Things got worse without Selassie. His successor Mengistu Haile Mariam would also be globally recognized. He led a communist government that attracted the attention of the Soviet Union, East Germany, Cuba, North Korea, and Libya. Stalin was long dead, but Mengistu followed his cookbook for ruthlessly eliminating perceived or real opposition, which included the highly educated. He also followed one of Mao's practices by implementing the wasted bullet tax, which had to be paid to obtain the dead body of a family member.

Like other communist leaders, Mengistu implemented collective agriculture. Food supplies plummeted, and famine struck in the eighties where an estimated 4 million died. Fewer would have died, but Mengistu was battling a second war, this one was a civil war (1974 to 1991)[11] and he was diverting international food aid to the military to maximize death to his opponents.[vi] Also consistent with Stalin's cookbook, Mengistu made atheism the official religion. Non-conforming Christians, rather than Muslims, bore the brunt of terror because Mengistu wanted to avoid the wrath of "radical Arab countries."[vii]

When the Soviet Union ended support for Mengistu in 1990 Ethiopia was teetering on failure. Per capita income in 1991 was lower than in 1975 and also lower than in 1950. In 2017 per capita incomes were $873.

Nigeria

In 1960 Nigeria became independent as a constitutional monarchy with the British monarch as head of state. In 1963 it became a democratic republic and in 1966 a military dictatorship. For twenty-nine of the next thirty-six years, Nigeria would have autocratic military rule.

The borders created for Nigeria enclosed more than 250 distinct ethnic groups. A Nigerian chief, Obafemi Awolowo said, "Nigeria is not a nation. It is a mere geographical expression. There are no 'Nigerians' in the same sense as there are 'English', 'Welsh' or 'French.'"[viii]

Nigeria was also religiously diverse. The north was predominantly Muslim and the south mostly Christian. Of the three dominant ethnolinguistic groups, the Muslim Hausa-Fulani live in the north. The Christian Igbo live in the south, and the Yoruba, who practice Christianity, Islam and indigenous religions are in the South west. Since independence the three have competed for power and consequently privilege. [12]

The first military dictator was an Igbo (Christian). He was assassinated. The second military dictator was a Hausa-Fulani (Muslim) on a mission to eliminate the Igbo living in the region of Biafra. An estimated 30,000 Igbo civilians were murdered before Biafra declared independence, and the Nigerian Civil War, also called the Biafran War (1967–1970) commenced. An estimated one to three million Biafran civilians died, most from a human-made famine used as a tool of war. The International Committee on the Investigations of Crimes of Genocide concluded that there was genocide against the Biafrans.[ix,13] The Igbo never got independence; instead, they have lived as marginalized people. Charged with national reconciliation by Nigerian President Sani Abacha (1993–1998), Chief Alex Akinyele said: "There are so many marginalized groups in Nigeria, but the case of the Ndigbo [Igbo] is too obvious. They are more marginalized than the others."[x]

Ethnic and religious conflict in Nigeria became worse when some states in the north adopted sharia law and, as is common, Islamic militancy appeared soon afterward.[xi] By 2009, Boko Haram,[14] a militant Islamist group promising to end corruption and eliminate western practices was inflicting mayhem on northeastern Nigeria. Boko Haram became globally recognized in 2014 when it kidnapped and enslaved 276 Christian girls from a high school and claimed an Islamic caliphate in its area of conquest. Boko Haram succeeded in eliminating western practices. Other outcomes were $9 billion in property damage, 20,000 dead, widespread malnutrition, and an unquantified number of refugees.[xii] Many questioned why the powerful military did not swiftly put an end to the mayhem. The answer: "Corrupt military officials have been able to benefit from the conflict through the creation of fake defense contracts."[xiii]

Political privilege in Nigeria extends to having special access to the fruits of corruption. These fruits expanded with rising oil production. During the 1980s kickbacks on contracts reached 50 percent. At this time, construction costs were 4X higher in Nigeria than in Asia. Political elites were pillaging national resources for personal use rather than building a nation that would benefit the masses.

In the post-Cold War period, there was hope that multi-party democracy would bring positive change to the masses. Hope turned to despair when the outgoing president annulled the first election, and General Sani Abacha became the next Nigerian president. More hopelessness followed. An early initiative in the transition to democracy was privatizing many state-owned industries. The buyers were mostly military, and the companies were priced to sell. The military became corrupt industrialists and increasing prosperity for the masses was again deprioritized.

Among Nigeria's most corrupt was Sani Abacha (1993–1998). He died after five years in power, but according to TI, he accumulated a personal fortune of $2–5 billion. It has been ordinary for corruption in this region to be accompanied by violent repression, and this was true of Abacha. Nobel laureate Wole Soyinka, said, "Abacha is prepared to reduce Nigeria to rubble as long as he survives to preside over a name." Abacha charged Soyinka with treason.

In 1960 Nigeria had about the same level of economic development as Singapore. And it had something Singapore did not have: abundant extractive resources. According to the IMF, in 2017 per capita income in Singapore was 29 times higher than in Nigeria.

The Democratic Republic of the Congo (DR-Congo) (formerly Belgian Congo and Zaire). When DR-Congo requested independence, the Belgians noted it was inadequately prepared, but honored the request. Resisting the request would have ignited a fiery response from the Congolese. Dating to the personal rule of Belgium's King Leopold (1885–1908), the Congolese had good reasons to despise the Belgians. Leopold's rule was characterized by land expropriations, forced labor, and executions. Estimates of the death toll under Leopold range from 3–15 million. The Belgians were however right, DR Congo was unprepared for independence.

Patrice Lumumba was the first prime minister of an independent DR Congo (1960). The locals were attracted to his anti-imperial and anti-white rhetoric. Upon arriving in office, he insulted whites, and condoned physical assaults against them, making it clear that it was in their interest to leave quickly. Within two weeks thousands of whites fled in panic and DR-Congo was bereft of skilled administrators for the government and the economy. Of the 1,400 civil servants at independence, just three were Congolese; the others were white and mostly Belgian. Without skilled foreign workers, the Congo was left with thirty Congolese college graduates, and no secondary school teachers, doctors, or military officers.[xiv] In record-breaking time Lumumba created a dysfunctional nation.

Like every new nation, DR-Congo needed foreign assistance, and Belgium was ready and willing to do this, but there was a condition; Belgium insisted on maintaining a military force to keep the nation secure. Lumumba rejected this and invited the Soviet Union to supply DR-Congo's military with arms, setting in motion the notion of a communist DR-Congo. Over sixty-seven days, Lumumba succeeded in making DR-Congo a pariah nation. The Belgians assassinated him.[xv]

The UN dispatched their Blue Helmet peacekeepers to restore order. Peacekeeping turned to peace enforcement. It was a troubling turn of events. UN official Brian Urquhart said: "the moment a peacekeeping force starts killing people it becomes part of the conflict it is supposed to be controlling and thus part of the problem." UN peacekeepers witnessed massacres and rapes, and many were killed. The UN would not launch another peacekeeping mission in this region until the 1990s.[xvi]

Right after Lumumba, Congolese governments were known for being weak and lawless. Then in 1965 Lieutenant General Mobutu Sese Seko came to power (1965–1997). He was not weak, but like others, he operated above the law. He worked closely with a richly rewarded military to ruthlessly eliminate the opposition. On his watch, there were reports of opponents being burned alive or beaten with sticks peppered with nails. Most of the atrocities are only known anecdotally. "Quantitatively, I think Zaire has the worst human rights record in Africa," said a UN official in Kinshasa. "In terms of social and economic rights and the number of state actors violating those rights, it's massive. And the bulk of human rights violations in this country never will be known. It's a black hole."[xvii]

Sese Seko was a first order despot, but he was also an ardent anti-communist, bordering two communist nations, Angola and Republic of the Congo.[15] This gave him the support of the First World, and most saliently Belgium, France, and the United States.

DR-Congo had the resources to fast track nation-building. It was the world's 11th largest country in landmass, it had incredibly rich stores of extractive resources, and it was a favored recipient of first-world foreign aid. But Sese Seko was more concerned with building his personal fortune and prestige on the world stage. The nightly news in DR-Congo began with a picture of Sese Seko descending through the clouds as if from heaven. In some years Sese Seko and his cronies stole the equivalent of 50 percent of the national budget.[xviii] He pocketed an estimated $5 billion.

After the Cold War, Sese Seko could no longer hold his primary donor nations (Belgium, France and the United States) hostage to foreign aid in return for his anti-communist stand. Future aid was now tied to multi-party elections. When DR-Congo's new prime minister forbade Sese Seko from withdrawing cash from the nation's central bank, Sese Seko dismissed him. He said, "The chief is the eagle who flies high and cannot be touched by the spit of the toad." In 1993 the chief was presiding over inflation near 9000 percent. Under 32 years of Sese Seko's misrule, DR-Congo's GDP had fallen 65 percent, and the DR-Congolese counted among the poorest people in the world.

After Leopold and Sese Seko, it may have seemed like things could not get worse for DR-Congo. But under Laurent Kabila (1997–2001) the nation became ground zero for the Great War of Africa (1998–2003) that directly involved nine African nations. An estimated 5.4 million died and 0.5 million were raped,[xix] but rape figures are truly unknown. A rape victim was asked if she reported her rape, she replied: "No, why? To be raped again."[xx]

Laurent's son Joseph Kabila (2001–2019) presided over a decade of relative peace (wars continued raging in eastern Congo) before DR-Congo was back at war. This time the war was triggered by Kabila refusing to leave office in 2016 upon expiration of his constitutionally defined term in office. There were reports of mass graves and massacres and the UN expressed concerns that the violence could escalate into ethnic cleansing.[xxi]

In 2017 half the countries in SSA had per capita incomes under $1,000. DR-Congo at $478, was low even by regional standards.

Notes

1. Exceptions include Liberia a colony of the American Colonization Society; Zanzibar (later part of Tanzania) ruled by Oman (1890–1963); and Ethiopia which did have a brief period (1936–1941) of rule by the Italian Empire that some characterize as an occupation.
2. In 1885 Belgium's King Leopold created a personal colony, the Congo Free State. Leopold's tyranny became well known, and in 1908 the Free State became the Belgian Congo, a colony of Belgium. It was renamed Zaire in 1971 and the Democratic Republic of the Congo in 1997.
3. According to Pew Research Center, in 2010, 57 percent of sub-Saharans were Christians and 29 percent were Muslims.
4. Namibia (formerly called South West Africa (1915–1990) and German South West Africa (1884–1915)) was made a League of Nation's mandate in 1920. South Africa was charged with oversight, but it effectively annexed Namibia in defiance of the UN and international pressure.
5. In 1989 Botswana, Gambia, and Mauritius were categorized as electoral democracies by Freedom House. These nations represented about 1 percent of the population of Africa.
6. This was under Nigerian President Shagari (1979–1983).
7. Sierra Leone was a British colony that in part had similar origins as a colony for freed slaves. Many early inhabitants were former slaves from the United States that had fought for the British in the American Revolutionary War.
8. Forced labor, a euphemism for slavery, was abolished in 1936.
9. Depending on different characterizations, Ethiopia was either a colony or occupied by the Italian Empire between 1936 and 1941.
10. The Eritrean War of Independence took place between 1961 and 1991.
11. Uniquely the belligerents were so-called communists for Mengistu and communists against Mengistu.
12. Throughout this region, the ruling tribal-ethnic group customarily receives privileges funded through the public purse in exchange for political support.
13. The committee also saw the British government defining borders for administrative convenience as a significant contributing factor to ethnic conflict in Nigeria.

14. Boko Haram is a commonly used name. The formal name is Group of the People of Sunnah for Dawa and Jihad. The group has also had other names.
15. To avoid confusion The Democratic Republic of the Congo is commonly called Congo-Kinshasa, and the Republic of the Congo is called Congo-Brazzaville.

References

i. Alesina, Alberto F., William Easterly, Arnaud Devleeschauwer, Sergio Kurlat, and Romain T. Wacziarg. *Fractionalization*. Harvard Institute Research Working Paper No. 1959, June 2002.

ii. Alence, Rod. "Democracy and Development in Africa." *The Journal of the International Institute* 16, no. 2 (Spring 2009).

iii. "The Best Money Can Buy." *Africa Confidential*, November 7, 2003.

iv. Ismi, Asad. "Impoverishing a Continent: The World Bank and IMF in Africa." *Halifax Initiative*, July 2004.

v. "Report of the Commission of Human Rights—Eritrea." *UN Office for the High Commission of Human Rights*, June 5, 2015.

vi. Franks, Suzanne. "Ethiopian Famine: How Landmark BBC Report Influenced Modern Coverage." *The Guardian*, October 22, 2014.

vii. Doulos, Mikael. "Christians in Marxist Ethiopia." *Biblicalstudies.org.uk*, 1986.

viii. Awolowo, Obafemi. *Path to Nigerian Freedom*. Faber & Faber, 1947.

ix. Nche, Ekwe. "Genocide Papers, Pt. 1." *Harvard-hwp.com*. Retrieved December 31, 2018.

x. Orji, Ema I. "Issues on Ethnicity and Governance in Nigeria: A Universal Human Rights Perspective." *Fordham International Law Journal* 25 (2001): 431.

xi. Bar, Shmuel. "The Religious Sources of Islamic Terrorism." *The Hoover Institute*, June 1, 2004.

xii. Olukayode Michael, and Yinka Ibukun. "Boko Haram Caused $9 Billion Damage in Nigeria's North, UN Says." *Bloomberg*, March 6, 2017.

xiii. "Corruption in Nigerian Army Weakens Boko Haram Fight, says Watchdog." *Africanews.com, Reuters*, May 18, 2017.

xiv. Meredith, Martin. "The Fate of Africa." *Public Affairs*, 2005.

xv. Ames, Paul. "Belgium 'Sorry' for Killing of Lumumba." *The Independent*, February 6, 2002.

xvi. Meisler, Stanley. *United Nations: A History*. Grove Press, 2011.

xvii. Dellios, Hugh. "Victims Describe Mobutu's Long Reign of Torture." *Chicago Tribune*, April 29, 1997.

xviii. Collins C. J. "Zaire/Democratic Republic of the Congo." *Foreign Policy*, July 1, 1997.

xix. Bavier, Joe. "Congo War Driven Crisis Kills 45,000 a Month: Study." *Reuters*, January 22, 2008.

xx. Glynn, Dearbhla. "Congo War: 48 Women Raped Every Hour at Height of Conflict." *Irish Times*, April 30, 2016.

xxi. Summers, Hannah. "Democratic Republic of Congo: 250 Killed in 'Ethnic' Massacres, says UN." *The Guardian*, August 5, 2017.

· 2 0 ·

THE MIDDLE EAST AND
NORTH AFRICA

Islamic empires ruled the Middle East from the 7th century until 1922, and North Africa until the 19th century. Most empires were Sunni and Arabic speaking and predated the Era of Empire.[1] The largest Sunni empire was, however, the Turkish/Ottoman-speaking Ottoman Empire and it was present for nearly the entire era. Unsurprisingly, MENA is overwhelmingly Muslim. Unusually, the Muslim population in the Middle East is a 50:50 mix of Sunnis and Shias.

The Safavids ruled the first major Shiite empire. Created in 1501 the Safavids embarked on an ambitious expansion spree setting in motion centuries of intra-Islamic wars with the Ottomans. When the Russian Empire (1721–1917) came into existence, it capitalized on the warring Muslim empires to annex huge swathes of land from the Ottoman and different Shiite empires.

The Shiite empires and the Sunni Ottoman Empire resolved some pointed differences, like ongoing boundary disputes in the 1746. Treaty of Kurdan and the two treaties of Erzurum (1823 and 1847). However, the seeds of future conflict were brewing in the nascent Saudi state. Its religious founder, Abd al-Wahhab was on a mission to purify Sunni Islam. Neither the Ottomans with their secular practices nor Shias (and Sufis) with their heretical practices were pure.

In MENA's North Africa region, Shiism was not a source of Muslim disunity because Shiite empires never penetrated the region. Christianity was also not a source of disunity until Europe's Christian empires replaced more than a millennium of Islamic rule in the 19th century. European empires established colonies or protectorates throughout North Africa.[2] Per usual practice, Muslims were subjugated to the Christians.

After WWI, Europe's empires were also controlling the Middle East. The Islamic community faced a strange reality; there were no Islamic empires, caliphate, or world powers. Instead, there were colonies, protectorates or mandates of Christian empires.[3] In the Middle East, former Ottoman lands were either British protectorates or League of Nation Mandates under French or British oversight. The British and French weren't present in the Middle East for very long, but they managed to cement their presence by selecting national leaders, condoning expansion of Saudi Arabia, overseeing the implementation of governments with secular and democratic practices, and facilitating the creation of borders that joined diverse ethnolinguistic and religious populations. Borders also defined who would have rich deposits of oil and gas. However, outside parts of Iran and Iraq, the presence of oil was not known with certainty during the border creation process.[i]

The Mandate for Palestine was particularly controversial. It was created with unanimous support from the League of Nations fifty-one members[4] to provide a future independent homeland for the Jewish people.[5] At this time, the League had no Arab members and opposition from Arab populations was forceful, and continuous. At a 1919 political convention in Damascus it was written: "We oppose the pretensions of the Zionists to create a Jewish commonwealth in the southern part of Syria, known as Palestine."[ii] During the history of the mandate, there were repetitive bouts of Arab-instigated social unrest. The message was clear, but so was the mission of the mandate and it gained additional urgency after WWII.

Generally, the purpose of any League mandate was to facilitate preparing nations for independence. For the overseers, it was essential that new nations provide for the peaceful coexistence of diverse religious, and ethnolinguistic populations. It was a tall order in a region with long histories of religious and ethnolinguistic discrimination and conflict. There were other challenges, like allocating governmental administration and control for the peripatetic Bedouins, the so-called desert nomads.[6]

The interwar period (1918–1939) was a fractious unideal time for nations to become independent, making the protection and oversight offered by

European empires valuable, even if resented. Saudi Arabia was still expanding its borders in the Middle East, and no one was sure where the leaders of the Soviet Union, Italy, Germany, or Japan were taking their ambitions, but the fear of conquest was real. In Iraq, the rejection of British rule was greater than fear of conquest and the British administration of Mandatory Iraq was cut short by independence in 1932. In WWII Iraq became an ally of the Axis powers making its rejection of Britain's ongoing oversight clear.[7]

After WWII the situation was very different. Ready or not, nations that wanted independence in the Middle East got it. Except for some small British protectorates on the Arabian Peninsula that voluntarily waited until 1969–1971, the composition of the Middle East was independent nations by 1948. In the 1950s and early 1960s independence came to North Africa. Most nations in this region achieved independence peacefully, but not Algeria. In 1962, after successfully waging a war for independence from France, Algeria became the last nation to gain independence in North Africa.[8]

Many national leaders in MENA were receptive to the democratic and secular practices promoted by their western overseers. In nations that knew or would know they had abundant extractive resources, they saw western oil companies as key to advancing their industries and nations. After their industries were operating, it was common to nationalize the oil and gas industries which increased the wealth accruing to their nations. The discovery and production of oil and gas in MENA transformed the region from being weak in power and receptive to western assistance, to one of global strategic significance and less receptive and even hostile to western influence. Oil and gas were harbingers of change.

Autocratic rule encroached on democratic practices, militaries expanded, and secularity began to be sidelined by overlapping church and state. The trend toward the latter became pronounced following the Arab defeat in the Arab-Israeli War (1967). Secularity was seen as a western imperial import and a significant contributor to the loss. More Islam was viewed as the solution. None of this had a positive impact on nation-building. However, European-defined borders and the influence of rejected western practices continued to shoulder the blame for stunted qualities of life. Credit to western powers for these outcomes was more generous than deserved.

Cold War-related conflicts that pitted advocates for communism against anti-communists tread lightly in this region. In 1970 South Yemen switched to a Soviet-supported communist government. This gave the Soviets unrestricted access to the highly coveted Port of Aden and an avenue to antagonize western interests in the region.[iii] It didn't, however, invite much of a response from the First World because they didn't see South Yemen's decision as persuasive in the region. Communism was appealing to many new nations, but not here. It would eliminate the wealthy like the region's royal families, call for atheism as an official religion, and make women comrades. The latter two are incongruous with Islam, and for Jordan and Morocco who are ruled by descendants of the Prophet Muhammad, so is the first.[9]

Outside South Yemen, MENA was a collection of mostly non-aligned nations, but this was a bit of a ruse.[10] Opportunistic exchanges of allegiance to the First or Second World were common. Clearly aligned with the Soviet Union were Egypt (until 1978), Iraq, Libya, and Syria. The Soviets supported the creation of Israel, but by 1956 they were militarily supporting these Arab nations in Arab-Israeli wars.[11,12] Iran (until 1979), Israel, Jordan, Turkey, and Saudi Arabia were aligned with the United States and other first-world nations, and national security was a big reason. A nation's alignment with the First or Second World in this region was so relevant it was a wedge issue that created the opposing parties for a mini-Cold War among Arab states.[iv]

Cold War alignment was partially evident in the Arab-Israeli wars, but not entirely. The Arab-Israeli wars gave Muslims in this region (and farther afield) a common cause to rally around, except Iran and Turkey. These two nations recognized Israeli sovereignty in 1950 and 1949 respectively, although Iran severed diplomatic ties with Israel and joined the common cause in 1979.

Iran didn't just join the cause; it became Israel's chief antagonist. Iran's new leader Ayatollah Khomeini was on a mission to unify Muslims under his rule. Being anti-Zionist was part of his appeal. There was nothing in Khomeini's mission that appealed to the rulers of Saudi Arabia. Khomeini's mission challenged Saudi Arabia's leadership in the Muslim world and brought to the foreground Wahhabist beliefs that the Shias were heretical Muslims.[xxiii]

Khomeini failed in his attempt to rule the Muslim community. Instead, he ignited or exacerbated intra-Islam, inter-religious, and geopolitical conflict in the region and beyond. This precipitated the never-ending Iran-Saudi proxy wars and the region's three most devastating wars: the 20th century's longest war, the Iran-Iraq War (1980–1988); the Gulf War (1990) which was instigated by the end of the Iran-Iraq war; and the Lebanese Civil War (1975–1990) where Iran supported Hezbollah and the radicalization of Lebanese Shias.

Khomeini was also instrumental in perpetuating conflict between Muslims and Israel. Sixteen years after he died, Iran's role as Israel's chief antagonist manifested itself in Iran-Israeli wars replacing a cessation of wars between Arab nations and Israel. Iran, acting through its proxies Shiite Hezbollah, Sunni Hamas, and the Sunni Palestinian Islamic Jihad (PIJ), and the Iranian Revolutionary Guard took the lead in a mission to destroy Israel.

MENA was one region where the end of the Cold War didn't bring any allusions of the long-awaited peace in the world. The post-Cold War period brought a resurgence in the competition for regional power and Islamic leadership. The Iran-Saudi rivalry secured additional people power from irregular "soldiers" returning home from the last major Cold War conflict: The Soviet-Afghan War (1979–1989).ˣˣᵛ Trained and experienced militants saw an opportunity with a defeated Second World, a First World blissfully believing democracy had won and world peace was at hand, and Iran and Saudi Arabia leveraging oil wealth to fund militants to fight their proxy wars. The latter instigated a vicious cycle of actions and reactions to uncontrollable stateless militants.

Islamic militancy spiked when the post-Cold War period began, but then it declined, before surging again after dictators were ousted in Egypt, Iraq, Libya, Syria, and Yemen during the Arab Spring (2011). Many westerners believed that a stronghold of autocratic rule would be transitioning to democratic systems with fundamental freedoms for all.

One thing that instantly became evident was the ousted autocrats were insanely corrupt. Next in evidence was that the west was naive—again. After democratic elections, wars broke out in Libya, Iraq, Syria, and Yemen. The latter three have large populations of Shias and Sunnis, and these wars doubled for red-hot Iran-Saudi proxy wars. Where there wasn't war in MENA, there were refugees seeking safety.

Wars, refugees, economic stagnation, and western intervention in the Arab Spring created a great environment for Islamists in different countries campaigning for more Islam as the solution to reach an expanded audience receptive to jihad by the sword. Islamic militancy soared inside and outside the region. The internet became a successful vehicle for recruiting militants from over a hundred countries. They were "inspired"[13] to terrorize innocent people in any nation where Muslims were allegedly marginalized, blamed for the loss of Islamic empires and the caliphate, or even participating in the Crusades. These nations included the former motherlands of European empires, the United States, China, and Russia. For some, militants murdering innocent non-Muslims were superheroes. Meanwhile, nation-building in MENA went sideways at best, the numbers living in poverty rose, and the dream of fundamental freedoms for all died again with the return of autocratic rule and increasing the overlap of church and state.

Cascading events from the Arab Spring also saw a new competitor for regional leadership. Aligned with western nations since independence, Turkey threw its hat into the ring. Just like the Era of Empire, there was one Arab-Sunni power, one Persian/Iranian-Shiite power, and one Turkish-Sunni power vying for power in MENA.

In MENA high levels of corruption are added to the problems of competitions for regional power, wars, and rising Islamic militancy. Serious levels of corruption are common to autocracies. It can be very high in nations at war or otherwise politically or economically unstable, and those with rich stores of extractive resources. In several suspect countries corruption is not that severe. At least that is the perception conveyed to TI.

By TI standards, Saudi Arabia counts among MENA's least corrupt. The Anti-Corruption Business Portal noted: "No law regulates conflicts of interest, and some officials engage in corruption with impunity … Gifts are regulated under Saudi law, but facilitation payments are not addressed." So, the definition of corruption is perceived differently in Saudi Arabia. With data censorship a priority in Saudi Arabia there is a chance that perceptions of corruption are also censored. This same set of circumstances may apply equally to the autocratic oil kingdoms of Kuwait, Qatar, and the UAE, which according to TI count among the least corrupt nations in the world.

Increasingly autocratic Turkey is also one of the least seriously corrupt. Or is it? "Turkey's government does not pledge to fight corruption, not even as lip service."[v] Corruption thrives in any country where it is basically legal.

Nation-building in MENA has faced and continues to face more challenges than most regions. Below are summaries of events in the early decades of independence for Turkey, Israel, Iran and Saudi Arabia, Libya and the Sudan.

Turkey

The British, French, and Italian occupation of Turkey after WWI was cut short by Turkey waging a successful war for independence. In 1923 Turkey, the center of Ottoman and Islamic power for more than half a millennium, became an independent nation. Mustafa Kemal Atatürk was the commander of Turkish forces during the war for independence, and now he was Turkey's first president (1923–1938). "Atatürk had contempt for his Arab coreligionists and took a disdainful view of religion in general."[vi],[14] He also admired some characteristics of the victorious Allied Powers and decided to implement a secular democratic form of government. He also changed the script used in Turkey from Arabic to Latin and politically and economically aligned Turkey with Western Europe—not MENA.

In 1952 Turkey cemented its pivot toward Europe by becoming a full member of NATO and in 1959 becoming an associate member of the European Economic Community, a predecessor to the EU. Turkey's 1974 invasion of northern Cyprus and their subsequent occupation and lone recognition of the independent state of the Turkish Republic of Northern Cyprus in 1983 damaged prospects for tighter integration with the European Community.[15]

Secular Turkey, with its recognition of Israel's sovereignty, steered clear of the regional conflicts with Israel and also the Iran-Saudi proxy wars. But it had its own conflicts. The occupation of northern Cyprus created a persistent source of conflict with the EU, and 1978 marked the start of a long-term armed conflict with separatist Kurdish rebels.

Turkey's alliance with the EU was strained by its occupation of northern Cyprus but otherwise reasonably healthy until the Arab Spring. This was when Turkey's Islamist President Erdogan accelerated a pivot away from Europe and secularity and toward MENA and Islam. This pivot met with mixed reactions from the west and within MENA. NATO was concerned about the implications of losing Turkey. MENA fretted that an alignment between Turkey and Iran would strengthen Iran and increase conflict with Saudi Arabia and its allies.[vii],[viii],[16] Turkey's shift was also a setback for gender equality, and potentially for Turkish non-Muslims and non-devout Muslims relying on freedom of religion.[ix]

Israel

When responsibility for the Mandate for Palestine shifted from Britain to the UN in 1947, it was decided that the mandated lands would accommodate a Jewish *and* a Palestinian nation. The Palestinian nation would receive 43.5 percent of the territory and the Jewish nation 56.5 percent.[17],[18] Jerusalem was designated as an internationally administered city to be shared by the Jews and Palestinians.[x]

On May 14, 1948, Israel became an independent nation. On May 15, 1948, a coalition of Arab nations attacked Israel from the territories allocated for a sovereign Palestinian nation. It was an ominous welcome for the Jewish state, although not wholly unexpected. Arabs had made their opposition to the creation of a Zionist state in MENA very clear. Their antagonism grew after a humiliating loss to a fledgling nation of people Muslims historically stereotyped as merchants—not soldiers.[xi,19,20]

Surrounded by Arab nations seeking its demise, Israel needed the UN to validate its sovereignty and deter Muslim nations from violating it. But this did not occur. Even after the Holocaust, sympathy for the Jews was a far cry from universal. Most developing nations in the UN General Assembly were anti-Semitic or anti-Zionist.[21] Israel also became caught in the crossfire of the Cold War when the Soviet Union saw it as another western ideological nemesis.[22]

The Soviets supported Arab nations in the Six Day War (1967), but Israel again defeated the Arab coalition. When this war ended, Israel was occupying lands allocated for a Palestinian nation. Israel said it hoped to trade lands for peace with their neighbors,[xii] but this was not to be. Egyptian President Nassar's call for the "liquidation of the consequences" became a joint slogan for Arabs and the Soviet Union. In 1967 the Arab League adopted the Khartoum Resolution, which included "the Three No's," "no peace with Israel, no recognition of Israel, no negotiations with it."[xiii] When Israel began building settlements on the lands allocated for Palestine, the same lands Israel ostensibly hoped to trade for peace, this ratcheted up the conviction of the Three No's.

Successive war losses to Israel encouraged Arabs to think of other ways to solve the problem of a Zionist state in MENA. If the Soviet Union would have agreed to join the military coalition instead of being a military advisor and supplier of military equipment, there may have been a greater appetite for more conventional wars, but the Soviets were unwilling to go to war with the United States over Israel. The solution became less secularity and conventional wars, and more Islam and guerilla warfare/Islamic militancy. The latter was supported by the former. Islamic sacred texts offered plenty of support to engage in militancy against enemies of Islam.[xiv] In 1972 Palestinian militants scored a major global headline when they massacred Israeli Olympians in Munich, Germany.

Sympathy for Israel remained in short supply. Soviet propaganda helped to cast Israel as an imperialist denying statehood to the Palestinians. Israel's needs for security from regular Arab (and Soviet) aggression was a muted topic. In 1975 the UN passed a resolution that declared "Zionism as a form of racism and racial discrimination." Some interpreted this as the UN denying a member's right to exist. An organization with a charter that included protecting the sovereignty of members and peaceful coexistence had become a pawn of Muslim aggression and Cold War politics. The UN was implicitly promoting the antagonization of Jewish Israel. It was only after the Cold War ended that the UN General Assembly voted to revoke this resolution.[xv]

The idea for Israel came from a desire to give the Jewish population a home where they would finally be free from negative perceptions that had led to so much persecution. Israel was an answer to Europe and Russia's Jewish Question. Jews would now have a homeland in another region. This effectively transferred the Jewish Question on the status and treatment of Jews to MENA, where it had been made clear that receptivity to a Zionist state was in short supply.

Israel-related conflicts have incurred substantial human costs. About 250,000 casualties were sustained prosecuting and defending the Arab-Israeli wars and associated terrorism, and millions have fled in search of refuge[23] in adjacent Jordan, Lebanon, and Syria. According to the UN, approximately 1.6 million Palestinians were living in refugee camps in 2016. Some have lived there since 1948, the year of the first Arab-Israeli war. About another 3.6 million refugees were living and working in Jordan, Lebanon, and Syria.[xvi]

The Jews may live relatively free from persecution within Israel, but they live with anti-Semitism or anti-Zionism around the globe, and they do not live in peace. Israelis live with the real fear of an imminent attack, but much of the world sees this as justified because many see the Jewish people as interlopers, aggressors, and the pawn of western imperialism.

In spite of living with regular wars and continuous conflict, Israel is the only non-oil-kingdom that has an advanced economy in MENA. In 2017 its per capita income was second to oil-rich Qatar.

Iran and Saudi Arabia

Ottoman rule over its vast empire was often loose. This was the case on the Arabian Peninsula where rule varied from nominal suzerainty to fully autonomous. The future nation of Saudi Arabia even had periods of complete independence in the 18th and 19th centuries. Success was however fleeting until the Ottoman Empire was declining and then dissolving. Between 1915 and 1932 Saudi Arabia became an expanding state with a cover of protection by the United Kingdom. In 1932 it became independent. [24]

The Safavids declared independence from Ottoman rule in 1501 and proceeded to build the Shiite Safavid Empire, centered in Iran (formerly Persia). Rule by Shiite Persian and Iranian dynasties continued until the Islamic

Republic of Iran was established in 1979. Iran maintained its independence except for brief occupations by Britain and Russia/Soviet Union between 1907 and 1918 and 1941 and 1946.[25,26] In 1908 a British company made the first major oil strike in the Middle East, and the Anglo–Iranian Oil Company was created on terms favorable to the British. By 1945 the British were earning three times that of the Iranians and Iranians wanted to renegotiate terms, including improvements in the slummy conditions provided for the Iranian workers. They lost patience with British intransigence and nationalized Anglo-Iranian in 1951.

During the Cold War, the nationalization of almost anything, like Anglo-Iranian, could be and often was construed as the actions of a communist, and the expansion of communism had to be prevented. First-world Britain and the United States with cooperation from the Shah of Iran engineered the coup of Iran's Prime Minister Mossadegh.[27] Now the most powerful man in Iran was Shah Mohammad Reza Pahlavi (1941–1979).

Pahlavi took a path similar to Atatürk; he ruled a pro-western nominally democratic and secular state. He also reduced the land and power of Islamic clerics, and improved the economy with initiatives, like expanding access to education, and giving women more influential roles in government and society.

The paths of Pahlavi and Atatürk were very different from Saudi Arabia; it had chosen an absolute monarchy with the complete overlap of Islam and state. The official religion was Wahhabism, a fundamentalist or Salafist version of Islam. Women were subordinate to their husbands and fathers, fundamental freedoms were limited, and outside religious education, education was not a priority. Ironically the different paths were both triggered by a desire to succeed where the Ottomans had failed. The Saudi's saw the secular leanings of the Ottomans as the source of its downfall. Leaders in Turkey and Iran saw governments weakened by too much religious influence.

In time the Shah increased his power in the manner of a corrupt autocrat. During a period of economic malaise, Ayatollah Khomeini, an outspoken cleric unhappy with the shah's reduction of clerical power, and secular directions including the expansion of female freedoms, organized a successful revolution in 1979. It ended Iran's 2500-year-old monarchy, and its secular, nominally democratic government.

If the expectations of the revolutionaries included freedoms: like speech, assembly, and from unlawful imprisonment; an end to executing political prisoners;[xvii] and improvements in the economy, they were disappointed.

Especially disappointed were Iranian women, but the clerics were generally pleased with the return of power.

Opponents were murdered *en masse* following Khomeini's 1988 fatwa: "It is decreed that those who are in prisons throughout the country and remain steadfast in their support for the Monafeqin (Mojahedin) [opponents] are waging war on God and are condemned to execution."[xviii] An estimated 20,000 were murdered.[xix]

The Shah had autocratic tendencies, but Khomeini was a totalitarian ruler. His rule was similar to that by the king of Saudi Arabia, with one primary difference; Iran was a theocracy. The most powerful person in Iran was a religious leader.

Khomeini cared naught about gender equality, political and economic freedoms, or the economy. He once said, "economics is for donkeys."[28] His disdain for economics was evident in Iran's economic performance. In 1979 per capita income was $2,314. In 1989 when the Ayatollah died, it was $1,642.[29]

His position on women was consistent with a strict interpretation of sharia, which was unhelpful for the economy and a disaster for women's rights. Women were purged from influential government positions, husbands decided if their wives worked, women lost rights to divorce and child custody, the legal age for females to marry was changed from eighteen to nine, and women were back to covering up.[30] The penalty for showing even strands of hair outside a head covering was seventy lashes or a steep monetary fine.[xx] Women in Iran now had similar rights, or lack thereof, to women in Saudi Arabia.

The Ayatollah preferred politics and in particular geopolitics over economics. He spent considerable efforts bashing the west, with a bullseye on the Great Satan, his nickname for the United States. He accused the United States of placing Israel in the Middle East as a Trojan Horse for the west.[31] He rejected secularity as a western and bad practice and held the west accountable for the roots of Iranian problems, like corruption, and what he saw as the exploitation of women.

Shortly after coming to power, Khomeini supported the eighteen-month detention of more than sixty American hostages seized from the US embassy in Tehran. In 1983 Khomeini, as leader of the military, supported the bombing of a US marine barracks in Lebanon. These actions led the United States to impose economic sanctions that limited trade and froze foreign assets.[32]

During the Iranian Cultural Revolution (1980–1983) universities were closed for curriculum retooling toward Islam. This was also when Iran became the principal supporter of Hezbollah,[33] soon known for inflicting terror on western targets, with a bullseye on Israel.

Khomeini's invective war with the west was anti-Christian, anti-American, anti-Israeli, and anti-imperial[34] and an important vehicle for gaining Muslim support. Khomeini was on a mission to lead Sunnis and Shias and return Islam to the world stage. Sowing the seeds for a global Islamic empire was ambitious, but for the leader of a Shiite-majority nation in economic decline, it was delusional. Throughout history, Sunni rulers saw the Shias as an inferior class and even as heretics. One Ottoman sultan, Selim I (1512–1520) said, "the killing of one Shia had as much otherworldly reward as killing seventy Christians." In 2017 one of Saudi Arabia's most highly regarded religious scholars said of the Shias, "they are not our brothers ... rather they are brothers of Satan ..."[xxi]

Instead of Muslims uniting on the world stage under Khomeini, the Ayatollah reinvigorated the Sunni-Shiite conflict from the Era of Empire. Khomeini's Islamic unification mission challenged the Saudi ruling family. The Saudi King was the Custodian of the Two Holy Mosques and held the de facto position of leadership in Islam.

In 1979 Islamic militants seized the Grand Mosque in Mecca and called for the overthrow of the Saudi monarchy. The militants were Saudi and Sunni, but Khomeini claimed they were pawns of the west. He leveraged this event to unite Muslims with propaganda that framed the militants as part of a western, imperial, Zionist plot.[35]

In blaming the United States, Khomeini also wanted to damage ties between Saudi Arabia and the United States. The two nations enjoyed a beneficial alliance since 1945 when US President Franklin Delano Roosevelt met with Saudi King Abdul-Aziz aboard the USS Quincy. It didn't work. The Saudi's didn't see Khomeini's accusations as credible. What they saw as reliable was Khomeini's affront to their position of Islamic leadership, and the possibility of losing control of their Shiite-majority Eastern Province, home to the Saudi's largest oil field and headquarters for Saudi Aramco, the national oil company.[36]

The importance of oil to Saudi Arabia could not be overstated. The government relied on oil receipts, and an increasingly important area for funding was supporting efforts to counter threats from Iran and local Saudi militants. After the Grand Mosque seizure, several new actions were implemented. The government further empowered religious leaders. There was increased funding for Islamic militants targeting non-fundamental Muslims, like Shias. They raised the intensity and volume of Wahhabist instruction in the kingdom and eliminated anything perceived as violating Islamic fundamentals. Music shops and cinemas were shut down, photographs of women in newspapers and television were banned, and there was elevated monitoring of the segregation of men and women in public by the morality police. To increase support for Saudi Arabia in the global Muslim community, the government increased investments in the construction and staffing of madrassas, mosques, and clerics that would teach and support Wahhabism in foreign countries.

With the Ayatollah encouraging and supporting Shias across the globe to revolt against Sunni oppression, and Saudi Arabia expanding the reach of Wahhabism, with its bias against unpure practices of Islam, like those practiced by Shias, the Muslim world was positioned for instability.

The competition between Iran and Saudi Arabia for the leadership of Islam and the region looked like a modified replay of the contest in the 16th to 18th centuries between the Safavids and Ottomans. One significant modification was employing guerilla warfare using state-sponsored or stateless Islamic militant groups. This contest for Islamic and regional leadership became an unstated contest for the biggest state sponsor of terrorism.[xxii]

Khomeini had more to worry about than the Saudis. Rallying Shias against Sunni oppression, like the Shiite-majority in Iraq, threatened the rule of Sunni Saddam Hussein. The Iran-Iraq war (1980–1988) resulted in mass carnage, heightened repression for Iraqi Shias, and widespread destruction for both nations, but no victor.

Instead of building a unified pan-Islamic empire the Ayatollah revived sectarianism in Islam and reinvigorated a belief that Shias were heretical Muslims.[xxiii] Sectarianism became a catalyst for Iran-Saudi proxy wars that were detrimental to nation building throughout the Muslim world, and unhelpful for perceptions of Islam and Muslims by non-Muslims around the world. Khomeini and his successors deflected blame for negative outcomes on Israel, the United States, and Western imperial powers, three targets of Khomeini's anti-rhetoric.

In the chaos of the Arab Spring Iran saw another opportunity to expand its influence. It became a principal financial and military supporter of Shiite militants, the Shiite-led government in the Iraqi Civil War (2014–2017), Shias in the Yemeni Civil War (2015–?), Shiite militants in Bahrain, and the Shiite-led government in the Syrian Civil War (2011–?). The Saudis saw a similar opportunity and supported the Sunni opponents in these wars. The support of Iran and Saudi Arabia increased and extended the impact of these wars.

The Iraqi Civil War (2014–2017) was unique because this is where the militant group, the Islamic State (IS) claimed a caliphate. Globally publicized "successes" ignited militant recruiting and standalone jihadists to inflict terror all over the world. This brought investment and tourism in many Muslim nations to a standstill. It also motivated many religious and secular leaders of Muslim nations to denounce incidents of terror, even those with histories of sponsoring militancy. Perhaps a turning point.

In the Era of Nation-States, no leader has had a greater impact in the Muslim world than Ayatollah Khomeini. It all began with an empire-like mission to unify Islam under his rule. Some would argue that this accolade belongs to the rulers of Saudi Arabia. Their conquest of Mecca and Medina (1924–1925) and the assumption of responsibility as the Custodian of the Two Holy Mosques, in conjunction with global leadership in oil production, made them the most influential Muslim-majority nation in the world. Their influence was, however relatively understated until Khomeini threatened their position of regional and Islamic leadership. Then the Saudi's spared no expense to neutralize Iranian outreach, marginalize followers of Shiite Islam, build valuable relationships with global powers in the world, and unofficially compete against Iran in an unstated contest for the biggest state sponsor of terrorism. It seems like both nations have been very influential and the other nations in MENA have been some combination of hostages or participants to the geopolitics of regional rivals.

Sudan

From 1899 to 1943 the British and Egyptians jointly ruled the Sudan. The northern province was predominantly Arabic speaking and Muslim. In the southern province, Britain introduced English and encouraged conversions to Christianity. In 1943 the provinces were united under British rule. The central government was in the north, and it gave scant representation to the south.

In 1955, one year before independence, the north and south were engaged in a civil war. Things did not improve at independence when the central government attempted to establish an Islamist state with Arabic as the national language.

Sudan experienced thirty-nine years of north-south civil wars between 1955 and 2005 where more than two million died from war-related causes.[xxiv]

It was a period of rampant murder and looting, the use of starvation as a tool of war, and the enslavement of "conquered" non-Muslims.

The intensity of fighting increased: with the discovery of oil in the south in 1978, with the application of sharia law to Muslims and non-Muslims in 1983, and in 1989 when Sudan became the second country after Iran to be ruled by Islamists. Religious law was so strictly applied non-relatives of the opposite sex were discouraged from looking at one another.

Sudan's President Omar al-Bashir (1989–2019) earned a reputation as a state sponsor of terrorism, although he preferred to think of himself as a benevolent ruler offering refuge to Arabs returning from the Soviet-Afghan War (1979–1989).[xxv] Among those given refuge was Osama bin Laden. By 1996, Sudan was labeled a rogue state and subject to US sanctions directed at oil transactions. Al-Bashir responded by clamping down on militants targeting foreign nations, but he supercharged militants operating in the south.

Sudan's civil wars entered another phase in 2003 with a war in the Darfur region between the government (Arab and Muslim) and the non-Arab Muslims living in Darfur who accused the government of practicing a system of apartheid. The International Criminal Court investigated allegations of genocide, war crimes, and crimes against humanity. Al-Bashir became the first sitting president wanted by the International Criminal Court (ICC). This did not deter the African Dignity Forum from honoring him in 2016 as an outstanding African leader.[xxvi]

In 2011 South Sudan gained its independence. This reduced religious-based conflict in Sudan, but tribal-ethnic conflict increased in South Sudan. This was an outcome of a northern strategy during the civil wars to create conflict between neighboring tribal-ethnic groups in the south.

Throughout its existence, Sudan has not experienced peace. It's been the Arab Muslims against anyone not Muslim or non-Arab Muslim.

Libya

Emir Idris exchanged crucial support to the Allied Powers during WWII for a commitment to independence. In 1951 Libya became a constitutional monarchy with Idris as the first (and last) king. Idris had his hands full. Libya was war-torn and had a per capita income of around $40,[xxvii] one of the poorest nations in the world. Idris solicited foreign aid and investment to build the nation's oil industries. After the Arab loss in the 1967 Arab-Israeli War,

Libya's alliances with the west came to haunt Idris. Muammar Gaddafi successfully painted Idris as a lackey of western imperialists, impugning his legitimacy to rule, and facilitating his overthrow in 1969 after Idris had increased per capita income by $2,128.[xxviii]

Idris had worked hard to attract western expertise and investment for Libya's oil industries. Gaddafi nationalized them, expropriated Italian assets, and expelled the entire Italian community. Idris has been described as the modest king of a democratic republic. Gaddafi was a megalomaniac consumed by total control. Libya's political system under Gaddafi was known as Jamahiriya, an autocratic sharia-influenced system invented by Gaddafi and modifiable at will.

Gaddafi was another MENA ruler who seduced supporters with anti-imperialist rhetoric while behaving like an imperialist wannabe trying to build a pan-Arab empire to fill the void left by the Ottoman dissolution. In 1972 Gaddafi facilitated the creation of the Federation of Arab Republics which combined Libya, Egypt, and Syria. Five years later it was disbanded. Gaddafi also tried to unify Libya, Sudan, and Egypt, but that failed for the same reasons. National leaders preferred sovereignty, and there was no common pan-Arab ethnicity.

Gaddafi undertook another empire initiative between 1971 and 1986. He attempted to build the Islamic Republic of the Sahel by annexing the northern region of Chad. It turned out that black Chadians were uninterested in rule by lighter-skinned Libyans known for racism.[xxix]

Gaddafi's empire forays gave him first-hand experiences into why attempts to revive an Islamic empire would face enormous challenges. During a meeting of the Arab League, he said, "How can we do that? We hate each other, we wish ill of each other and our intelligence services conspire against each other. We are our own enemy."[xxx]

When Gaddafi wasn't empire building, he was causing mayhem. He obsessively interfered in the sovereignty of other nations. Libyan oil money was used to sponsor terrorists to disrupt western governments, of which the United States and Israel figured prominently. He had Libyan exiles in Europe assassinated and authorized the shooting down of US and French commercial jetliners and attacks on Italian and Austrian airports. He sponsored communist revolutionaries in Latam and Africa and assisted terrorists in Northern Ireland. Dartmouth University professor Diederick Vanderwalle said, "Terrorism was also a cheap alternative that would enable [Gaddafi] to emerge as a ... leader in the Arab World."[xxxi]

Gaddafi interfered with Arab nations too. He targeted national leaders in MENA and sub-Saharan Africa if they had alliances with western nations (including Israel), or because he saw them as weak and ineffectual. His obsession with interfering in other nations ultimately branded Libya as a rogue nation.[xxxii]

Gaddafi started rethinking the mayhem he was inflicting in the world in the early 2000s and gave indications that he was reforming. For example, he decommissioned his weapons of mass destruction and condemned Al Qaeda.

In 2008 he was able to realize an imperial ambition when he was crowned King of Kings in a ceremony with 200 African tribal kings; something else bought and paid for with Libyan oil money. He was proud of his title. In 2009 he said, "I am an international leader, the dean of the Arab rulers, the king of kings of Africa and the imam of Muslims ..."[xxxiii]

Within Libya, Gaddafi's rule endured in part because Libyans enjoyed the highest standard of living in Africa, and in part because there was no room for dissent. His surveillance organization employed 10–20 percent of the population.[xxxiv] Perceived opponents met brutality swiftly, and there were plenty of opponents. He instituted laws that made it easy for the state to expropriate assets that were given to political cronies.[xxxv]

Corruption under Gaddafi was off the charts. The "royal" family squandered the nation's wealth to enjoy lives of considerable luxury that included things like a personal Airbus A340, and a private coastal resort.

After forty-two years in power, simmering dissent exploded into a rebellion and then civil war. In 2011 Gaddafi was ousted with the support of three nations that Qaddafi's regime had terrorized, but subsequently created friendly relations: France, the United Kingdom, and the United States.

By the time he died in 2011, Gaddafi had diverted billions from Libya's national treasury to his personal account. The Los Angeles Times estimated that in 2011 Gaddafi was worth an estimated $200 billion. Libyan GDP in 2010 was estimated to be $75 billion.

With Gaddafi gone, Libyans hosted democratic elections, but the outcomes, per democratic protocol, were not respected. Among the losers was an Islamist party that set up a second government and made it impossible for the winners to form an effective government. Libya had its second civil war in three years. The ensuing chaos became fertile ground for Islamic militancy sending scores of Libyans in search of refuge and suffocating economic output. Per capita income plunged 40–65 percent between 2010 and 2015. In 2015 GDP was estimated at $29 billion.

Notes

1. Saudi Arabia's conquest of polities on the Arabian Peninsula is sometimes categorized as the work of an Arab empire and sometimes as the work of a unifier.

2. The future independent nations of Algeria, Djibouti, Libya, and Sudan were colonies. Egypt, Morocco, Mauritania, and Tunisia were protectorates. Morocco became a French protectorate in 1912, with Spain becoming the protector of a northern portion including Ceuta and Melilla, which to this day remain autonomous cities of Spain.

3. Iran and North Yemen were independent. North Yemen had just gained its independence when the Ottoman Empire dissolved.

4. At the time this was nearly every sovereign in the world, in addition to some Dominions of the British Empire. The only Muslim-majority member was Iran.

5. This mandate offered a solution to Europe and Russia's long-standing Jewish Question.

6. In 1900 the Bedouin population in the lands of the future nations of Saudi Arabia was about 40 percent, Iraq 35–40 percent, and Libya 25 percent.

7. The French Mandate for Syria and Lebanon became Vichy French Syria and Lebanon after France surrendered to the Germans in 1940. This surrender really altered perceptions of the value of French protection.

8. The Western Sahara was a colony of Spain that was annexed by Morocco in 1975. There have been many calls for independence, but it remains, in UN parlance, a non-self-governing territory of Morocco.

9. Eliminating the king of Saudi Arabia who is the Custodian of the Two Holy Mosques would have created a very unwanted void in the Islamic community.

10. With a shared border and contentious history of conflict with the Russian Empire, and a shift toward secularity and greater industrialization, Turkey saw the Cold War differently. It feared Soviet and communist encroachment. It became the only Muslim-majority nation that was part of the First World and a member in NATO. Once the Soviets aligned with Arab nations against Israel, Israel chose alignment with the First World.

11. After 1948 the United States supported Israel in the Arab-Israeli wars.

12. The Soviets supported the Arabs in the 1956, 1967 and 1973 Arab-Israeli wars. The Arab-Israeli conflicts in 1982 and 2006 are also called the 1982 and 2006 Lebanon wars. The Soviet Union did not support these wars. In 1982 Lebanon was supported by its occupying power Syria (1972–2005). In the 2006 war, the United States supported Israel. The primary opponent was Iranian-backed Hezbollah: a Shiite Lebanese political party and militant group.

13. Inspire is the name of a magazine published by al-Qaeda that encouraged jihad.

14. During Turkey's Kemalist period (1923–2002), the betrayal of the Arabs in the Arab Revolt was highlighted as a reason the Ottoman's lost WWI.

15. Cyprus signed an association agreement with the EU's predecessor organization, the European Economic Community in 1973. Cyprus has been a member of the EU since 2004.

16. The alignment of Sunni Turkey with Shiite Iran against Sunni Saudi Arabia was an illustration that the Iran-Saudi proxy wars were not purely about leadership of Islam or Shiite-Sunni conflict. The political leadership of MENA was a powerful driver.

17. According to the Jewish Virtual Library, Jews represented 30 percent of the population of Mandatory Palestine in 1946. In 1948 they were 82 percent.

18. There are many disputed claims that the Jews received a disproportionate share of arable land.
19. Many Jews were merchants, but Judaism also sees war as defensive.
20. The Israelis did have help from the Soviet sphere; Czechoslovakia shipped them arms.
21. In 1975 the UN General Assembly passed resolution 3379 with 72 votes for, 35 against and 32 abstentions. The resolution declared Zionism as a form racism.
22. Western nations are defined here to include the nations of Western Europe, the United States, Canada, Australia, New Zealand, and Israel.
23. Following the 1948 Arab-Israeli war, there was an equal number of Jewish and Arab refugees. Jewish refugees came from all over MENA.
24. The Treaty of Darin (1915–1927) and the Treaty of Jeddah (1927–1932) offered protection to Saudi Arabia from the United Kingdom, even though Saudi Arabia was not yet a recognized nation. In exchange, Saudi Arabia agreed to refrain from conquering other British protectorates on the Arabian Peninsula that included the future nations of Kuwait, Oman, Qatar and the United Arab Emirates.
25. Americans participated in the WWII occupation. They were viewed as a moderating force that would ensure the return of independence, instead of being colonized by the British or Soviets.
26. After WWII the Soviets refused to leave until compelled to do so by the United States with the support of the UN. Called the Iran Crisis (1946) some consider this to be the first Cold War-related conflict.
27. Mossadegh was not a communist. He had been the leader of a democratically elected parliament committed to constitutional government. He nationalized Anglo-Iranian because he believed it was the right thing to do for Iranians.
28. Khomeini ruled according to sharia, where economics is virtually a mute topic.
29. Decreased income was affected by a few factors: changes in the price of oil, the Iran-Iraq war, decreases in oil production, and unhelpful economic policies.
30. According to Nobel Prize winner Iranian Shirin Ebadi, professional Iranian women supported the rise of Khomeini. They had not contemplated this could plunge women's rights into the dark ages.
31. It was inconvenient truths that: Britain was the first nation to openly support a Jewish homeland, League of Nation members including Iran unanimously approved the Mandate for Palestine, and it was the UN General Assembly in Resolution 273 that recognized Israel as a sovereign nation.
32. Iranian President, Mahmoud Ahmadinejad (2005–2013) could take credit for passage of a UN resolution in 2006 authorizing more sanctions on Iran for violating the nuclear non-proliferation treaty.
33. Hezbollah later became a Lebanese political party with a military/militant arm.
34. Iran's imperial arch nemeses had been the Ottoman Empire and the Russian Empire, but this anti-imperial wrath was directed at western powers.
35. Khomeini knew the United States had engaged in several coups, including one in Iran in 1953. He saw an opportunity to blame them. "It is not beyond guessing that this is the work of criminal American imperialism and international Zionism." His position fueled anti-American demonstrations by Muslims throughout the world.
36. Saudi Arabia completed the nationalization of Saudi Aramco in 1980.

References

i. Hobbs, Mark. "Oil Maps of the Middle East." *British Library*. Retrieved November 19, 2018.

ii. McHugo, John. *A Concise History of the Arabs*. New York: The New Press, 2013.

iii. Russell, Michael. "Marxism and Islam in South Yemen." Graduate school paper for Air Command and Staff College Air University, 1988.

iv. Harrison, Ross. "Shifts in the Middle East Balance of Power: An Historical Perspective." *Al Jazeera Center for Studies*, September 2, 2018.

v. Kucuksahin, Sukru. "Has Turkey Given up fighting Corruption." *Turkey Pulse*, June 8, 2016.

vi. de Bellaigue, Christopher. "Turkey's Hidden Past." *The New York Review of Books*, March 8, 2001.

vii. "Saudi Prince Says Turkey and Iran part of a 'Triangle of Evil.'" *Bloomberg*, March 7, 2018.

viii. Clarke, Colin P., and Ariane M. Tabatabai. "Is Major Realignment Taking Place in the Middle East?" *Foreign Policy Magazine*, October 31, 2018.

ix. Baran, Zeyno. "Is Kemalism Dead in Turkey." *Hoover Institute*, December 13, 2010.

x. "UN Partition Plan." *BBC.co.uk*, November 29, 2001.

xi. Uyar, Mesut, and Edward J. Erickson. *A Military History of the Ottomans*. Greenwood Publishing Group, 2009.

xii. Brown, Cameron. "The Six-Day War and the Middle East Peace Process." *Sixdaywar.co.uk*, April 19, 2007.

xiii. Ro'I, Yaacov, and Boris Morozov. *The Soviet Union and the 1967 Six Day War*. Stanford University Press, 2008.

xiv. Bergen, Peter. "Does Islam Fuel Terrorism?" *CNN.com*, January 13, 2015.

xv. Meisler, Stanley. *United Nations: A History*. New York: Grove Press, 1995.

xvi. "Palestine Refugees." *UNRWA.com*. Retrieved January 1, 2019.

xvii. Abrahamian, Ervand. *Tortured Confessions*. Berkeley: University of California Press, 1999.

xviii. Lamb, Christina "Khomeini Fatwa Led to Killing 30,000 in Iran." *The Telegraph*, February 4, 2004.

xix. "Judgment Time?" *The Economist*, October 30, 2012.

xx. Esfandieri, Haleh. "The Women's Movement." *The Iran Primer: United States Institute for Peace*. Retrieved September 23, 2016.

xxi. Maida, Adam. "They are not our Brothers." *Human Rights Watch*, 2017.

xxii. Weinstein, Adam. "The Real Largest State Sponsor of Terrorism." *Huffington Post*, March 16, 2017.

xxiii. Shuster, Mike. "As Iran Exported Its Shiite Revolution, Sunni Arabs Resisted." *NPR*, February 14, 2007.

xxiv. Deng, Francis M. "Sudan—Civil War and Genocide: Disappearing Christians of the Middle East." *Middle East Quarterly*, Winter, 2001.

xxv.   "Interview: Omar Hassan Ahmed al-Bashir." *PBS*. Retrieved September 20, 2017.

xxvi.   "Sudan: African Initiative for Pride and Dignity to Honor President Al-Bashir Friday in Addis Ababa." *Allafrica.com*, July 28, 2016.

xxvii. "Libya." *Encyclopedia.com*. Retrieved March 10, 2017.

xxviii. Vandewalle, Dirk. "Libya Since 1969." *The History Reader*, March 25, 2011.

xxix.   King, Matthew. "NYT Wakes up to Racism against Africans in Libya." *The American Interest*, September 12, 2017.

xxx.   "Gaddafi Condemns Arab leaders." *Al Jazeera*, March 29, 2008.

xxxi.   Obeidat, Sara. "Muammar Gaddafi and Libya's Legacy of Terrorism." *Frontline*, *PBS.org*, October 13, 2015.

xxxii. Obeidat, Muammar Qaddafi.

xxxiii. "Gaddafi as Orator: A Life in Quotes." *Al Jazeera*, October 20, 2011.

xxxiv. Eljahmi, Mohamed. "Libya and the U.S.: Qadhafi Unrepentant." *The Middle East Quarterly*, 2006.

xxxv.   Worth, Robert. "Thousands of Libyans Struggle with Recovery of Property Confiscated by Qaddafi." *New York Times*, May 13, 2012.

· 2 1 ·

SOUTH ASIA

Every major empire/group influenced this region. The Portuguese established the first permanent European settlement in Goa, India (1505–1961). When they did Islam was already present on the subcontinent. The reach of the Chinese tributary empire extended to Bhutan,[1] Nepal, and Sri Lanka. The first foreign empire to dominate South Asia in the Era of Empire was the Islamic Mughal Empire (1526–1858). Before domination, the Safavids and other Persian empires battled for control of today's Afghanistan, Pakistan, and northern India.[i] The British Empire succeeded the Mughals in 1858. The Russians were the last. The Russian Empire wanted to extend its borders to control Afghanistan, but Russian influence was delayed until the Cold War. Then it was strongly felt during the Soviet-Afghan War (1979–1989).

All empires, except the Chinese tributary empire, left their marks: Islamic Empires brought Islam to the region and a painful history of discrimination against Hindus; the British brought borders, the English language, and democratic forms of government; and the Soviets created the setting for the first national breeding ground for Islamic militants. All of the empires/groups have also left postscripts, like Cold War conflicts and Iran-Saudi proxy wars.

The Islamic empires altered an overwhelmingly Hindu and Buddhist region to one with the largest regional Muslim population, including a significant Shiite minority. Afghanistan, Bangladesh, Pakistan and the Maldives have Muslim majorities, and India has the second largest Muslim population in the world. They also left behind the memory of forced conversions and the Hindu Holocaust.

The British had good intentions in 1947 when they partitioned British India into independent India and Pakistan. They were trying to minimize Hindu-Muslim conflict that was an aftermath of the predecessor Islamic empires. Good intentions turned into calamity when the partition instigated a cross migration of 10–14 million Muslims and Hindus, of which an estimated 1–2 million died,[ii,iii,2] many from religion-oriented violence. Nationhood for India and Pakistan began in a crisis; actually, two and both were related to borders. Two months after partition the Indian state (a Union Territory as of 2019) of Jammu Kashmir (Kashmir) was invaded by Pakistani Pashtun militants looting, setting fires, raping women, destroying infrastructure and blockading essential supplies.[iv] They believed Muslim-majority Kashmir should be part of Pakistan. Soon the ongoing Indo-Pakistani wars commenced.

About twenty-five years later another border-related crisis arose. Pakistan was created with two geographically distinct areas called West and East Pakistan, with a thousand miles of India in between. The population was overwhelmingly Muslim, with ethnolinguistic differences. This may not have been a problem but the Punjabi-speaking population in the west was in charge of the government, and they implemented discriminatory policies against the majority Bengali-speaking population in the east.[v] The Bengalis expressed their displeasure.

In 1971 the Pakistani army launched Operation Searchlight to eliminate a growing Bengali separatist movement. Soon enough there was a civil war, the Bangladesh Liberation War. During the war, Hindus in East Pakistan were targeted and some ten million fled to India. In combination with West Pakistani air attacks, this led India led to fully support East Pakistan and tipped the balance in their favor. Nine months after the war began, West Pakistan unconditionally surrendered, and independent Bangladesh was born. An estimated 200,000 to 3 million died in the war.[vi] In Bangladesh the official figure is 3 million.[vii]

In this region, only Afghanistan was engaged in a Cold War-related armed conflict, but Cold War politics really took a toll on the region. The ongoing dispute between Pakistan and India created an opportunity for first- and second-world nations to take sides and insert their influence into South Asia. Pakistan aligned with the United States, and "non-aligned" India with the Soviet Union.

The Soviet Union and India signed the Indo-Soviet Treaty of Friendship in August of 1971. In December India entered the Bangladesh Liberation War with assurances from the Soviet Union that if the Chinese or US military engaged in the war, the Soviets would support India. The Soviet Union also exercised its veto to prevent the UN from demanding a ceasefire and the withdrawal of Indian and Pakistani militaries. These actions facilitated the strengthening of Soviet-supported India and by extension East Pakistan.

A negotiated settlement in Kashmir may have occurred if not for Cold War politics. The UN had been actively involved in resolving this conflict and appeared to be making progress. However, US support for Pakistan and Soviet support for India, weakened the resolve of both nations to comply with UN resolutions. In 1972 a cease-fire line was converted to a Line of Control (LOC), or a temporary boundary that divides Kashmir between India and Pakistan. It didn't end the conflict it simply moved it to the LOC,[viii,ix] where it remains.

India's relationship with the Soviet Union influenced the development of its economic system.[x] A socialist economic system and a democratic political system was an odd combination, and it became an economic disaster—not just for India, but the entire region. India could have been a regional economic locomotive, but it was not. In 1991 per capita income in India was $318. In Israel, which became independent one year after India it was $13,320. In the post-Cold War period, China's economy was soaring. This motivated India to introduce capitalist weighting and lessen its socialist leanings. Economic improvement in India helped to upgrade the region's economic performance.[xi]

The year 1979 holds a lot of significance in the Muslim world. It is the year of the Iranian Revolution and the seizure of the Grand Mosque. It is also the first year of the Soviet-Afghan War, which was the first civil war between a government and Islamic militants. During the war, Al-Qaeda and the Taliban were formed, and their role in defeating the Soviet Union was globally recognized, albeit overstated. It was also the year that Pakistan's President Zia-ul-Haq shifted the nation toward Islamism, following a Salafist version of Sunni Islam that was anti-Shia. With Iran exporting its Shiite revolution to Pakistan, it was a perfect storm for Shiite-Sunni conflict. "The year 1979 was a turning point for international terrorism in Pakistan."[xii]

Zia was another despot that found favor with the United States during the Cold War. He was a useful ally against the Soviets in Afghanistan, but his methods were unconventional and the United States condoned them. Zia presided over a Pakistani state sponsoring Islamic militancy in Afghanistan and Pakistan.[xiii-xv]

Pakistan and Afghanistan regularly top the Global Terrorism Index,[3] and they are two of the most dangerous nations in the world. Nearby India, with a long history of Hindu-Muslim conflict, including volatile Kashmir, has not been spared. According to the Global Terrorism Database, prior to 1979 annual Islamic militant acts in India numbered zero or one. In the 1980s incidents reached a high of 339. In 2011 it reached 643 and 882 in 2015.

Terrorism of this magnitude really hurts economic development, and so does corruption. Corruption generally affects autocracies harder than democracies, but in South Asia autocracies and democracies alike have serious problems with corruption. Afghanistan, Bangladesh, and Pakistan characteristically sit near the very bottom of TI's corruption rankings.

In Afghanistan an estimated $3 billion was paid in bribes in 2016.[xvi] This was down from $3.9 billion in 2012.[xvii] To get a feel for the seriousness of this problem, GDP in 2016 was $19.22 billion. In Pakistan corrupt police have the company of corrupt politicians and judges.[xviii] A cozy relationship between these three is found in many countries with serious corruption problems. It's a perfect configuration for unchecked corruption.

India ranks in the middle. It is telling that even in the middle there are so many corrupt politicians, they are assumed to be corrupt. So are many in the public sector, and this includes educators, and health care administrators. Corruption is everywhere in India. In a 2016 survey 54 percent of Indian respondents said they paid a bribe in the past twelve months.[xix] That is less than Bangladesh where it was 66 percent. Like Pakistan the police are perceived to be among the most corrupt, but public officials rank at the top.[xx]

Geographically adjacent China has been a source of challenge and opportunities. The Chinese trading juggernaut has facilitated economic growth but also increased its influential role in the region, at the expense of India. According to the World Bank in 1978, the year China began economic reforms, the economies of India and China were similar in size: $135 billion and $149 billion respectively. In 2016 they were worlds apart: $2.3 trillion and $11.2 trillion respectively.

South Asia is one of two very underdeveloped regions; the other is sub-Saharan Africa. In 2017 half the countries in sub-Saharan Africa had per capita incomes under $1,000, and in South Asia 95 percent of the population had per capita incomes under $2,000.

Conflict with ties to religion has been a significant contributor to poor economic performance. Most, but not all, have been between Hindus and Muslims. In Sri Lanka, a conflict between Buddhist Sinhalese and Hindu

Tamils led to twenty-six years of civil war. Many conflicts in South Asia are tied to the rule of empires, but religious conflict has also been exacerbated by under-skilled and misguided leaders. Some of this is politically motivated. National leaders have also introduced setbacks by condoning or doing too little to address corruption. The greatest setbacks are because too many leaders are just not up to the job of nation-building.

The rest of the South Asia section goes into more details on the trajectory of nation-building in Afghanistan, Bangladesh, and Pakistan.

Afghanistan

Afghanistan was at a nexus of empires expanding Shiite and Sunni Islam in the 16th and 17th centuries. In the 19th century Afghanistan became a British protectorate (1878–1921). In the 20th century it became a client of the Soviet Union (1978–1989). Uniquely, the influence of each of these empires/groups can be seen in the multiple and different decisions made on political systems.

Afghanistan has been governed with absolute and constitutional monarchies, as a democratic republic, under communism, and as an Islamist state. None succeeded because the politics that have prevailed are those of the indigenous territorial warlords: some Sunni and some Shia. The warlords have been described as warriors and gangsters. During Afghanistan's many wars some warlords became mujahedeen leaders, and some became known as mujahedeen warlords or mujahedeen gangsters.[4]

From 1964 to 1973 Afghanistan had a constitutional monarchy with equal rights for men and women and universal suffrage.[5] This was its period of greatest stability. When Afghanistan began transitioning toward communism in 1978 notions of stability were gone.[6] The warlords were very unhappy with land confiscations, severe repression, and female comrades. They called for jihad.

With the survival of the government at risk, the Soviet Union intervened, and the Soviet-Afghan War took place (1979–1989). This was a Cold War conflict where successor nations from the Chinese, European, Islamic and Russian empires were involved.[7] The warlords were supported by mujahedeen,[8] and the mujahedeen were supported by the United States, Turkey, Pakistan, China,[xxi] France, Iran, the United Kingdom, Saudi Arabia and other Arabian Peninsula monarchies. Iran's supportive role was nuanced by the unfathomable notion of an alliance with the United States.[xxii]

Military casualties in this war are estimated at around 120,000, but Afghan civilian casualties have been estimated at 1.5 million.[xxiii] This high civilian casualty toll has been attributed to a Soviet-led campaign to suppress massive resistance, and so is the mass rape of Afghan women.[xxiv,9]

The Soviets pulled out in 1988 and 1989.[10] Jihadists were winners in the last major Cold War conflict.[11] The Soviets/Russians continued support for government forces that were battling mujahedeen coalitions until 1992. When Russian support ended the government conceded defeat and yielded to a mujahedeen coalition that paradoxically wasn't interested in joint decisions.

In 1992 one civil war ended and the next one began. This one was between mujahedeen coalitions. It was in part another Iran-Saudi proxy war. At least one Shiite group was supported by Iran, and the Sunni Taliban was supported by Saudi Arabia and Pakistan's intelligence service.[xxv] When this war ended in 1996 the world had its first Islamist government ruled by Islamic militants, the Taliban, and they were intolerant of the Shias because they saw them as heretics.

In 1996 a new civil war commenced where the Taliban supported by al-Qaeda fought Afghanistan's United Front (or the Northern Alliance), a group of tribes, warlords, and political parties united in opposition to Taliban rule. In 2001 the Taliban was routed from Afghanistan, by a UN supported, US-led coalition.[12] Most members of the Taliban travelled across the Pakistani border and into the arms of fellow Pashtuns, where they became a disruptive force in Pakistan too.

Afghanistan's continuous wars were an ongoing training ground for militants coming from, and returning to or relocating to different nations. There is irony in the last major Cold War conflict creating a source of instability around the world in the post-Cold War period, and the major powers, including the five permanent Security Council members charged with keeping peace in the world, being instrumental in this outcome.

Escaping the instability of being a global training ground for Islamic militancy has not been easy for Afghanistan, even with the help of NATO. It has been said that no one ever completely defeats the warlords in Afghanistan. In April 2017 the Taliban, long considered another warlord, was controlling about 11 percent of Afghanistan's territory,[xxvi] and maintaining a target on Afghani Shias. Meanwhile other warlords were doing their best to keep the Taliban in check.

It cannot be surprising that Afghanistan, with a per capita income of less than $600 in 2017 remains one of the poorest countries in the world.

Bangladesh

Bangladesh was born in the aftermath of the Bangladesh Liberation War (1971). The nation was in shambles, million had died, and even more had become refugees. The Pakistani military's targeted extermination of the people most capable of facilitating nation- building created another giant setback for the fledgling nation.

Amidst challenges aplenty, the nation's leaders have not always focused on nation-building. Since 1991 only two people have served as prime minister. Two women from rival political dynasties have gained global notoriety for pursuing personal vendettas that have left many dead, and seriously disrupted effective governance and economic development. They have facilitated or condoned vote rigging, trumped up criminal charges against each other, extrajudicial killings, labor strikes, street protests, and boycotts.[xxvii]

Bangladeshi's pay the price. In 2017 per capita income in Bangladesh was $1,602. South Asian neighbor Sri Lanka became independent in 1972 and endured a civil war of twenty-six years. It's per capita income in 2017 was $4,084.

Pakistan

Pakistan was founded as a democratic and secular nation for Muslims. Pakistan's founder, Muhammad Ali Jinnah said, "You are free; you are free to go to your temples. You are free to go to your mosques or to any other places of worship in this State of Pakistan. You may belong to any religion, caste or creed—that has nothing to do with the business of the state."[xxviii] Pakistan didn't stay democratic or secular, and people didn't remain free to go to their religious establishment of choice.

Pakistan is another nation filled with national leaders making modest progress toward nation-building. Since 1947 military leaders have ruled for thirty-three years. This is in part justified by an existential threat from India, and from the prominent presence of Islamic militancy. Ironically, the latter was exacerbated by the decisions of military rulers to leverage Islamic militancy to combat India's threat to national security.[13] With or without military rule the military has played a weighted role in the government and the economy, for which it has sometimes received high marks and other times not so much.[xxix,xxx]

President (General) Muhammad Zia al-Huq (1977–1988), a follower of the fundamentalist Sunni Deobandi movement felt differently from Jinnah about freedom of religion. He wanted to create an Islamist state. Pakistan's large Shiite population objected to the imposition of aspects of Deobandi religious law. This ended up being a catalyst for intra-Islamic intolerance,[xxxi] sectarian conflict, and an Iran-Saudi proxy war. Sunni militants were funded by Saudi Arabia and they operated with impunity on a mission to temper Iran's influence over local Shias.[xxxii]

Zia was a catalyst for increasing militancy in a second way. He supported the mujahedeen during and after the Soviet-Afghan War. When the war ended trained jihadists streamed across the porous border dividing Afghanistan and Pakistan.[14] Now Pakistan had a very serious militant problem in the Federally Administered Tribal Areas (FATA).[15,16] Pakistani author Ahmed Rashid called President Zia's approach to governance, "the Islamization of criminal activity and the criminalization of segments of Islam."[xxxiii]

Things were about to get worse in Pakistan. Saudi Arabia and Iran began funding hundreds of madrassas that created a feeder system for Islamic-militant recruiters. In 1980 Pakistan had 800 madrassas. By 2015 there were 20,000. Some estimate that *just* 20 percent of madrassas teach hate. In Pakistan that's 4,000. Actually, most teach hate; Saudi-supplied textbooks promote anti-Semitic, anti-Christian, and anti-Shiite and -Sufi ideas. Iranian-supplied textbooks teach hatred of the Jews.[xxxiv]

Pakistan has an overwhelming Sunni majority and teaching hatred in school has taken serious tolls on people following minority faiths. Shiite and Sufi Muslims, and non-Muslims have experienced the destruction of their houses of worship and shrines, numerous murderous acts of terror; and the prosecution of honor killings and honor rapes against women perceived to violate interpretations of Deobandi religious law regarding modesty and chastity. A country created to respect religious freedom had become a death trap for non-Sunni or -Islamist Muslims and non-Muslims.[17] According to the IMF, in 2017 per capita income in Pakistan was $1,541.

Notes

1. Bhutan disputes this.
2. Many speculate that if Mahatma Gandhi had not been assassinated the death toll would have been reduced.
3. The Global Terrorism Index reported that 66 percent of all terrorist attacks in 2013 were attributed to al-Qaeda, Boko Haram, the Islamic State, and the Taliban. All but Boko Haram are present in Afghanistan and Pakistan.
4. The term mujahedeen refer to Muslims engaged in jihad by the sword.

5. Afghanistan had its first constitution in 1923 and a second one in 1931. However, uncharacteristically these did not limit the power of the monarch.
6. Unusually for a communist state, Islam remained the state religion.
7. The Soviet Union was a primary belligerent. The involvement of the others was in opposition to the Soviet Union and consisted of support in the forms of training and supplying financial and military aid. Much of the support was covert.
8. The most famous mujahedeen are Osama bin Laden and Ayman al-Zawahiri, the founders of al-Qaeda.
9. These women then faced a life of dishonor because they had sex outside wedlock.
10. Many tie this devastating and expensive war to the final nail in the Soviet coffin.
11. Jihadists were a minor percentage of the victorious forces but it was their victory that was publicized.
12. The Taliban, like Sudanese President al-Bashir, made the error of giving Osama bin Laden (and al-Qaeda) sanctuary.
13. The strategy to leverage Islamic militancy was part of a military doctrine called Bleed India with a Thousand Cuts.
14. The border is called the Durand Line. It was defined in 1893 between an Afghan emir and a diplomat from the British Empire. The border divides Afghanistan and Pakistan and also the Pashtun ethnic group.
15. In 2018 FATA, which had been ruled semi-autonomously, was merged with the government in the Pakistani province of Khyber Pakhtunkhwa.
16. The Pakistani Taliban in FATA sheltered Osama bin Laden until he was captured and killed in 2011.
17. According to Human Rights Watch, Hindus, Christians, and Ahmadis have faced "unprecedented insecurity and persecution."

References

i. Axworthy, Michael. *A History of Iran*. New York: Basic Books, 2008.
ii. Dalrymple, William. "The Great Divide." *The New Yorker*, June 29, 2015.
iii. Bates, Crispin. "The Hidden Story of Partition and its Legacies." *BBC*, March 2011.
iv. Singh, Hari. "Maharaja Hari Singh's Letter to Mountbatten." Government of India, October 26, 1947.
v. Asadullah, Mohammad. "Educational Disparity in East and West Pakistan, 1947–1971: Was East Pakistan Discriminated Against?" *Oxford University*, July 2016.
vi. "Bangladesh sets up War Crimes Court." *Al Jazeera*, March 25, 2010.
vii. Bergman, David. "Questioning an Iconic Number." *The Hindu*, July 29, 2016.
viii. "UN's Failure in Kashmir: A Factual Survey." *The Economic Weekly*, October 2, 1965.
ix. Ahmad, Wajahat. "Kashmir and the United Nations." *Countercurrents.org*, August 27, 2008.
x. Mehrotra, Santosh. *India and the Soviet Union: Trade and Technology Transfer*. Cambridge: Cambridge University Press, 1991.

xi. "South Asia Should Remove Trade Barriers for Mutual Economic Gains: New World Bank Report." *The World Bank*, September 24, 2018.

xii. Moore, John. "The Evolution of Islamic Terrorism: An Overview." *PBS.org*, Retrieved November 11, 2018.

xiii. Shams, Shamil. "Pakistan's Islamization—before and after Dictator Zia-ul Haq." *DW.com*, August 17, 2016.

xiv. Nasir, Abbas. "Zia's long shadow." *Dawn*, July 6, 2012.

xv. "Modern Sunni-Shia Tensions 1979–2017." *Council on Foreign Relations*. Retrieved October 14, 2018.

xvi. Gul, Ayaz. "Survey: Afghans Pay $3 Billion in Bribes Annually." *VOA.com*, December 8, 2016.

xvii. "Corruption in Afghanistan: What Needs to Change?" *Transparency International*, February 16, 2016.

xviii. "Global Corruption Barometer." *Transparency International*, 2003.

xix. Burke, Jason. "Corruption in India: 'All your Life you Pay for Things that should be Free.'" *The Guardian*, August 18, 2011.

xx. Hardoon, D., and F. Heinrich. "Daily Lives and Corruption: Public Opinion in South Asia." *Transparency International*, 2011.

xxi. Hilali, A. Z. "China's Response to the Soviet Invasion in Afghanistan." *Central Asian Survey* 20, no. 3 (September 2001): 323–351.

xxii. Nader, Alireza, and Joya Laha. "Iran's Balancing Act in Afghanistan." *The Rand Corporation*, 2011.

xxiii. "Soviet War in Afghanistan." *Findthedata.com*. Retrieved December 14, 2016.

xxiv. Cummins, Joseph. *The War Chronicles: From Flintlocks to Machine Guns*. Beverly: Fair Winds Press, 2009.

xxv. Carpenter, Ted Galen. "Terrorist Sponsors: Saudi Arabia, Pakistan, China." *Cato.org*, November 16, 2001.

xxvi. "Global Terrorism Index 2017." *Institute for Economics and Peace*, 2017.

xxvii. "The Battle between Bangladesh's two begums is over." *The Economist*, December 7, 2017.

xxviii. "Muhammad Ali Jinnah's first Presidential Address to the Constituent Assembly of Pakistan (August 11, 1947)." Source: G. Allana, Pakistan Movement Historical Documents. *Columbia.edu*, Retrieved January 3, 2019.

xxix. Pervaiz, Faisel. "Pakistan's Military -Democracy Complex." *Stratfor*, February 2, 2016.

xxx. "Military Dictatorship vs. Civilian Rule." *Business Recorder*, August 7, 2017.

xxxi. Ispahani, Farahnaz. "Pakistan's Decent into Religious Intolerance." *Hudson Institute*, 1 March 2017.

xxxii. Riedel, Bruce. "Why do Saudi Arabia and Iran Compete for Pakistani Support." *Brookings.edu*, January 11, 2016.

xxxiii. Rehman, I. A. "Zia-ul-Haq: Master of Illusion." *The Herald*, August 23, 2016.

xxxiv. Posner, Alexander. "Exporting Intolerance." *The Yale Globalist*, April 21, 2015.

· 2 2 ·

SOUTHEAST ASIA

All empires/groups influenced Southeast Asia, but most rule was indirect until the 19th century. The Chinese Empire exacted tribute until the 19th century. The Islamic empires exerted indirect influence through Arab-Muslim traders, Indian-Muslim traders, and Muslim rulers beginning in the 7th, 12th and 14th centuries respectively. The Soviet's rule was also indirect, but this was in the 20th century when they supported communist parties and their Vietnamese client (1978–1988).

It was only the European and Japanese empires that exercised direct rule in this region, and for the Japanese, it was in the form of war-time occupations. Between 1520 and 1800 the Portuguese, Dutch, and Spanish established colonial settlements in East Timor, Indonesia, and the Philippines respectively.[1] In the 19th century, the British and French colonized the rest of the region excluding Thailand. However, all European empires lost control of their colonies when they failed to defend them from Japanese conquests and Thai annexations during WWII. This failure diminished the perceptions colonials had for their imperial protectors.

A long and diverse history with empires and long periods of little or no direct empire rule explains why the nations in this region share so little in common when it comes to politics and religion. This is the only region with a mix of atheist, Buddhist, Christian, and Muslim majority nations, and a mix of political systems that include democracies and autocracies, of which the latter takes the forms of communist, non-communist, and Islamist.

Colonies in Southeast Asia were among the first to secure independence in the Era of Nation States. Those from Britain and the US came by it peacefully. Colonies of France and the Netherlands did not. For all, when independence arrived, the honeymoons were short-lived. Bordering second-world China; in proximity to first-world Australia; having historical colonial ties to first-world Britain, France, the Netherlands, Portugal, and the United States; and China and the Soviet Union's interest in cultivating leftist movements, turned this region into a Cold War hot spot. There were communist insurgencies, anti-communist purges, and armed-Cold War conflicts.

Cold War conflicts in Cambodia, Laos, and Vietnam followed the Indochinese wars for independence from France (1946–1954). Communist insurgencies occurred in Malaysia, Myanmar, the Philippines, and Thailand. Anti-communist purges took place in East Timor, Indonesia, and Thailand; in Indonesia, the death toll is counted in hundreds of thousands. In East Timor, the perceived threat of communism led to its invasion and annexation by Indonesia in 1976. East Timor had to wait for the Cold War to end to become independent.

When the Cold War ended, like many other regions there was hope that conflicts over political ideologies and global powers competing for influence would be over. That didn't occur. The end of the Cold War was the end of one chapter in an ongoing story of great power rivalries.

In the post-Cold War period, this region has seen rising interest in Islamist parties, and sporadic increases in Islamic militancy. Some tie this to outreach by Saudi Arabia.[i] With three Muslim-majority nations and four nations with significant Muslim minorities, Islamism as an alternative system for governing, would be appealing to some. An appeal that is not helped by Islamic militancy, which is not widely applauded. The region has a firm commitment to extinguishing this threat.[ii] Interest in Islamist political systems is also tempered by the region's diverse religious populations and a long history of religious pluralism.

Corruption has been an ongoing threat to nation-building. According to TI, only democratic Singapore, and autocratic Brunei, do not have histories of serious corruption. But TI measures *perceptions* of corruption. Brunei is a country where royals tend to see national assets as personal assets, and only a soon-to-be-locked-up criminal would question that belief. It's a crime to say anything bad about the royal family—like they are corrupt. The Sultan of Brunei lives in a 1700-bedroom palace. He has a harem of 40–50 women who are allegedly richly rewarded for their services—all from the national till.[iii] One source said that concubine compensation could be tallied with seven figures.[iv] The royal family also has the world's most expensive private car collection. Numbering 7,000 cars, it includes 600 Rolls Royce's, 11 McLaren F1s, and 300 Ferraris. Estimates of the value of the collection are as high $5 billion.[v] These are all very expensive outlays for a nation with a GDP of $12 billion in 2017, which is less than Forbes' estimate of $20 billion in 2011 for the Sultan of Brunei's net worth.

According to TI, Cambodia is the region's most corrupt nation. Cambodians with no faith in the police or the judiciary created a new law in 2015. To discourage police from taking bribes for voiding traffic tickets, fines were increased, and police get a 70 percent cut.[vi]

A judicial mafia is a term used by a lecturer and lawyer at the University of Indonesia to describe corruption in Indonesia. Corruption "is in the whole system, from the investigation process, to the trial, to the prisons." Corrupt officials can be leveraged to drop cases or increase the punishments. Corruption is so common most people assume that paying bribes is how "justice" is served and business is done.[vii]

Drivers In Myanmar in 2015 were not yet required to have insurance. In the event of an accident, the drivers involved negotiated a settlement. Calling the police was seen as silly because all that did was add a person requiring a fee for doing—well nothing.

Indonesia and the Philippines have national leaders that rank among the world's greatest thieves. Indonesia's Suharto had a heist of $15–35 billion, while the Philippine's Marco was about $8 billion. Philippine President Joseph Estrada (1998–2001) was forced to resign and sentenced to life in prison for allegedly plundering $80 million. He was later pardoned and elected Mayor of Manila.

The economies in Southeast Asia have experienced healthy growth since the Cold War ended. Peace, WTO memberships, and economic reforms in Cambodia, Laos, Malaysia, and Vietnam, in addition to neighboring China and India have contributed to these outcomes.

China's influence has not just been economic. China's return to the world stage has brought back memories of a hegemonic Chinese Empire. China's annexation of small islands in the South China Sea legally demarcated to other countries, and Chinese leaders expressing a desire to recover the sphere of influence captured in the Era of Empire has sharpened memories. In turn, this has encouraged many in the region to build up their militaries and to seek security assurances from the United States. Some academics wonder if China has abandoned its practice of conducting foreign policy on a tributary basis.[viii]

Below is a closer look at the nation-building paths for Cambodia, Myanmar, and Singapore.

Cambodia

Cambodia was part of French Indochina. It was occupied by Japan and Thailand during WWII and returned to French rule afterward. One year later Cambodians were fighting the French for independence in the First Indochina War (1946–1954). A period of peace was followed by the Cambodian Civil War (1967–1975), a Cold War conflict that pitted the US-supported government against the Khmer Rouge's communist revolutionaries supported by China.

For most, the communist win didn't yield the euphoric feeling of victory. Under Prime Minister Pol Pot (1975–1979) perceived and potential opponents were eliminated, "re-educated," imprisoned, or forcibly migrated. An estimated 20–40 percent of Cambodia's population died from torture, execution, imprisonment, or starvation. Mass graves became known as the killing fields, and the collective exterminations, the Cambodian genocide. Pol Pot had another genocide in mind when he targeted the Vietnamese-Cambodians for elimination. This instigated the Cambodian-Vietnamese War (1977–1991) that ended Pol Pot's rule and brought Cambodia, as the People's Republic of Kampuchea (1979–1989), into the orbit of the Soviet Union.

After the Cold War, Cambodia transitioned to a democratic form of government. Beginning in 1992, the UN effectively ran the government for eighteen months with a focus on building a stable foundation for nation-building. Cambodia restored its monarch in 1993 and officially became a constitutional monarchy. Then came a period of brief applause for Cambodia as a UN success story.

In 1998 Cambodia unofficially became a dictatorship under Prime Minister Hun Sen (1998–?).[2] Hun Sen gained a reputation for human rights abuses, serious corruption, and unfree and unfair elections. In 2011 he said, "I not only weaken the opposition, I'm going to make them dead … and if anyone is strong enough to try to hold a demonstration, I will beat all those dogs and put them in a cage."[ix] In 2017 Hun Sen threatened military action if his party did not win elections in 2018.[x] The promise of Cambodia in the 1990s was detoured by Hun Sen.

Cambodia, Laos, and Vietnam traveled similar nation-building paths before 1991. In 2017 per capita income in Cambodia was $1,390, or about 70 percent less than in Laos or Vietnam.

Myanmar

The borders of British Burma, the future Myanmar,[3] enclosed Burma proper and several "frontier areas" that were contiguous with China, Bangladesh, and Thailand. Nearly half the population lived in the frontier areas, and most were ethnic minorities. Under British rule, there was self-government in Burma proper and also the frontier areas, and they coexisted reasonably well.

As a British colony, Myanmar supported the Allied Powers in WWII, but this did not include the support of Major General Aung San. When the Japanese occupied Myanmar (1942–1945) support for the Allied Powers officially ended. Some ethnic groups in the frontier areas, and significantly the Karen, continued fighting with the Allied Powers against the Japanese and Burmese armies.[4] This instigated inter-ethnic conflict that persisted after the war.

Success for the Allied Powers was looking increasingly likely in March 1945 when Major General Aung San abandoned his pro-fascist position to support the Allied Powers. After the war, he negotiated Myanmar's independence with the British,[5] concluded an agreement with several ethnic minorities to build a unified Myanmar and was on deck to be the nation's first prime minister. Five months before independence, he was assassinated. Instead of a democratic government and ethnic unity at independence (1948), there was ethnic conflict and a communist insurgency. In 1962 conflict was halted by the installation of a repressive military dictatorship, under Ne Win (1962–1988) that turned Myanmar into a hermit kingdom. In 1988, fed up with repression, isolation, and poverty hundreds of thousands marched against the regime. Thousands of protesters were killed and imprisoned, but they succeeded in bringing change to Myanmar, but nothing permanent or welcome.

Elections were finally held in 1990 and the daughter of Aung San, Aung San Suu Kyi, convincingly won. The military responded by annulling the results, doubling its size and increasing repression. They also minimized the chance of future protests. Universities provided the forum to organize protests, so they were closed between 1988 and 1990, and again between 1996 and 1999.

It would be another twenty years before Myanmar hosted another election. If Myanmar's neighbors weren't experiencing so many post-Cold War improvements in quality of life, it might not have occurred. In 2010 the government changed to a presidential democracy, with the twist of the military maintaining a constitutional guarantee to occupy 25 percent of parliamentary seats. In 2014 Myanmar hosted direct elections, and the party of Aung San Sui Kyi again won overwhelmingly, and this time the results were honored.

Ms. Sui Kyi, like her father, was committed to solving ethnic conflict. Unlike her father, she faced the challenges of being a civilian leading a military "partner" unaccustomed to a subordinate role, and decades of ethnic conflict. Among the most intractable ethnic conflicts are with the Karens[6] and the Rohingyas. The latter is a Bengali-speaking Muslim population that migrated to Myanmar when it was part of British India (1858–1937).

Nearly fifty years after independence Myanmar had a fresh start at nation-building. There are challenges aplenty, like subduing the military, building a democracy, advancing the economy, and establishing peace among Myanmar's ethnic groups. Still, there is much more promise than when Myanmar was a hermit kingdom.

Singapore

Singapore's path to independence was unique. In 1963 it was incorporated into Malaysia because it was thought too small to economically prosper or defend itself against a communist takeover. Singapore's landmass is only 42 km (26 mi.) long and 22.5 km (14 mi.) wide. As part of Malaysia, Singapore's leaders accepted that Malays would have political preferences as long as the Chinese would not be handicapped economically. When the preferences expanded into education, positioning the Chinese (and the Indians) for economic disadvantages, Singapore's leader Lee Kwan Yew tried to build a political coalition to bring political equality to all citizens. Not only did he fail, Singapore was ejected from Malaysia. It became independent in 1965.

Unlike Malaysia, tiny Singapore had no extractive resources to facilitate nation-building. What it had was: access to the sea; people that were Chinese, Indian and Malaysian living with constitutional commitments for political equality; Lee Kwan Yew; and the Cold War. Opportunities from the Cold War became key to nation building. Singapore's economy relied on exporting military supplies and renting land for air bases to the British and Americans. In 1967 receipts from Britain and the United States were 35 percent of Singapore's national income.[xi]

Lee had to endure the wrath of others in the region that accused him of perpetuating colonialism. Among his western supporters, he bore the criticism of being a benevolent dictator. Lee and Singaporeans could laugh all the way to the bank. In record-breaking time Lee oversaw the transformation of an agrarian developing nation into one of the most economically advanced nations in the world. In 2017 per capita incomes were nearly six times higher than in Malaysia.

In Southeast Asia, it's easy to see how different variables, like the Cold War, political systems, and national leaders influenced nation-building. Lee, presiding over an illiberal democracy, leveraged opportunities with first-world nations in the Cold War to fast track Singapore's trek to becoming a prosperous nation. Second-world supported despotic communist Pol Pot followed by autocratic Hun Sen share in the uncelebrated achievement of relatively impoverished Cambodia. Equally poor, completely isolated Myanmar was ruled by the military dictator Ne Win while remaining neutral in the Cold War.

Notes

1. The United States acquired the Philippines from Spain in 1898. It was a US colony between 1898 and 1946.
2. Hun Sen was also prime minister between 1985 and 1993 and second prime minister between 1993 and 1998.
3. Burma was renamed Myanmar in 1989 to create a name that did not emphasize the Burmese majority.
4. The Karen ethnic group has Myanmar's largest Christian population. About 20 percent of Karens are Christian. The Karen were reliably loyal to the British.
5. This was quite a step up. During WWII Churchill called Aung San, a "traitor rebel leader."
6. During WWII, Karen fighters played an important role in the defeat of the Japanese. After the war, some thought the British would champion an independent Karen state. It did not occur, and the Karen have been fighting for independence since 1949. This conflict is dubbed "the longest running civil war."

References

i. Ignatius, Dennis. "Wahhabism in Southeast Asia." *Asia Sentinel*, March 27, 2015.
ii. "SE Asia Boots Fight Against 'Real and Present' Militant Threat." *The Star.com*, October 21, 2018.

iii. Moulton, Emily. "Sex, Lies and Sharia Law: The Secret Life of the Sultan of Brunei." *News.com.au*, April 27, 2015.

iv. Lauren, Jillian. *Some Girls: My Life in a Harem*. Penguin, 2010.

v. "Sultan of Brunei Net Worth." *Bornrich.com*. Retrieved January 3, 2019.

vi. Frauenfelder, Mark. "Cambodia Legalizes Police Corruption." *Boingboing.net*, July 29, 2015.

vii. "Judicial Mafia: Corruption as a Barrier to Justice in Indonesia." *International Bridges to Justice*. Retrieved May 30, 2017.

viii. Hevia, James, L. "Tribute, Asymmetries, and Imperial Formations." In *Rethinking Relations of Power in Eastern Asia*. University of Hawaii Press, 2010.

ix. Adams, Brad. "30 Years of Hun Sen: Violence, Repression, and Corruption in Cambodia." *Human Rights Watch*, January 20, 2011.

x. "Hun Sen Hints at Military Action If He Loses Cambodia's Election." *Radio Free Asia*, February 22, 2017.

xi. Ngoei, Wen-Qing. "Lee Kuan Yew's Singapore Bloomed in the Shadow of the Cold War." *The Diplomat*, March 28, 2017.

· 2 3 ·

EASTERN ASIA

The Chinese Empire completely dominated this region until the mid-19th century. But every empire/group had a presence. Islamic empires influenced the region through multiple channels: Arab- and Indian-Muslim traders introduced Islam along the Silk Road; Muslims were encouraged to immigrate by the Mongol rulers of the Yuan Dynasty (1271–1368); and Muslim-majority Xinjiang (formerly Chinese Turkestan) was annexed in the 18th-century.

Excluding the influence of Islamic empires and Portugal's rental of Macau between 1557 to 1887,[1] the presence of other empires came during the Century of Humiliation (1842–1949). There were humiliations aplenty. The Chinese lost Hong Kong to the British Empire. The European, Russian, and Japanese empires and the United States operated self-ruling treaty ports. The Russian Empire permanently annexed Outer Manchuria, including the maritime port of Vladivostok, and attempted to conquer Xinjiang.

The Japanese Empire (1868–1945) existed only briefly, but it had an out-sized impact in this region. In 1895 the Japanese colonized Taiwan and the Liaodong Peninsula. In 1910 Japan colonized the Chinese Empire's long-time tribute Korea. During WWII the Japanese occupied most of Mainland China. Their brutality as occupiers has been compared to the Nazis, complete with concentration camps and vivisections. During this occupation estimates for the combined soldier and civilian fatalities are between 15 and 20 million. Internal refugees are estimated at 90 million.[i]

A fresh start or two was on deck for all Eastern Asian nations in the 20th century. In 1911 China became a republic and in 1949 a people's republic, a designation common to communist governments.[2] Mongolia declared its independence from the Chinese Empire in 1911. Then in 1921, with Soviet support, it declared independence from the Republic of China, effectively becoming a Soviet satellite until 1991. In 1945 Japan abruptly transitioned from an autocratic empire to a constitutional monarchy. In 1945 Korea became independent from Japan, but by 1948 North and South Korea were operating independent governments; the north was a people's republic and the south a republic.

The first armed-Cold War conflict was the Korean War (1950–1953). Two permanent Security Council members, China, and the Soviet Union supported North Korea. The other three permanent members, France, the United Kingdom, and the United States supported South Korea. Atypically, China, rather than North or South Korea, incurred the highest number of military deaths.[ii] This reflected Mao's dogged determination to win this Cold War conflict and to claim victory over the United States.

The Cold War's deadliest episode occurred in this region, but not in a conventional war. Up to sixty-five million Chinese died from communist programs and policies, including the killing of perceived opponents, during the ongoing transition to communism under Mao (1949–1976).[iii]

The estimated 1–3 million that perished in North Korea during the decades of implementing communism from 1954–1987, and then another estimated 3 million dying in a famine between 1994 and 1998[iv] might seem trivial compared to China, but in 1954 China's population was 69 times larger. The 100,000 that died during Mongolia's transition to communism between 1921 and 1944 might also seem trivial, but Mongolia's population was about 1 million.[v]

After the Cold War, most nations abandoned communism, but in this region only Mongolia did. China's implementation did change in the late 1970s when it introduced some capitalist weighting. North Korea remained a totalitarian communist state. Since this time Mongolia and China have prospered and North Korea remains an impoverished nation. After the Cold War, South Korea also changed its government. It became a democratic republic and joined the exclusive club of democratic nations with advanced economies, just like its regional neighbor Japan.

The impact of China's economic reforms reached far beyond China. An economic underachiever for most of the Cold War, China became an economic superpower propelling economies throughout eastern Asia and beyond.

Excluding Japan and South Korea, corruption has been a regional deterrent to economic advancement. In spite of a massive crackdown that indicted more than 1.5 million Chinese Communist Party officials from 2012–2015, a 2016 report by TI indicated little progress on the perception of corruption in China. China does rank higher than Mongolia, and nearly a hundred spots higher than North Korea.

North Korea has been ranked at the bottom, among virtually lawless countries like Somalia, South Sudan, Syria, Yemen, and Libya. Corruption in North Koreas takes less traditional forms. The government's desperation for hard currency led it to hack into banks in seventeen countries.[vi]

A brief review of nation-building in China and North Korea follows.

China

The Chinese Revolution (1911) ended the Chinese Empire and began China's history of non-monarchical rule. Disagreements over governing were immediately apparent, and civil war broke out between the communists and nationalists. The war was placed on hold in 1936 to unite[3] against their common enemy in the 2nd Sino-Japanese War (1937–1945).[4]

The civil war fully resumed in 1946. Supported by the Soviet Union, Mao Zedong was leading the fight for communism. His opponent Chiang Kai-shek, the leader of the Republic of China (1928–1949), was tepidly supported by the United States. The United States saw Chiang's political ideology as unclear, unlike his leadership style, which was clearly autocratic. They also saw the communists as superior in capturing the hearts and minds of the masses. Still, the United States couldn't stay fully aloof and let China adopt communism without a fight.

After twenty-three years of civil and world wars, a combined military and civilian death toll between 17 and 27 million or 3–5 percent of the population, and two tumultuous hyperinflationary years, 1947 and 1948, victorious Mao Zedong was Chairman of the communist People's Republic of China (PRC). Chiang fled to the Republic of China (ROC) also called Taiwan where he became an elected dictator.

Mao's mission was to make sure China was never humiliated again. To him, this meant re-engineering China's political, economic, and social-cultural systems. He saw the implementation of communism as crucial to achieving this, and this involved some grand initiatives. Between 1958 and 1961 Mao launched the Great Leap Forward, an initiative to fast track the economy by industrializing and collectivizing agriculture. It could have been called the Great Leap Backwards because the economy regressed and 15–43 million died from starvation in the Great Famine (1959–1961).

The Cultural Revolution took place between 1966 and 1976. Its purpose was to purge the country of anything old and to eliminate the bourgeoisie who were accused of exploiting the masses. The Red Guard, composed of children of middle-school age, was encouraged to attack the four olds: old culture, old customers, old ideas, and old habits. The guards destroyed thousands of priceless artifacts and assaulted anyone educated, or that had some amount of wealth, which could be something as small as a trinket. These were the so-called bourgeoisie. Millions ended up imprisoned, tortured, or killed.

The young people in the Red Guard weren't truants. Only a fraction of children attended middle schools. In 1965 110 million children attended primary schools and 14.4 million attended middle schools. This was 14.4 million more than attended in 1966. During the Cultural Revolution middle schools and universities were closed. Many primary and middle schools stayed shut until 1969. Universities remained closed until 1970 or 1972.[vii] Young people were the focus of another initiative. During the Down to the Countryside movement in the 1960s and 1970s, some 17 million "privileged" urban youth were exiled to the countryside. These two initiatives left the legacy of an undereducated generation that grew up believing the government prioritized rebellion and rustication over education.

In the PRC's first twenty years the combined death toll from the: imprisonment or murder of real or perceived opponents, like the bourgeoisie; famines instigated by collective agriculture; and 600,000 killed in the Korean War, was up to 65 million. Not even tens of millions of dead Chinese would stand in the way of Mao's modernization mission.

In Taiwan, things were not much better. When Chiang ruled Taiwan (1950–1975) it was under martial law and the White Terror. There were persecutions of tens of thousands of government opponents. Most were perceived to be communists, but most were not communist. The government had a slogan: "It is better to capture one hundred innocent people than to let one guilty person go free."[viii,ix] Economically, however, Taiwan left China in the dust. In the 1980s it was grouped as one of the four Asian tigers. The other three tigers were Hong Kong, Singapore, and South Korea. In 1980 per capita income in Taiwan was $2,139. By 1990 it had risen to $7,672.[5] In China, it was $312 in 1980 and $345 in 1990.

The poor state of the economy was a worry for some Communist Party officials, and plenty of Party members disagreed with Mao's policies, although publicly doing so would have been very stupid. When Mao died in 1976 China's economic development was decades behind neighbors like the Asian Tigers and Japan, and per capita income was between 1/5th and 1/49th. The world's most populous nation had the tenth largest economy.

Something had to change, and that something was an injection of capitalism. This was a remarkable turn of events. Mao had once contrasted capitalism with communism as, "a dying person who is sinking fast" versus a system "full of youth and vitality." Improvements in the economy were at first gradual, but they were supercharged following China's membership in the WTO in 2001.

In 2001 China had the world's sixth largest economy. In 2010 it was the second largest. China had returned to the world stage, and it was making its position known by making claims to lands it said were formerly part of the Chinese Empire. In 1914 the British and independent Tibet (1912–1951) agreed to the McMahon Line as the border between India and Tibet. In 2008 China claimed the entire Indian state of Arunachal Pradesh as part of Tibet. At a similar time, China claimed the Diaoyu islands in the East China Sea. These islands called the Senkaku by the Japanese have been controlled by Japan since the end of the First Sino-Japanese War (1895). Other islands in the South China Sea where China claims ownership are also claimed by Vietnam, the Philippines, and Taiwan. [6]

In 2001 China signed the Treaty of Neighborliness, Friendship and Cooperation with Russia. This was intended to resolve Russia's acquisition of Outer Manchuria during the Century of Humiliation. But Chinese students are still taught that the Russians stole this land from them, and leaders of China have said this land will return to China.[x]

Like any world power, some events can cause the aggrandizement of power to pause or regress. A couple that could have an outsized impact on China in the 21st century is its political system, a declining population, and income inequality. China is pioneering the use of a communist political system and a capitalist-weighed economic system. World-beating inequality[xi] in an allegedly classless political system has been one outcome of this unusual combination, and income inequality is a known source of social instability.

The UN has forecast declining populations for many nations in the 21st century, but none are of China's magnitude. The decline is forecast to be 330 million. That's 2–3 times greater than the reductions expected in the EU, Russia, and Japan combined. If this decline materializes, it will produce an aging population that will create challenges for a diminishing labor population to support.

China's pace of economic advancement in the 21st century has been extraordinary. It has risen from a poor country to an economic superpower, although it is not yet a wealthy country. This status is reserved for nations with the higher per capita incomes (pci) that come from having an advanced economy. In 2017, the United States pci was $59,792, Singapore's was $57,713, Hong Kong (SAR of China) $46,080, Japan $34,448, South Korea $29,938, Taiwan $24,318, and China $8,643.

China's current status as an economic superpower relies on having the world's largest population. In 2017, the US GDP was 58 percent greater than China's, but the United States had only a quarter of the population. Japan with 1/10th of China's population, had 40 percent of its GDP. China's upward trend has though been swift and positive. Declining and aging populations could however affect this trend and so could political or social instability.

Korea

Korea became independent from Japan after WWII, but it was occupied until elections could be held. The communist Soviet Union occupied the north above the 38th parallel, and the democratic United States occupied the south. Before elections were held, the Korean War (1950–1953) commenced. The north was led by Kim il-Sung, a former major in the Soviet Red Army, and supported by China and unofficially the Soviet Union. The south was supported by a UN-backed coalition, with nations from every inhabited continent, led by the United States. There were nearly 3 million fatalities, and unusually civilian fatalities at 1.6 million exceeded military deaths. But there was no victor. Independent North Korea would have a communist system under Kim. Independent South Korea's ruler, Syngman Rhee, would be anti-communist, but not democratic.

North Korea

Kim il-Sung ruled throughout the Cold War (1948–1994). Under his leadership, millions died of unnatural causes, including one million from the Korean War.[xii] North Korea became known as the Hermit Kingdom. There is a real shortage of information known about the nation, beyond it being a totalitarian state guilty of oppression, mass human rights abuses, and an economy stunted by self-imposed isolation.

The North Korean economy relied on trade, concessions, and aid from the Soviet Union until 1991. The dissolution of the Soviet Union was politically and economically devastating to North Korea. In 1994 a new Kim led the country, and he was soon presiding over a famine that killed an estimated three million. Kim Jong-il called the famine another Arduous March and called on North Koreans to endure bouts of "fighting against thousands of enemies in 20 degrees below zero braving snowfall and starvation." Thousands of enemies? The famine is generally attributed to the loss of Soviet aid, failures in central planning, and floods.[xiii]

Without Soviet support and oversight, a nation struggling to feed its people oversaw a strategy of using nuclear tests to terrorize neighbors and then the world.[7] Threats would be dialed-back in exchange for aid. To rein in this rogue nation, the UN began imposing sanctions in 2006 but not all nations participated, and North Korea continued developing its nuclear program and terrorizing its neighbors.[xiv]

The government hasn't worried about popular revolts because it employs draconian punishments for even trivial offenses. Men work without being paid to avoid punishment, although supervisors are known to accept bribes to overlook absences from workers that have other jobs that pay. The North Korean government does something similar so they can earn hard currency. They send workers to foreign locations and confiscate their wages.[xv,xvi]

The world had misplaced hope when thirty-four-year-old Kim Jong-un succeeded his father in 2016. The Kims seem determined to cement their reputations as erratic and menacing. The regular threat of igniting nuclear bombs and warheads as a negotiating tactic, and cyber-attacks, including bank heists on foreign governments count among the most disturbing, but there are others. The government has "abducted hundreds of foreign nationals, sold weapons to rogue Middle Eastern states, manufactured drugs to earn hard currency, and printed counterfeit foreign banknotes."[xvii]

North Korea is counted among history's most repressive regimes. Being accused of a crime is the same as being convicted, and punishment includes the imprisonment of the convict's nuclear family and their offspring; the intention is to annihilate a bloodline. Death is said to be a preferred outcome to prison. A report the from UN said, "The gravity, scale of [human rights] violations reveal a State that does not have any parallel in the contemporary world."[xviii] One report detailed the fate of a baby conceived during a prison guard's rape of a female political prisoner. The baby was tossed to dogs. Another report described the extermination of populations by depriving them of food, so their deaths were slow and painful.[xix]

"About 70 percent of North Korean's lack secure access to food, and nearly one-third of children under five have stunted growth."[xx] Per capita incomes in 2010 were less than they were in 1980.[xxi] In the dismalness of insufficient food and repression North Koreans worship in front of pictures of their Dear Leaders daily. If they are caught doing otherwise, there are consequences.

Notes

1. Between 1887 and 1979 Macau was a Portuguese colony.
2. Taiwan, Hong Kong, and Macau are part of Eastern Asia, but none are recognized by the UN as sovereigns. Macau and Hong Kong became SARs of China in the 1990s. Taiwan's sovereignty is unrecognized, primarily because China maintains that it is part of the PRC. These three polities did not select communist systems.
3. The opposing communists and nationalists continued to engage in battles throughout WWII.
4. When China officially joined WWII's Allied Powers in 1941, this war became part of WWII's Pacific theatre.
5. All data on per capita income is from the World Bank and IMF, except Taiwan. Taiwan is not a UN recognized nation. This data is from the National Development Council of Taiwan.
6. Signs of a resurgent Chinese Empire have led many nations to fortify their militaries. According to the Stockholm Peace Research Initiative, the nations with the greatest arms build-up from 2011–2015 include China's neighbors South Korea, Vietnam, and Australia along with China.
7. During the Cold War, the Soviet Union used its influence to keep client states from engaging in activities that could provoke war with the United States. This check ended after the Cold War.

References

i. Mitter, Rana. *China's War with Japan 1937–1945: The Struggle for Survival*. London: Allen Lane, 2013.

ii. Millett, Allan. "Korean War." *Encyclopedia Britannica*. Retrieved November 15, 2018.

iii. Edwards, Lee. "The Legacy of Mao Zedong is Mass Murder." *The Heritage Foundation*, February 2, 2010.

iv. Rummel, R. J. The Democidal Famine in North Korea. Orthodoxytoday.org, February 12, 2004.

v. Sandag, Shagdariin, and Harry H. Kendall. *Poisoned Arrows: The Stalin-Choibalsan Mongolian Massacres 1921–1941*. Boulder, CO: Westview Press, 2000.

vi. "North Korea Hacking Banks in Nigeria, 17 Other Countries To Fund Nuclear Program." *Punch Nigeria*, April 7, 2017.

vii. Saywell, William. "Education in China Since Mao." *The Canadian Journal of Higher Education* 10, no. 1 (1980).

viii. Wu, Julie. "Remembering Taiwan's White Terror." *The Diplomat*, March 8, 2014.

ix. Gold, Michael. "Help! I'm a Taiwanese Communist: Taiwan went through a Mass Killing of its Communists. Today the Country is Opening up about this Dark Past and Communists Face a Freer Environment." *Sage Journals* 46, no. 2 (June 19, 2017): 55–57.

x. Wall, David. "Chinese reoccupying Russia." *Japan Times*, May 5, 2016.

xi. Jain-Chandra, Sonali. "Chart of the Week: Income Inequality in China." *IMFBlog*, September 20, 2018.

xii. Rummel, R. J. *Statistics of Democide: Genocide and Mass Murder Since 1900*. Transaction, Rutgers University 1997.

xiii. Noland, Marcus, Sherman Robinson, and Tao Wang. "Famine in North Korea." *Institute for International Economics*, 2001.

xiv. "North Korea." *Nightwatch*, January 26, 2017.

xv. "North Korea: Economic System Based on Forced Labor." *Hrw.org*, June 13, 2012.

xvi. Higgins, Andrew. "North Korean Workers in Russia Work 'Basically in the Situation of Slaves.'" *Independent.co.uk*, July 15, 2017.

xvii. "North Korea at 70: Seven Turbulent Decades of Repression, Murder and Nuclear Brinkmanship." *The Telegraph*, December 14, 2016.

xviii. "North Korea: UN Commission documents wide-ranging and ongoing crimes against humanity, urges referral to ICC." *Ohchr.org*, February 17, 2014.

xix. "Report of the Detailed Findings of the Commission of Inquiry on Human Rights in the Democratic People's Republic of Korea." *UN Human Rights Council*, February 7, 2014.

xx. "Under Kim Jong Un, North Korea's Children Suffering Severe Malnutrition." *International Business Times*, January 26, 2016.

xxi. Kin, Cheon-koo. "North Korea's Per Capita GDP Comparison with South Korea." *Hyundai Research Institute*, March 14, 2014.

· 2 4 ·

CENTRAL ASIA

The Chinese, Islamic, and Russian empires influenced Central Asia. The Chinese Empire's influence was comparatively minor. During the 19th century running of the Great Game, the Chinese Empire was busy defending territory on its western edge that was coveted by Britain and Russia. The influence of Islamic empires began in the 8th century from Muslim traders traveling the Silk Road and invading Arab armies. Later influence came from rule by Turkic or Persian-speaking empires or khanates,[1] many of which were local to the region. The rule of the Russians and Soviets was a little more than 100 years, but they were last in, only exited in 1991, and introduced some profound changes including borders, atheism as the official religion, and encouraging sedentary lifestyles. The presence of significant nomadic populations always complicated ruling Central Asia until the Soviets implemented formal governance that prompted stationary ways of living.

Central Asia was one of the last three regions to gain independence. Like Central and Eastern Europe, this was triggered by the dissolution of the Soviet Union. Upon independence, these nations embarked on a transition from communism to a democratic form of government with capitalism. Some transitions dragged on, and others were abandoned. Only the two Christian-majority countries of Armenia and Georgia, and more recently Tajikistan have demonstrated a commitment toward a democratic form of government.

A BRIEF HISTORY OF INTERNATIONAL RELATIONS

A return to the old days of repressive rule should have been expected; the entire history of formal government in this region was with the Russian Empire and the Soviet Union. The first leaders of independent nations were commonly former communist party apparatchiks that maintained close ties with Moscow. When Moscow began abandoning democratic practices so did many former Soviet republics.

Other things could have been anticipated. The Central Asian region borders China, Russia, Iran, and Turkey. The EU and Saudi Arabia are nearby. All of the above curry favor. A general in China's People's Liberation Army calls Central Asia "the thickest piece of cake given to the modern Chinese by the heavens."[1] Meanwhile, Central Asia is seen by the Russians as part of its near abroad; the EU as key to energy security; and the United States as a strategic location for global military security. Iran and Saudi Arabia are competing for influence in this predominantly Muslim region to increase influence in the global Muslim community.[2] All this interest has been good for attracting foreign investment, but it has also fueled corruption.

Similarly, foreseeable was the unraveling of ethnic bonhomie once the Soviet policies of atheism and internationalization were gone. Also predictable was the return of religion in a controlled fashion. Practicing religion became permissible, but with the church clearly subordinate to the state like it had been in the Russian and Soviet empires. This time the motivation was at least in part different. A region sharing long borders with Iran with its large Azeri population, and Afghanistan where many are ethnically Tajik, Uzbek or Turkmen, ethnicities common to Central Asia, could not be indifferent to the possibility of rising Islamic militancy.

High levels of corruption in an autocratic region where some nations have plentiful stores of extractive resources were also predictable, with or without foreign investment. The degree of corruption less so. In extractive rich Turkmenistan, their megalomaniac ruler, his Excellency Saparmurat Niyazov Turkmenbashi the Great (1990–2006), made securing his place in history a national priority. Rich stores of extractive resources helped finance his ego. Tributes to himself include a 250-foot Neutrality Arch with Niyazov on top and in gold. The arch rotates so that his face is always with the sun. The presidential palace was made in gold-plated white marble. To remind his current and future countrymen of his greatness: statues of gold and other materials have been placed throughout the capital city Ashgabat; months and days of the week have been named after himself, family and friends; the national anthem was created to glorify yours truly, and a 50-foot statue of his book

Ruhnama was created. Ruhnama is mandatory reading in all grades at school and university.[ii]

Under Uzbekistan's President Karimov (1991–2016) it was said that "corruption is used both for self-enrichment of elites and also as a means of maintaining political control through a hierarchical system of patron–client networks."[iii] One self-enriched elite included Karimov's daughter who was the alleged recipient of $114 million in bribes from a Dutch telecom company.[iv]

Azerbaijan is another nation with significant extractive resource wealth. Running the country is said to be a family business and the head of the family is a role model. In 2012 the Organized Crime and Corruption Reporting Project awarded Azerbaijan's President Aliyev corruption person of the year.

At least the populations cheated by corruption and the scourge of national leaders unfocused on nation building are limited. About 1 percent of the global population lives in Central Asia.

A summary of nation-building in Azerbaijan and Tajikistan follows.

Azerbaijan

When the Russian Empire acquired Azerbaijan from the Shiite Qajar Dynasty (1789–1925) in 1813, they divided the land of the Azeri ethnolinguistic group between the Russian Empire and Iran. This became a long-term source of conflict between Iran and Azerbaijan.

Iran contains more Azeris than Azerbaijan, and Iranian leaders have targeted Azerbaijan "as the most appropriate target for exporting the Islamic revolution."[v] This has not gone over well in Azerbaijan. Azerbaijan is a sovereign nation with a distinct nationality and a secular government. Half of Azeris, the highest percentage for any Muslim-majority nation and one of the highest in the world self-categorize as irreligious.[vi] In Iran apostasy from Islam is punishable by death.

The Soviet Union created another problem for Azerbaijan. The borders for the Soviet Republic of Azerbaijan enclosed Muslim Azeris who speak Azerbaijani, with Armenian-speaking Catholics from Nagorno-Karabakh.[3] At independence Nagorno-Karabakh voted to become part of Catholic Armenia and war broke out between Armenia and Azerbaijan (1988–1994). This war evolved into an Iran-Saudi proxy war, with an odd twist that belies the proxy wars as a contest between Shias and Sunnis for Islamic leadership. Saudi Arabia supported Shiite Azerbaijan, and Shiite Iran supported Catholic Armenia.[4]

Azerbaijan has the good fortune of being an extractive rich state that has attracted significant investment from a who's who list of global players: China, the EU, Iran, Russia, Saudi Arabia, and the United States. But autocratic rule and serious levels of corruption limits investments in nation-building and also limits the private sector's motivations and interests in innovation.[vii]

Tajikistan

In 1991, Tajikistan had its first directly elected president. In less than a year, he was ousted. Dictatorial rule followed, and so did a civil war that officially lasted until 1997. The Soviet-defined borders for Tajikistan enclosed a mix of diverse ethnicities, and this war was fought above all to determine which ethnicities and regions would control the institutions and modest assets of Tajikistan.

Different ethnic groups allied with either the Russian-supported secular government or the odd combination of Islamists and democratic reformers aided by al-Qaeda and the Taliban. The presence of these militant groups was logistically simple; Tajikistan has a 1300 km (810 mi.) long border with Afghanistan. Having these militant groups in Tajikistan brought them geographically closer to Russia, motivating Russian involvement.[vii]

The combination of war and fleeing refugees led to economic collapse. When the war ended Tajikistan became the region's only country to allow Islamist political parties, but this did not last. Fearing a rise in Islamic militancy, it became illegal for children under the age of 18 to participate in religious activities. Islamist parties were banned, and the previously legal Islamist Islamic Renaissance Party (IRPT) was designated a terrorist organization, and the party's leaders arrested.[viii]

Fearing Islamic militancy is not unfounded. Tajikistan shares borders with three regions or nations besides Afghanistan with histories of Islamic militancy: Kashmir in India, Pakistan, and China's Xinjiang province. Neighbors with instability problems, being one of six landlocked nations in the region, and having 93 percent mountainous terrain makes Tajikistan geographically unlucky. None of this helps nation building. At $824 in 2017, Tajikistan's per capita income was the lowest in the region.

Notes

1. A khanate is generally defined as land ruled by descendants of Genghis Kahn's empire.
2. Unusually for a region of mostly Muslim-majority nations, in 1992 all recognized Israel.
3. Nagorno-Karabakh has declared independence, although the UN does not recognize it. A similar situation exists with South Ossetia and Abkhazia that are officially part of Georgia. These conflicts are called zones of frozen conflict.
4. Wahhabism is a Sunni Islam movement practiced in Saudi Arabia that sees Shias as heretics. Catholics in Iran face government-sponsored discrimination.

References

i. Pantucci, Raffaello. "China Must Get Along with Regional Powers to Make its New Silk Road Work." *China in Central Asia*, August 21, 2017.
ii. "Badass of the Week." *Badass.com*. Retrieved October 1, 2016.
iii. Lewis, David. "Tackling Corruption in Uzbekistan: A White Paper." *Open Society Foundation*, June 2016.
iv. Goldstein, Jeff. "Uzbekistan's Perfect Storm of Corruption." *Open System Foundation*, May 26, 2016.
v. "Azerbaijan-Iran Relations: Challenges and Prospects." Belfer Center for Science and International Affairs, Harvard Kennedy School, November 30, 1999.
vi. Noack, Rick. "Map: These are the World's Least Religious Countries." *The Washington Post*, April 14, 2015.
vii. "Tajikistan Civil War." *Factsanddetails.com*. Retrieved January 29, 2017.
viii. "Tajikistan 2017 International Religious Freedom Report." *US Embassy in Tajikistan*. Retrieved November 18, 2018.

· 2 5 ·

EASTERN EUROPE

Eastern Europe was ground zero for the Russian Empire and the Soviet Union after that. It is the influence of these two empires that dominate the region. This is the only region where all nations have an Eastern-Orthodox majority. All nations also have a significant Russian minority or an outright majority, in the case of Russia. All nations experienced long histories of autocratic rule under the Russian and Soviet empires that created extra challenges for post-Cold War transitions from state-directed communism to democracy and market-driven capitalism.

Islamic and European empires were also present in the region. In 1812, the Russian Empire annexed Moldova from the Ottoman Empire. Ukraine was a political hot potato. Between the 16th and 20th centuries, excluding war-time occupations, all or parts of it were ruled by the Polish-Lithuanian Commonwealth, and the Ottoman, Austrian and Austria-Hungary empires. The Polish Lithuanian Commonwealth ruled Belarus into the 18th century. Aftermaths from these empires are, however, less obvious.

Nations in this region had to wait for independence until after the Soviet Union dissolved in 1991. When it came, there was a backdrop of years of declining growth from a failed experiment in communism.

Communism performed well economically until the 1970s. This was when unmotivating aspects like repression, equal rewards for unequal performance, and shortages of essential items worked their way into the system. The only people with monetary incentives were Communist Party members, but these were rewards for engaging in corruption not for superior performance. Party members were profiting from their monopoly of control over goods, services, and information.

Many years of woeful performance were concealed to the outside world by censorship and propaganda until the Berlin Wall came down. Now it was visibly clear that communism was not superior to democracy and capitalism.

Eastern Europe, like Central Asia and Central Europe, pioneered both the implementation of communism in the first half of the 20th century, and the post-Cold War transitions from state-directed communism to market-driven capitalism. Results for the latter varied by region, and the outcomes in Eastern Europe reflected poorly executed transitions or outright abandonment.

When Mother Russia declared the nations of Eastern Europe part of its near abroad, it resumed domination of the region and gave a green light to those in its clutch to return to autocracy, just like Russia. There was a resumption or continuation of government repression and corruption that has deterred nation-building throughout the region. Belarus has done a better job of controlling corruption, or at least the perception of it, but Belarus holds its own when it comes to repression.

Corruption was supercharged when nations executed privatization initiatives. The sale of state industries created a new crop of wealthy elite called the oligarchs. In Ukraine, oligarch corruption has been an enormous deterrent to democracy and capitalism. A Ukrainian parliamentarian summed up this problem: "As a class, oligarchs represent as great a danger to the community as does the external enemy [Russia] on our eastern border. [1] They are the sources of corruption ... And most important, it is they who are least interested in the building of a new country."[i]

In 2015 it was reported that $1 billion had disappeared from three prominent banks and the national bank in Moldova. Dubbed the "theft of the century" for stealing an amount equal to about 15 percent of GDP, the thefts are tied to Moldovan oligarchs and high-ranking politicians.[ii]

Russia's oligarchs keep political officials on the payroll as an insurance policy against prison time. Is Russian President Putin on the payroll? A lifelong servant of the people Putin's net worth has been estimated at $40 billion, and the collective net worth of his close friends at $200 billion.[iii] Another source estimated Putin's net worth at $200 billion.[iv]

The return of a dominant Russia has not been applauded universally in the region. In the early 21st century Moldova and Ukraine wanted a change; they wanted to align their nations with the EU where member states enjoy protected individual freedoms, improved quality of life, access to a much greater market,[2] and respect for their sovereignty. Russia emphasized to Ukraine what it meant to be part of Russia's near abroad by annexing lands and instigating a war. Moldova has been luckier, so far.

Covered below are summaries of nation-building in Russia and Moldova post-Soviet dissolution.

Russia

Russia's transition to democracy was marred from the beginning. The masses saw their lives under the Russian version of democracy and capitalism as worse than communism. In 1992, annual inflation reached 2,333 percent. From 1993–1995 inflation was counted with three digits. Per capita income plunged 40 percent between 1991 and 1998.

National industries that had allegedly been held in common by the masses under communism were auctioned off with the appearance of being rigged for political insiders. The winning bidders became the new Russian elite class—the oligarchs. In 2008 Russia's fifty richest oligarchs controlled an amount of wealth comparable to 35 percent of GDP.[v]

The masses welcomed a return to something historically familiar—another strongman. When their lives improved so did the welcome, and they didn't care if the real reason was the rising price of oil. When Vladimir Putin came to office in 1999, the cost of a barrel of crude oil was $17.58; in 2008 it reached $127.47. Russians were enjoying more social programs and a military re-fortification that put Russia back on the world stage. In 2014 Russia annexed the Crimean Peninsula, a sovereign territory of Ukraine, and then supported rebel troops in eastern Ukraine in their bid for succession. Both actions violated international laws. With Russia holding a Security Council veto, it was impossible to uphold Article 2 of the UN Charter prohibiting the "use of force against the territorial integrity … of any state."

Many western nations did what they could to express their disapproval. By coincidence, the markets did far more. In 2016 the price of crude oil had fallen below $30, and according to the World Bank, the poverty rate in Russia increased by more than 15 percent. Incredibly, Putin's approval rating skyrocketed, but the propaganda machine was reworking familiar messages describing economic setbacks as the work of western democracies trying to destroy Russia. To support the disinformation, Russia flaunted its military power at the west. "The more Putin acts like a mad dog in the global pit, the better the Russian electorate admires him."[vi]

Russia placed a bullseye on the west. It also took an aggressive position in the Syrian War in defense of the murderous despot Bashar al-Assad, who is a Shia (Alawite). When a Russian jetliner exploded in 2015 in Egypt killing everyone aboard, the Sunni Islamic State said it was retaliation for Russia's role in the Syrian War. The Russian propaganda machine, however, blamed the west.[vii] In 2016 the Russian Ambassador to Turkey was assassinated in plain sight at an art exhibition by an Islamic militant shouting, "God is great. Do not forget Aleppo. Do not forget Syria." This too was painted as a murder masterminded by the west.[viii]

Russia was new to having Russians targeted by Islamic militants abroad. It was more familiar with militants at home, and Russian support for Shiite Assad didn't facilitate bonhomie with Russia's predominantly Sunni Muslim population. Cordiality with Russia's Muslims had already been in short supply from a long history of discrimination against Muslims in the Russian and Soviet empires in Kazan, Chechnya, Ingushetia, and Dagestan in the Caucasus, in addition to the rejection of independence for Chechnya in 1991.[3] Discrimination continued in the post-Cold War period. In 2004 Ingush and Chechen militants retaliated by massacring nearly four hundred children in a school in Beslan, Russia.

Islamic militancy will be a threat as long as Muslims perceive discrimination. It is, however unlikely to be an economically disastrous problem for Russia. Official state religious leaders support Russian policies and can be more persuasive than the leaders of militant groups. Autocratic rule, an economy overweighted toward extractive resources, and a population expected to be 25 percent smaller by 2100 pose greater challenges.[4]

Will Russia with smaller economic heft be less prominent on the world stage? Russia's position has always been based on instilling fear through the projection of military power, and this continues, but relative economic strength may matter. To match the US spending 3.5 percent GDP on the military in 2017, Russia would have had to spend 44 percent of GDP. Then again, a "mad dog" Russian president can be persuasive beyond reason.

Russia's military-first strategy has been working. In 2014 Russia annexed Crimea and began exercising massive military drills. In 2015 Russia began promoting its military role in the Syrian War. In 2018 Russia, with China's assistance executed its grandest war game in forty years. To grasp the impact this has on perceptions consider that in spite of Russian GDP being similar in 2008 and 2018, most Russians and Americans see the importance of Russia increasing on the world stage. Meanwhile, US GDP increased 31 percent between 2008 and 2018 and the United States was outspending Russia 8 to 1 on military expenditures. Still only a third of Americans and Russians saw its influence increasing.[ix]

Moldova

In 1940 Transnistria and Moldova were joined to form the Moldovan Soviet Socialist Republic. Transnistria's population was 60 percent Ukrainian, Russian, and Belarussian.[x] Moldova was predominantly Moldovan. In 1990 Moldova and Transnistria individually declared independence. Ostensibly in support of its Russian population, Russia supported Transnistria's unsuccessful war for independence (1990–1992). Two years of war on top of decades of economic stagnation created an inauspicious beginning for independent Moldova that would soon be compounded by inflation.

Transitioning to an independent currency didn't go smoothly; it often does not. Annual inflation reached 487 percent in 1994, and the new currency collapsed. "The extent of Moldova's economic collapse exceeded that of all the former Soviet republics following the break-up of the Soviet Union. Only Tajikistan approached the scale of decline experienced in Moldova."[xi]

Beginning in 1998 nation building in Moldova was aided by strengthening ties with the EU. In time the EU was able to offer access to its common market, financial assistance for upgrading infrastructure and institutions, and support for an amicable solution to the Transnistrian conflict.[xii] Receiving these benefits is contingent on Moldovans demonstrating a commitment to democratic government and a market economy.

Transnistria, which had closer ties to Russia than Moldova threatened to secede if Moldova became an EU member. It had a change of heart when Russia interfered in the sovereignty of its Ukrainian neighbor, and it realized that the Transnistrian economy had become reliant on trade with the EU.[xiii]

Uniquely, this Russian near-abroad member's shift to the EU has thus far taken place without a consequential backlash from Russia. In 2017 Moldova had about 3.5 million people and a GDP of $8 billion. Moldova's security may be based on not being interesting enough for Russia to generate a global backlash.

Notes

1. In 2015 oligarch, Igor Kolomoisky used his private army to seize the headquarters of the state oil company, UkrTransNafta.
2. In 2017 Russian GDP was 7 percent of the EU's. The Russian military does dwarf the EU's, but it does not overshadow the combined militaries of NATO.
3. In 1991 Chechnya declared independence as the Chechen Republic of Ickheria. Russia rejected this, and the Chechens went to war. The war ended in 2000.
4. Russia had the world's 9th largest population in 2017. It is forecast to have the 21st largest in 2100.

References

i. Shapiro, Jeremy. "Of Oligarchs and Corruption: Ukraine Faces its own Demons." *Brookings*, March 24, 2015.
ii. Coffey, Luke. "A Tangled Web of Corruption Is Strangling Moldova." *The National Interest*, August 29, 2016.
iii. Dawisha, Karen. "*Putin's Kleptocracy: Who Owns Russia*. New York: Simon and Schuster, 2015.
iv. Interview by Fareed Zakaria with Bill Browder. *CNN*, February 2, 2015.
v. Kuzio, Taras. "Oligarchs Wield Power in Ukrainian Politics." *Eurasia Daily Monitor*, July 1, 2008.
vi. "Service, Robert. "Russia Wrestles with Islam." *The Hoover Institution*, August 1, 2017.
vii. Whitmore, Brian. "Egypt Plane Crash: The Russian Media Veers into Conspiracy." *The Atlantic*, November 10, 2015.
viii. Scott, Alev. "Why Turkish Media Is Blaming the CIA for the Russian Ambassador's Assassination." *Newsweek*, December 21, 2016.
ix. "6 Charts on how Americans and Russians see each other." *Pew Research Center*, October 4, 2018.
x. "Reconsider Russia and the former Soviet Union: Moldova and Transnistria overview." *ReconsideringRussia.org*, April 2014.
xi. Hensel, Stuart, Anatol Gudim. "Moldova's Economic Transition: Slow and Contradictory." *Center for Strategic Studies and Reform*, 2004.
xii. "EU-Moldova relations." *European Union External Action*, 2017.
xiii. De Waal, Thomas. "An Eastern European Frozen Conflict the EU Got Right." *Politico.eu*, February 16, 2016.

· 2 6 ·

CENTRAL EUROPE

Central Europe was a central battleground in the competition for empire. The Habsburg, French, Ottoman, Russian/Soviet, and Swedish empires and the Polish Lithuanian Commonwealth ruled tracts of Central Europe. One aftermath of empire diversity is religious diversity. This is a region that uniquely has nations with Muslim, Roman Catholic, Eastern Orthodox, and irreligious majorities.

One aftermath of regular wars and treaties changing borders was the alteration of population diversity. Between 1772 and 1795 Poland was partitioned three times. Each time the Polish people were separated into multiple states. The former Yugoslavia and Czechoslovakia intentionally combined diverse ethnicities from multiple states to help secure and defend independence after WWI. During WWII Poland, Latvia, and Lithuania lost more than 10 percent of their populations. Jews, Slavs, and gypsies disproportionately suffered.

Most nations in this region experienced independence more than once. For some, the first came in the 18th and 19th centuries after winning wars for independence from the Ottoman Empire.[1] Czechoslovakia, Hungary, the Second Republic of Poland, and the Kingdom of Yugoslavia gained independence after WWI. All Central European nations would experience independence, in many cases again, between 1989 and 2008.

The post-WWII commitment to self-determination should have restored independence to the nations of Central Europe in 1945. But Joseph Stalin's Soviet Union was occupying most of the region and Soviet forces weren't letting go. All nations in this region except Yugoslavia[2] and Albania[3] lost their sovereignty to the Soviet Union between 1945 and 1989–1991. Some became Soviet republics and others satellites. The satellites of Hungary and Czechoslovakia unsuccessfully tried to regain sovereignty. In 1956 the Soviets brutally suppressed the Hungarian Revolution. In 1968 Czechoslovakia declared its independence and the Soviets invaded it.

After the Soviet dissolution, Soviet satellites and republics secured independence peacefully. Ironically, it was Yugoslavia, a nation that had avoided direct rule by Moscow, and whose ethnic composition and borders were an outcome of planning by southern Slavs, rather than being imposed by empires, that imploded. It turned out that southern Slavs were not a cohesive class, and different ethnic groups sought independent states.

Among the highest national priorities after independence was securing protection from Russian re-annexation and interference. Most sought alignment with the EU and membership in NATO. This fast-tracked nation building. Enforcing the EU requirements of liberal democratic governments and a functioning market economy prevented backsliding, like that occurring in Central Asia and Eastern Europe. The security of the EU and NATO encouraged western multinationals to set up operations throughout the region. EU aid provided substantial funds for building infrastructure and institutions. EU aid allocated just to Poland for the period 2008–2020 was $318 billion.

The results have been astounding. In 2018 three nations from this region had advanced economies, and all nations had been advancing more rapidly than fellow Soviet sphere nations in the Russian near-abroad regions of Central Asia and Eastern Europe.

Hungary is an EU member nation that has defied its commitment to liberal democracy. This has been disappointing, but it illustrates some of the challenges the EU accepted when agreeing to enlarge its union to include nations geographically proximate, but less closely aligned historically, politically, economically, and socially than those in Western Europe.[i] Much of Central Europe was part of the Ottoman Empire until the late 19th century, and the Russian Empire held all or parts of some states in the north until it dissolved. While states in Central Europe were parts of agrarian empires ruled by autocrats, states in Western Europe were industrializing and exploring democratic rule. Then came forty plus years of communism during a time when Western European political and economic systems rapidly advanced to become a collection of wealthy, stable developed nations.[4]

Below is a closer look at nation-building in Yugoslavia and Bosnia.

Yugoslavia

Yugoslavia's history of independence was different. To become and stay independent, the Kingdom of Yugoslavia[5] needed size, and this was achieved by intentionally amalgamating diverse ethnic and religious populations. In 1918 the Kingdom began with a democratic form of government but like others in the interwar period changed to autocracy. WWII was a period of severe crisis for Yugoslavia. It was dismembered, endured civil war, and experienced cross genocidal campaigns against targeted groups.

In spite of WWII's hellish period, Yugoslavia remained intact after the war. In 1945 it abandoned its monarch, became a republic, and independently selected a communist government. Initially, there was a friendly relationship with Moscow, but it rapidly deteriorated because Yugoslavia's President Tito didn't yield to Stalin.

In 1961 Yugoslavia became a founding member of the non-aligned movement, which rejected alignment with the First or Second Worlds. Doing business with and accepting different forms of aid were different. Quite unusually for a communist nation, Yugoslavia had alliances, aid, and trade relationships with first- and second-world nations.

Under the leadership of Tito (1953–1980), diverse populations lived in peace, but when the Cold War ended, there was an ethnic implosion that instigated the Yugoslav Wars (1991–1999). The outcome was seven independent nations: Bosnia and Herzegovina (Bosnia), Croatia, Kosovo, Macedonia, Montenegro, Serbia, and Slovenia. The recognition of Kosovo as a UN sovereign is still pending.[6]

The EU has affiliations with all of Yugoslavia's successor nations, and this has been helpful to nation-building. Yugoslavia's previous exposure to alliances with western nations has also been beneficial. Slovenia and Croatia have already developed advanced economies, although their per capita incomes dwarf those in most Western European countries.

Bosnia and Herzegovina

Like many nations in the Balkans, the diverse influences of the European and Islamic empires, and the Byzantine Empire before that has resulted in an ethnically and religiously diverse population.

Bosnia's first president, Alija Izetbegovic, was an Islamist presiding over a population that was 44 percent Muslim Bosniaks, 31 percent Serbian Orthodox Catholics, and 17 percent Roman Catholic Croats.[ii] Izetbegovic against the warnings of the Serbian population declared independence and war broke out pitting the Serbs against a Croat-Bosniak coalition (1992–1995).

The Serbs rationalized their belligerence to the world by saying they were fighting Islamic fundamentalists, even though the Bosniaks were moderate and secular. Their ploy backfired. The Croat-Bosniaks received support from Pakistan, Iran, Saudi Arabia, NATO, and foreign jihadists (many of which previously fought in the Soviet-Afghan war). Both sides experienced horrific outcomes but the Muslim Bosniaks were victims of Serb ethnic cleansing[7] and their women were targeted for rape.

Post-war bedlam and lingering jihadists created an opening for Saudi Arabia to fortify its influence by investing in madrassas, mosques, and preachers oriented toward Wahhabism. To encourage mosque attendance, an estimated 10,000 widows from the war were offered a monthly allowance for life in exchange for covering up and sending children to Saudi-run madrassas.[iii]

In 2017 the population in Bosnia was 52 percent Christian and 45 percent Muslim, and Muslims remained overwhelmingly moderate. Forty-six years of communist atheism, living in a region of secular and mostly Christian countries, a history of residing among diverse religious populations, and very importantly the desire to be an EU member creates a foundation for religious moderation for people of all religions.

Notes

1. Albania, Bosnia-Herzegovina, Bulgaria, Greece, Montenegro, Macedonia, and Serbia won wars for independence. All are Central European countries but Greece (WE).
2. Yugoslavia was unusual unusual among Central Europe's communist states. Yugoslavia was not "liberated" by the Soviets during WWII, they voluntarily determined a communist system, and they were never puppets of Moscow.
3. Albania broke ranks with the Soviet Union in 1961. Between 1961 and 1978 Albania became the only European communist country to form an alliance with the People's Republic of China. This ended in 1978 with the rapprochement of China and the United States.

4. Developed nations are generally defined as having advanced economies *and* democratic political systems. This is the definition used in this book.
5. From 1918 to 1929 the name was the Kingdom of Serbs, Croats and Slovenes.
6. To be recognized by the UN all five permanent Security Council members, and 2/3^{rds} of all members must vote in favor of recognition. Russia has remained opposed to recognizing Kosovo.
7. In 2015 ten Security Council members voted to classify this ethnic cleansing as genocide, but Russia vetoed the resolution.

References

i. Berend, Ivan, and Bojan Bugaric. "Unfinished Europe: Transition from Communism to Democracy in Central and Eastern Europe." *Journal of Contemporary History*. 50 no. 4 (2015): 768–785.
ii. Taylor, Alan. "20 Years Since the Bosnian War." *The Atlantic*, April 13, 2012.
iii. Prothero, Mitchell. "Feature: Bosnia's Muslim Aid Hard to Resist." *UPI*, May 16, 2002.

· 2 7 ·

WESTERN EUROPE

For centuries Europe was a backwater compared to Asia. Europeans looked up to the progressive accomplishments taking place in China and the Middle East. In the 15th century that began to change. The Ottoman's had motivated Europe to wake-up from its long slumber in the Middle Ages.

It was a powerful awakening. No empire/group played a more active role in the competition for global supremacy than Europe's empires. They conquered and colonized more land and subjugated more people than any other empire/group. Between the 15th and 18th centuries, overseas conquests were centered in the New World, where sparsely populated, lightly fortified lands were easier prey than the more heavily populated, fortified lands in the Old World. That changed in the 19th century when nations in Europe became leaders in industrial revolutions driven by capitalism.

Economics was always a driver of empire expansion, but it moved to the fore as the primary driver of Europe's empires. Profit-driven industrial capitalists were stoking interest in expansion, and there were plenty of profits to be made in the Old World. The 19th and 20th centuries saw Europe's empires expanding all over Asia and Africa and engaging in the grandest battles ever fought on European turf.

The global reach and impact of Europe's empires are why history courses around the world teach aspects of European history. Everyone's history includes the presence and influence of Europe's empires.

European empires inflicted many visible scars on Europe. The Thirty Years War (1618–1648) completely devastated dozens of polities in Western Europe. The Napoleonic Wars (1803–1815) wreaked havoc across Western and Central Europe and beyond. Napoleonic France left behind other aftermaths that were positive for Europe, although not for its ruling classes. The notion of the divine right of absolute monarchs to rule and the institutionalized privilege of a noble class was shaken to its core. Some rulers hung on, but over the next century, power was reduced when absolute monarchs became constitutional monarchs. Others were ejected for republican and democratic forms of government.

There were many other wars, but the grandest battle scars in Europe from Europe's empires were branded during WWI and WWII. WWI's battling empires inflicted devastation all over Europe. Unprecedented death tolls were counted in the millions. Then came WWII. The year 1945 is dubbed Year Zero. In Western Europe, tens of millions died, and major cities were leveled. Left for posterity were the deep scars of genocides and ethnic cleansings. The economic impact of the physical damage would have been worse but economic recovery was aided by an unforeseen imperative. The Soviet Union was not done with the competition for global supremacy, and Western Europe wore a bullseye. It had the appearances of a susceptible target. From the time Karl Marx and Friedrich Engels published the Communist Manifesto in 1848 there was interest in communism. Europe had a long history of hereditary ruling classes and social immobility. The masses had been receptive to communism's promise of social equality. However, a lot had changed since 1848. Democratic forms of government with capitalist-weighted economic systems had learned from the mistakes of the interwar years. They had made a comeback, and Europe was prepared to defend these systems against communism.

By the time the Era of Nation-States arrived, Western Europe could say been there, done that. For all but two nations, Cyprus and Malta, this was a region of independent nations in 1945. Tiny San Marino's independence dates to 301, France to 486, England 927, Denmark 958, and Portugal 1139. Not all nations are more than 500 years old. Germany became independent in 1871, and so did Italy. This is one reason these two were among the last to embark on building an empire. The Roman Catholic Irish defensively merged with Protestant Britain in 1801, but they were never content with their second-class status. Between 1919 and 1921 the Irish fought a partially successful war for independence.

Ireland was partitioned into the Irish Free State (Ireland), and Northern Ireland. The latter has remained an integral part of the United Kingdom.[1]

After WWII, it wasn't nation-building that was on the agenda; it was rebuilding nations. The European Reconstruction Plan also called the Marshall Plan, provided the 2018 equivalent of $100 billion to aid recovery after WWII. The Marshall Plan "has been repeatedly praised as the most successful initiative of U.S. foreign policy and the most effective reconstruction program in history."[i] Key to reconstruction was the re-integration of West Germany. Most Europeans wanted nothing to do with Germany but the thought of leaving it vulnerable to Soviet appeals or coercion, and aid being contingent on re-integration were compelling.

Integrating the economies of Western Europe soon became the region's strategy to maintain power and peace in the Era of Nation-States. An economically integrated Europe would replace the political and economic power lost by dissolving colonial empires and open the possibility for a collection of relatively small and mid-sized nations to remain on the global stage.

In 1952 the EU's first predecessor organization was established, and regional integration was underway. Fundamental to EU membership was a commitment to democracy and capitalist-weighted economies. The latter is also referred to as market-driven economies. These bottoms-up flexible systems were by and for the benefit of the masses and viewed as crucial to building a union of politically and economically stable nations. Four decades of preparations and negotiations later the EU was established in 1993 with twelve members. Serendipitously its inauguration closely coincided with the dissolution of the Soviet Union. This presented the EU with the uncontemplated opportunity of expanding its sphere of influence into the former Soviet sphere. By 2011, the EU included eleven former Soviet sphere communist nations and more were preparing for membership.[2] It also included Cyprus and Malta.

Cyprus and Malta didn't become independent until 1960 and 1964 respectively. Nation building for Cyprus was rocky from the start and problems were rooted in their history with empires. Cyprus was part of the Ottoman Empire from 1571–1878. During this time, Turkish Muslims were transported into Cyprus. At independence, the British Empire facilitated the apportionment of political representation between Muslims and Christians. The decisions made became a source of conflict that necessitated UN peacekeepers. Then in 1974 Turkey invaded Cyprus ostensibly to protect the Turkish minority, and the Turkish Republic of Northern Cyprus declared its independence.[3] UN peacekeepers have continued their long-term stay on the divided island.

Incredibly Cyprus has developed an advanced economy. So has Malta. But this never would have happened without membership in the EU. The model of the EU requires all members to have a similar level of economic development. They achieve this by having richer members subsidize development in less advanced nations.[4] Largesse by the richer members is not without controversy. During the financial crisis that began in 2008, Portugal, Italy, Greece, and Spain needed extra funding and were nicknamed the PIGS. One front-page headline in Germany read: Sell the Acropolis. Controversies notwithstanding, this subsidization formula has created something unique: an entire region of advanced economies where people enjoy an average quality of life that rivals the best in the world. It has also facilitated making the EU an economic power whose strength is equal to or greater than China, Russia, Iran, Saudi Arabia, or the United States.

A region with a history of regular wars, with the help of NATO, has avoided conventional wars since 1945, but it has not been completely conflict-free. Among the most unsettling have been several brazen, devastating acts of Islamic terrorism that have done their job—terrified millions. This somewhat unexpected turn of events beginning in the early 21st century has ties to the Era of Empire. After WWII many nations in Europe had a level of population homogeneity they had not had in decades. They also had labor shortages. Non-white, non-Christian immigrants and guest workers, primarily from current and former colonies and protectorates in Africa and Asia began arriving into a region with a historical reputation for seeing white, Christian populations as superior. Many nations have managed diversity by implementing multicultural policies that have encouraged new populations to live in separate communities. The public rationale for this was to allow immigrants to maintain their cultures. That sounds nicer than requiring assimilation, but populations that retain their differences will face a higher probability of discrimination, and this will translate into unequal opportunities and unhappy people.

The EU has become the headline for this region in the Era of Nation-States. For good reasons. Behind the scenes, the EU has been creating a region of nations that are democratic with advanced economies. It is the combined performance of the EU (and NATO), rather than any nation that keeps this region politically and economically on the world stage. But there would be no EU if member nations did not agree to sacrifice some aspects of sovereignty for the chance to stay relevant on the world stage. Something like this was never done before and never since.

There is a giant headwind blowing in Western Europe's direction. The region is experiencing dramatic population and demographic changes that may affect its place on the world stage. In 1900 Europe represented 25 percent of the global population.[ii] According to the UN it was 12 percent in 2015 and is expected to drop to 7 percent by 2050. Population declines will take a greater toll on Christians than Muslims, due to higher fertility rates for Muslims.[iii] The population of Muslims was 4.5 percent in 2016 but is expected to grow to between 7.6 and 14 percent by 2050.[iv] This is an extraordinary news item for a region once called Christendom. Without addressing the problems of discrimination that are inherent in multiculturalism, it will generate other news streams. It's possible, however, that the boldest 21st-century headline will read: Europe is economically suffering from too many pensioners and not enough workers.

Notes

1. Between 1535 and 1542 Wales was merged with the Kingdom of England. In 1707 Scotland joined England and Wales to form Great Britain. In 1801 Ireland merged with Great Britain to form the United Kingdom of Great Britain and Ireland. In 1922 the Republic of Ireland became independent, but Northern Ireland remained, and the United Kingdom of Great Britain and Northern Ireland was formed, more commonly called the United Kingdom or the UK.
2. In 2016 there were twenty-eight members, but the UK passed a referendum to exit the union and was expected to leave in 2019.
3. Only Turkey recognizes the Turkish Republic of Northern Cyprus. This recognition became a major impediment to Turkey's accession into the EU.
4. An article in the EU Observer (28 July 2014) by Valentina Pop showed that the biggest giver to EU aid and the nation whose GDP has increased the most from the EU's single market is Germany.

References

i. "Rebuilding Austria—The Marshall Plan." Austrian Press & Information Service in the United States, Washington, D.C., February 14, 2007.
ii. "The World at Six Billion." United Nations: Department of Economic and Social Affairs Population Division, 1999.
iii. Sherwood, Harriet. "Muslim population in some EU countries could triple, says report." *The Guardian*, November 29, 2017.
iv. "Europe's Growing Muslim Population." Pew Research Center, November 29, 2017.

· 2 8 ·

LATAM

The Spanish and Portuguese were the dominant European empires in Latam. By the early 1800s, most colonies won their independence. Unlike the renegade Americans in the north, colonies in Latam closely followed in the footsteps of the Spanish and Portuguese empires. Beyond practicing Roman Catholicism and speaking Spanish and Portuguese, these nations were led by autocrats that hierarchically ordered populations. From the Era of Empire to the Era of Nation-States, it was more of the same with the addition of armed-Cold War conflicts, the Dirty Wars, drug cartels, liberation theology, populist movements, and communism.

The Soviets weren't initially targeting Latam because it was geographically close to the United States. When Fidel Castro's Cuba implemented communism, Castro volunteered to handle communist outreach and to be the chief antagonist of the United States; the Soviets became interested.

Castro had a lot to work with. Communism with its pitch of redistributing the land and wealth from political elites to the poor masses was attractive in a region of social immobility and vast inequality. Three nations in Central America: Guatemala, Nicaragua, and El Salvador fought Cold War conflicts where communists were supported by some combination of Cuba and other nations in the Second World, and the United States and first-world allies supported anti-communists. Every war lasted over ten years, and at some level, the communists were victorious in each conflict.

There were other Cold War-related conflicts in Latam, but they weren't conventional wars. The Dirty Wars pitted leftist revolutionaries, some communist, and some supported by the Soviet Union against entrenched oligarch-supported rightist dictatorships. The Soviets wanted to supplant US influence in the region,[i] but this was unpalatable to political elites and other oligarchs who saw communism as a system that would confiscate their wealth, and place targets on their foreheads.

Government-managed security forces engaged in extra-judicial killings to make real and perceived communist agitators and sympathizers disappear. Between 1968 and 1989 a coalition of right-wing dictators from Argentina, Bolivia, Brazil, Chile, Paraguay, Uruguay, Peru and Ecuador engaged in US-supported Operation Condor to eliminate perceived communists. Rounded up were labor union leaders, student activists, priests, nuns, and avowed communists. Operation Condor was responsible for up to 60,000 murders.[ii] Far more were tortured. Argentina alone had four hundred torture camps.[iii]

The United States' support of right-wing dictators is part of its controversial history in this region. U.S. Secretary of State, John Foster Dulles, (1953–1959) remarking on the presence of American supported anti-communist dictators famously said, "If he is a bastard, at least he is our bastard." One bastard was Paraguay's President Stroessner (1954–1989) who ruled ruthlessly and by decree. Perceived opponents lived in prisons described as concentration camps. Thousands were tortured and an estimated 3–4,000 killed.[iv] Stroessner left Paraguay among the most impoverished nations in the Americas. Other bastards were Papa Doc and Baby Doc Duvalier, the rulers of Haiti from 1957–1985. The Duvalier's oversaw the rape, torture, and murder of tens of thousands of opponents, sometimes communist, other times not.

Peru also engaged in an overt war against the Cuban-supported Shining Path,[v] an organization committed to communism, of a Maoist variety.[1] Its mode of persuasion was terror. The Shining Path inflicted a reign of terror on Peru from 1980–1992. Peruvian President Alberto Fujimori (1990–2000) made the Shining Path enemy number one and disbanded the group in 1992.

Beginning in 1964 Colombia became embroiled in a battle with the Cuban-supported Revolutionary Armed Forces of Colombia (FARC), a guerilla/terrorist group that claimed to be devoted to Marxism-Leninism. The FARC terrorized Colombians for decades and severely hampered economic development into the 21st century. Like the drug cartels, the major funding for the Shining Path and the FARC came from drug cultivation and trafficking.

Inspired by receptivity to communism's promise of social equality two alternatives emerged. Latam's version of populism and Liberation Theology that saw the church as the leader liberating the poor masses through political activism.

Latam's populist politicians have the sound of modern-day Robin Hoods stealing from the wealthy oligarchs and foreign corporations and giving to the poor masses.[2] With world-beating income inequality, this message resonates, even if Robin Hood-type policies have historically shown their footing is a house of cards. Populist policies have led to high inflation, and even hyperinflation, increased corruption, lowered real wages,[vi] and increased political instability. Populists have set economic development back in Argentina, Brazil, Chile, Peru, Mexico, Nicaragua, and Venezuela.[vii]

When the Cold War ended, it was evident that communism, liberation theology, and populism had done little to change inequality in the region. Change, however, was afoot. Dictators could no longer count on the financial support of nations from the First or Second Worlds. Foreign aid was only available to those adopting democratic forms of government. This instigated a regional trend that included leftist/communist governments in Guatemala, El Salvador, and Nicaragua re-selecting democratic forms of government. After more than 150 years, dictators supported by oligarchs that left the masses in poverty seemed to be fading into Latam's history—almost everywhere.

It was easy for corruption to root in nations ruled by autocrats with or without the support of oligarchs. Unrooting it remains a regional problem. Following a devastating earthquake in 2010 foreign aid poured into Haiti, and media reports poured out questioning where the money had gone. How corrupt is a country where officials steal foreign aid earmarked to lessen the impact of cholera, tuberculosis, and other infectious diseases?

In 2017 Venezuela's TI score was eleven spots lower than Haiti. It ranked 169th out of 180 nations. Venezuela was not always this corrupt. Bolivarian socialism was implemented when Hugo Chavez came to power in 1999. The nationalization of industries and increasingly autocratic rule followed, creating a great foundation for rising corruption. In 1999 Venezuela ranked 75th on the TI index.

Corruption in Latam facilitates organized crime and vice versa. It also encourages murder. Latam's homicide rate of 24 per 100,000 is four times the world average.[viii] In 2015 UNDOC reported that it was nearly ten times the global average in Honduras. Meanwhile, in Venezuela in 2017 it was twenty times the average. Between 2007 and 2014 Mexican drug cartels were responsible for killing 83,000 people.[ix] According to the Mexican Institute for Competitiveness, criminal conviction rates have been less than 2 percent. In 2016 it was reported that drug cartels were paying bribes of $100 million monthly to Mexican police officers. Known as the silver or lead decision police have the option to take a bribe or get killed for enforcing the law.[x] When organized crime operates with impunity, mayhem is a natural outcome.

Organized crime is a more recent homegrown problem tied to the drug cartels, but it is also an outgrowth of the centuries of dictatorial rule that empowered law enforcement and the military to control the masses, while "legitimizing" autocratic rule. There are many other problems in this region with ties to the perpetuation of empire aftermaths by misguided and under-qualified leaders. In the post-Cold War period, the nations of Latam began addressing some of the most damaging aftermaths of empire, like autocratic rule, income inequality, social immobility, and other discriminatory practices. Latam was embarking on a long-delayed journey to modernity. Out with dictators supported by oligarchs, and in with democratic leaders responsible to the masses, and capitalist-weighted economic systems that help to spread the wealth. Progress has at times been sidetracked, for example by populists and the nouveau oligarchs running organized crime. Still, slowly nations in the region have been moving forward. These aftermaths didn't become entrenched overnight, and they will take time to undo; providing the people are willing to make it clear that this is what they really want.

The rest of this section zeroes in on the two nations, Cuba and Venezuela, that rejected democratic rule and capitalist-weighted economic systems. During the Cold War, Cuba chose a communist political system and alignment with the Soviet Union; afterward, it remained committed to communism. In the post-Cold War period, Venezuela traded a democratic system with a capitalist-weighted economic system for Bolivarian socialism.

Cuba

When Fidel Castro came to power in 1959 Cubans believed they had a leader that would adhere to promises to end corruption and restore political freedoms, like the freedom to elect government leaders. By 1961 Castro was an avowed communist, and there were no political or economic freedoms. In 1961 he banned political elections saying he had insufficient time for a low priority task, he expropriated church property and made atheism the official religion. In an overwhelmingly Roman Catholic country, he thought better than to bar religious practice, but anyone practicing religion was banned from the communist party.

Castro was not a disciple of Marx. He "turned to communism because it was a useful tool of the absolute power of a kind enjoyed by no run-of-the-mill strongman, coming as it did, with the shield of Soviet protection,"[xi] (plus Soviet weapons and oil). The turn to communism eliminated ties with the US government, which was fine for Castro. His new sponsor was the Soviet Union.

When the Cold War ended Cuba continued carrying a dictatorial communist torch, and it wasn't easy without Soviet support. Castro's Cuba found a new source of income—drug trafficking. According to a former bodyguard Castro viewed trafficking in cocaine as a "weapon of revolutionary struggle."[xii] In 2002 Castro secured another benefactor.

Venezuela

Oil-rich and independently wealthy Venezuela was trading in its democratic and capitalist-weighted economic system for populism and autocracy. Their new president became Cuba's new patron.

Campaigning on a populist platform, Hugo Chavez became President of Venezuela in 1999. He introduced a Stalinesque version of communism—called Bolivarian socialism. He nationalized industries, confiscated assets, and delivered rich social welfare programs to the masses. In possession of immense revenue from oil and gas, Chavez in the fashion of a nouveau Soviet leader dished out copious amounts of foreign aid to Bolivia, Cuba, Ecuador, Nicaragua, and Iran in exchange for unofficially being part of his coalition of enemies of the United States.

The unskilled local managers running the nationalized oil and gas industries saw revenue plunge, but not nearly as much as when the price of oil plummeted. Declining revenues, rising outlays of foreign aid, and rich social welfare programs led to funding shortages. The government looked to the populist's handbook and began printing money.

Venezuela was in a state of chaos. In 2018 inflation was measured with seven digits. Minimum wages were being adjusted monthly. In August 2018 they were hiked sixty-fold. There were shortages of everything from toilet paper to milk, and crime had skyrocketed. Venezuelans were dying because they couldn't access ordinary medicines. Millions fled the country. Chavez turned a productive capitalist-weighted economy into unproductive Bolivarian socialism, and his successor Nicholas Maduro turned it into a failed state. Populism's track record remained awful. The masses were again worse off.

Venezuela's plunge into an economic abyss was a catastrophe for Cuba.[xiii] In desperation it reluctantly engaged in conversations to establish relations with the United States. This chapter in Cuban-American history is TBD.

Notes

1. Marxism-Leninism, Stalinism, Maoism are all communist variations.
2. Populism is sometimes equated to politicians that pander to the concerns of the masses to improve popularity; this is not the populism of Latam.

References

i. "Soviet Policies and Activities in Latin America and the Caribbean." The US Central Intelligence Agency, June 25, 1982.
ii. Rohler, Larry. Exposing the Legacy of Operation Condor. *New York Times*, January 24, 2014.
iii. Daniels, Alfonso. "Argentina's Dirty Wars: The Museum of Horrors." *The Telegraph*, May 17, 2008.
iv. Vargas, David. "Paraguay: Stroessner's Crimes Under the Microscope." *Inter Press Service News Agency*, July 24, 2007.
v. "Fidel Castro's Communist Utopia." *Wall Street Journal*, November 27, 2017.
vi. "The Return of Populism." *The Economist*, April 12, 2016.
vii. Dornbusch, Rudiger and Sebastian Edwards. *The Macroeconomics of Populism in Latin America.* University of Chicago Press, 1991.
viii. "Stop the Carnage." *The Economist*, February 25, 2017.
ix. Grillo, Ioan. *Gangster Warlords: Drug Dollars, Killing Fields, and the New Politics of Latin America.* Bloomsbury Press, 2016.
x. "Mexico: Cartels Pay Corrupt Cops $100 Million a Month." *Latin American Herald Tribune*. Retrieved October 3, 2016.
xi. "Briefing Fidel Castro." *The Economist*, December 3, 2016.
xii. Sanchez, J. R. *The Double Life of Fidel Castro.* St. Martin's Press, 2015.
xiii. Whitefield, Mimi. "Study: Cubans Don't Make Much, But Its More Than State Salaries Indicate." *Miami Herald*, July 12, 2016.

· 2 9 ·

ENGLISH-SPEAKING NORTH AMERICA

Many European empires had colonies in English-speaking North America, but in the end, virtually all colonies were ruled by the British Empire or incorporated into the United States. This is how the region came to be overwhelmingly English-speaking and named English-Speaking North America (ESNA). Language isn't the only empire aftermath; every nation has a Christian-majority, and the diversity of populations reflects historical immigration from Europe, Africa, and Asia. The latter two were slavery and indentured servant labor sources between the 16th and 19th centuries.

In 1776 the Thirteen Colonies declared independence from the British Empire. The United States was the first overseas colony to declare and permanently keep its independence. Next in the region was Canada, and this would not occur for more than a hundred years.[1] For the ten small island nations in the Caribbean, it was yet another hundred years. Other small island polities voluntarily retained ties to France, the Netherlands, the United Kingdom, or the United States.

ESNA has two huge nations, Canada and the United States, but the US population and economy are about ten times larger than Canada's. The other ten nations are much smaller.

It is easy to forget that the British Empire once dominated this region because the United States eclipsed its power long ago, and then went on to surpass it. Below are some highlights of the United States as a global power in the Era of Nation-States.

The United States

The United States pioneered the implementation of a democratic political system with a capitalist economic system. These systems became the vehicles for propelling this former colony onto the world stage in the early 20th century. Thus far, an unmatched feat.

WWI was America's coming out party. The United States had already been providing significant war-related financing to Britain, France, and Italy,[i] before joining as an Allied Power in 1917. The United States joined under the condition that the people living in the losing empires would have the right to self-determination. As a Big Four participant in the Paris Peace Conferences, US President Wilson ensured that his fellow allies honored this commitment.

The United States cemented its status as a global power during WWII. It distributed $50.1 billion (nearly $700 billion in 2018 dollars) of aid to China, Britain, France, and the Soviet Union; 16 million Americans served; and the United States supplied more military ships, planes, and vehicles than any other nation. When victory seemed assured it took the lead in overseeing the creation of the United Nations as a vehicle to halt the competition for empire and facilitate independence for subjugated people everywhere. The United States had earned a position on the world stage among the Era of Empire's greatest powers.

After WWII, the United States economy was much stronger than any other. It had the world's most powerful military, and it was the only state with atomic weapons. As an uber champion of the UN Charter, and a stalwart believer in the goodness of capitalist-weighted, democratic systems it was the only nation capable of presenting a credible defense against the Soviet Union's dismissal of the UN Charter in pursuit of an expanding communist empire. The United States became the leader of the First World during the Cold War.

It wasn't long before the nation once admired as a David that had beaten the goliath British Empire was taking on the aura of a new Goliath. It wasn't an imperial power annexing territory, but that didn't matter. It was a superpower with the unwanted inheritance of Europe's imperial history. Many in the

Second and Third Worlds, encouraged by second-world propaganda, painted it as a hegemonic imperial power picking up where Europe's empires left off, a neo-imperial power imposing democracy and capitalism on the world, a hypocrite supporting anti-communist despots, and an unwanted meddlesome global cop.

After the Cold War things were supposed to be different. US Ambassador to the United Nations, Jean Kirkpatrick, wrote an article in 1990 called "A Normal Country in a Normal Time." She said it was time for the United States to "focus again on its own national interests." These sentiments echoed US President Warren Harding's direction for a "return to normalcy" after WWI.[ii]

Then an ominous threat to global peace began surfacing. In 1996 the leader of al Qaeda, Osama bin Laden, issued a fatwa: the "Declaration of War against the Americans Occupying the Land of the Two Holy Places." The occupation referred to the United States honoring a request by the Saudi monarch to maintain an American military presence to help protect Saudi Arabia during and after the Gulf War (1990–1991). A fatwa was something new in the common lexicon of non-Muslim nations, and so were the names Osama bin Laden and al-Qaeda. The fatwa was classified as a non-credible threat. In 1998 bin Laden directed a pair of terrorist actions against US embassies in Africa that killed 224 people.

Three years later on September 11, 2011, forever remembered as simply 9/11, Islamic militants under the direction of bin Laden hijacked planes and flew them into New York's World Trade Center, and the Pentagon in Washington D.C. killing nearly 3,000 innocent civilians. The world was generally aghast, but some Muslims were filmed rejoicing. The juxtaposition of Muslims rejoicing, while most mourned a deplorable mass murder was incomprehensible. Over and over again rejoicing Muslims from the Palestinian territories beamed across televisions around the world. The credibility of the threat from bin Laden, and al-Qaeda was no longer in doubt.

As the lone superpower, the United States again found itself in a leading position defending an unfamiliar enemy. A militant form of Islamism was as incomprehensible to American values as communism. Militant Islamism was not the only threat to global peace and American power in the world. In a similar timeframe, familiar foes from the Cold War, Russia and China, violated the sovereignty of some nations in contravention of international law and they were intimidating others. Russia and China were in the process of rebuilding power in the same spheres of influence as their predecessor empires.

There was mounting evidence that the United States had not passed into a normal time where it could be a normal country. There was still a need for a global cop, and no one suitable was stepping forward to take America's place.

The United States endeavored to stay away from the wars of empires outside the Americas. Then it took a very decided stand against empires in WWI and WWII. After the world wars, it ended up inheriting angst for imperial actions that were more appropriately directed at Europe's empires and carrying disproportionate responsibility for preventing sovereign infringement in the Era of Nation-States. To do this, it has disproportionately engaged in infringing sovereignty. However, much of the world and many Americans too only see the United States as a belligerent, unchecked hegemon. No question America's place in the world is complicated, and unlike most other global powers, its place is debated vigorously inside and outside the United States and extra energetically by competitors for global power.

Note

1. In 1867, Canada became a self-governing dominion in the British Empire. In 1931 it became legislatively independent of Britain, and in 1982 Britain could no longer amend Canada's constitution. It was now independent beyond the ties it voluntarily retains by having Britain's monarch as its head of state.

References

i. Mulder, Nicholas. "War Finance." International Encyclopedia of the First World War 1914–1918. Retrieved November 19, 2018.
ii. Kagan, Robert. "Superpowers Don't Get to Retire." The New Republic, May 26, 2014.

· 3 0 ·

OCEANIA

Oceania is like ESNA in having: two large countries that were former British colonies; several smaller island nations, of which most were former British colonies; some island territories that have voluntarily retained ties to former European empires or the United States; nations with Christian majorities; and in all but one English is the national language. The large nations are Australia and New Zealand. Australia is the larger of the two; its economy is about seven times larger, and its population is about five times larger. Both nations became virtually independent in 1901 and 1907 respectively, but not entirely independent until 1986 and 1947 respectively.[1] Independence came to the twelve smaller nations between 1970 and 1994.

The colonies of Australia and New Zealand underwent a long process of attaining progressively more responsibility for governing. At virtual independence, they had mature political institutions and battle-tested military forces. Both nations were essential contributors to the Allied Powers during WWI and WWII.

Half a world away from other nations in the First World, Australia and New Zealand were charter and committed members defending democracy during the Cold War. Located in the South Pacific close to conflicts in Southeast and Eastern Asia made them indispensable. Like other first-world nations they were breathing a sigh of relief when the Cold War ended, but they quickly grasped that the post-Cold War period was not a "normal" time and they had to remain vigilant in assessing and managing external threats that have ties to Era of Empire postscripts.

Australia and New Zealand are the regions only two advanced economies. The next largest nations, Fiji and Papua New Guinea have struggled with nation-building, and misguided national leaders are a significant reason why. For decades Fiji has been grappling with an ethnic conflict between indigenous Fijians, and Indo-Fijians that trace their descent to indentured servants arriving from India during the Era of Empire. There have been four military coups since independence in 1970, and each time at issue is ethnic conflict. Corruption is also a serious problem in Fiji although not as grand as Papua New Guinea where the government is "notorious for corruption, and ever runs the risk of turning the state into a fully-fledged kleptocracy."[i]

Like Fiji and Papua New Guinea, the rest of Oceania's small nations have struggled with nation-building. Sometimes this is purely a function of size. Three nations have populations under 25,000; they are no more populous than a large town in most nations. Nauru and Tuvalu have landmasses of 21 and 26 km² (8.1 and 10 mi²). Nearly 300,000 of either of these nations could fit inside Australia.

The subjugation of women hurts economic development everywhere, but here the problem is particularly terrible. Excluding Australia and New Zealand, this region has a reputation for domestic violence. Depending on the nation, 60–80 percent of women have experienced physical or physical and sexual abuse. Many of their first experiences were as children.[ii]

China has become a jumbo engine of growth for this region bringing Australia and New Zealand economically closer to the Middle Kingdom. Harkening back to China's penchant for nations pledging tribute to its empire, China has applied pressure to alter foreign policies,[iii,iv] putting these two in tough positions. Historically, militarily, politically, and culturally Australia and New Zealand are aligned with their fellow western nations.

Note

1. Australia and New Zealand (like Canada) ended rule by the British Empire in stages. Both countries have retained the British monarch as their ceremonial head of state.

References

i. "Near Neighbors, Worlds Apart." *The Economist*, August 8, 2011.

ii. "Violence Against Women in the Pacific." UN Population Fund Pacific Sub-Regional Office, January 1, 2013.

iii. "Meddle Kingdom." *The Economist*, June 17, 2017.

iv. Kwok, Jackson. "Chinese Media Responds to the Defense White Paper." *The Interpreter*, September 11, 2017.

CONCLUSION

Facilitating the transition from empires to nation-states was given considerable thought. The best-laid plans can be undone, and this happened here. When the Cold War commenced the world's grandest transition became an un-navigated muddle.

New nations had the benefit of IGOs like the UN, World Bank, and GATT, but assistance was often squandered by inexperienced, misguided leaders in an environment of limited oversight. They also had access to expedient generous global powers. In exchange for allegiance first- and second-world powers proffered financial and military aid. But global powers were not supposed to be leveraging opportunities afforded by the flood of newbie nations and national leaders to rebuild spheres of influence. It was, in the end, a fool's errand. Allegiance to first- or second-world powers was as durable as the last tranche of squandered aid.

Decades and billions of development dollars later there was little to show for it. At best, nation-building in the Second and Third Worlds made modest progress. For the First World, things were different. They experienced decades of unprecedented prosperity. The democratic/capitalist First World, the communist Second World, and the unaligned Third World could now be described as the rich First World, the poor Third World, and the poor-to-less-poor Second World.

The environment for nation building was expected to be better for everyone in the post-Cold War period. The Red Scare had ended, there were expanded opportunities for trade, global powers would surely meddle less, and nations had to be in better and safer hands with a bench of skilled government leaders applying prudent reasoning.

Expanded trade opened up opportunities for everyone and gave global powers a vehicle to extend their influence and meddle more. They focused on their historical spheres of influence, where there were common histories, religions, languages, and political systems. Some sovereign leaders were receptive, while others rejected a trap door to nouveau subjugation while seeking cover in a less intrusive sphere of influence. For many, the dream of true independence remained an illusion.

By 1991 most nation had decades to build a bench of qualified leaders. For many, the bench remained empty. Billions of people still had under-skilled misguided national leaders and nations bore the telltale signs of mismanagement—poor qualities of life, underdeveloped infrastructure and institutions, repression, and unchecked discrimination. There was nothing anyone outside voters, rebellious masses, or organized opponents, perhaps supported by global powers, could do about the perpetuation of problems from lousy governance. These were sovereign nations, and these were internal issues. It was just as well that coups mismanaged by foreign powers were globally repudiated. Perhaps this attitude reflected one thing that was virtually achieved in the Era of Nation-States: a widespread belief that sovereignty was sacrosanct, just like the UN Charter envisioned it.

This was a good omen for the continued plodding of an Era of Nation-States. There might be underperforming nations all over the world, but almost everywhere qualities of life have been improving. It was a natural outcome when making the switch from colonies as captive suppliers of raw materials to industrializing nations and also from subjugation and foreign rule to sovereign nations with indigenous rule. There is plenty more to do, but a return to empires, virtual or real, is not a cure for anything that ails countries today. Cures are found in skilled, experienced, benevolent national leaders, including those from global powers, that are committed to peaceful coexistence, fundamental freedoms for all, and encouraging superior qualities of life.

APPENDICES

APPENDIX A

Countries by Region

Note: Territories are distinguished by noting the parent nation in parenthesis, for example, Anguilla (UK).

Central Asia (CA)
Abkhazia (unrecognized by the UN)
Armenia
Azerbaijan
Georgia
Kazakhstan
Kyrgyzstan
South Ossetia (unrecognized by the UN)
Turkmenistan
Tajikistan
Uzbekistan

Central Europe (CE)
Bosnia and Herzegovina
Albania
Bulgaria
Croatia

Czech Republic
Estonia
Hungary
Kosovo (unrecognized by UN)
Latvia
Lithuania
Macedonia
Montenegro
Poland
Romania
Serbia
Slovak Republic
Slovenia

Eastern Europe (EE)
Belarus
Moldova
Russia
Ukraine

Eastern Asia (EA)
China
Hong Kong, SAR of China
Japan
Macau, SAR of China
Mongolia
North Korea
Taiwan/Republic of China (Unrecognized by the UN)
South Korea

English-Speaking North America (ESNA). Divided by the Mainland and the Caribbean.

Mainland
Canada
United States

The Caribbean
Anguilla (UK)

Antigua and Barbuda
Aruba (NL)
The Bahamas
Barbados
Bermuda
British Virgin Islands (UK)
Caribbean Netherlands (Bonaire, Sint Eustasius, Saba)
Cayman Islands (UK)
Curacao (NL)
Dominica
Grenada
Jamaica
Montserrat (UK)
Puerto Rico (US)
Saba (NL)
St. Barthelemy
St. Kitts and Nevis
St. Lucia
Saint Martin/Sint Maarten (FR and NL)
St. Vincent and the Grenadines
Trinidad and Tobago
Turks and Caicos Islands (UK)
US Virgin Islands (US)

Latin America (Latam). Divided in four: Mexico, Central America, South America and the Caribbean.

Mexico

Central America
Belize
Costa Rica
El Salvador
Guatemala
Honduras
Nicaragua
Panama

South America
Argentina
Bolivia

Brazil
Chile
Colombia
Ecuador
Falkland Islands (UK)
French Guiana (FR)
Guyana
Paraguay
Peru
Suriname
Uruguay
Venezuela

Caribbean
Cuba
The Dominican Republic
Guadeloupe (FR)
Haiti
Martinique (FR)

The Middle East and North Africa (MENA). Divided into the Middle East and North Africa.

Middle East
Bahrain
Iran
Iraq
Israel
Jordon
Kuwait
Lebanon
Oman
Palestinian territories (UN permanent observer)
Qatar
Saudi Arabia
Syria
Turkey
United Arab Emirates
Yemen

North Africa
Algeria

Djibouti
Egypt
Libya
Mauritania
Morocco
Sudan
Tunisia
Western Sahara (disputed territory of Morocco)

Oceania (O) (Only inhabited islands.)
American Samoa (US)
Australia
Cook Islands (NZ)
French Polynesia (FR)
Fiji
Guam (US)
Kiribati Islands
Northern Mariana Islands (US)
Marshall Islands
Micronesia (the Federated States of)
Nauru
New Caledonia (FR)
New Zealand
Niue (NZ)
Norfolk Island (AU)
Palau
Pitcairn Islands (UK)
Papua New Guinea
Samoa
Solomon Islands
Tokelau (NZ)
Tonga
Tuvalu
Vanuatu
Wallis and Futuna (FR)

Southeast Asia (SEA)
Brunei
Cambodia
East Timor/Timor-Leste
Indonesia

Laos
Malaysia
Myanmar
Philippines
Singapore
Thailand
Vietnam

South Asia (SA)
Afghanistan
Bangladesh
Bhutan
India
Nepal
Maldives
Pakistan
Sri Lanka

Sub-Saharan Africa (SSA). Divided by geographic region.

West
Benin
Burkina Faso
Cape Verde
Côte d'Ivoire (Ivory Coast)
The Gambia
Ghana
Guinea
Guinea-Bissau
Liberia
Mali
Niger
Nigeria
Senegal
Sierra Leone
Togo

East
Burundi

Comoros
Eritrea
Ethiopia
Kenya
Madagascar
Malawi
Mauritius
Mayotte (FR)
Mozambique
Réunion (FR)
Rwanda
Seychelles
Somalia
South Sudan
Tanzania
Uganda
Zambia
Zimbabwe

Middle
Angola
Cameroon
The Central African Republic
Chad
Democratic Republic of the Congo
Equatorial Guinea
Gabon
Republic of the Congo
São Tomé and Príncipe

South
Botswana
Eswatini (Renamed in 2018. Formerly Swaziland.)
Lesotho
Namibia
St. Helena (UK)
South Africa

Western Europe (WE)
Aland (FI)
Andorra
Austria
Belgium
Cyprus
Denmark
Faroe Islands (DK)
Finland
France
Germany
Gibraltar (UK)
Greece
Greenland (DK)
Guernsey (UK)
Iceland
Ireland
Isle of Man (UK)
Italy
Jersey (UK)
Luxembourg
Liechtenstein
Malta
Monaco
The Netherlands
Norway
Portugal
San Marino
Spain
Sweden
Switzerland
Turkish Republic of Northern Cyprus (unrecognized by the UN)
United Kingdom (England, Northern Ireland, Scotland, Wales)
Vatican City (UN permanent observer)

APPENDIX B

Designations for Groups of Countries

Anglo countries: United States, Canada, the United Kingdom, Ireland, Australia, and New Zealand

Balkan states: Albania, Bosnia and Herzegovina, Bulgaria, Croatia, Greece, Kosovo, the Republic of Macedonia, Montenegro, Romania, Serbia, Slovenia and Turkey.

Baltic states: Latvia, Lithuania, and Estonia.

Benelux countries: Belgium, the Netherlands, and Luxembourg.

Greater China: Peoples Republic of China (PRC), Hong Kong a Special Administrative Republic (SAR) of China, Macau a SAR of China, and the Republic of China (Taiwan).

Horn of Africa: Djibouti, Ethiopia, Eritrea, and Somalia.

Nordic countries: Scandinavia, Finland, Iceland, and the associated territories of Greenland, the Faroe Islands and the Aland Islands.

Scandinavian countries: Sweden, Denmark and Norway.

The United Kingdom and Great Britain (UK): England, Northern Ireland, Scotland, and Wales.

Vicegrad countries: Poland, Hungary, the Czech Republic, and Slovakia.

INDEX

P

Pahlavi, Reza Mohammad (Shah of Iran), 196

Pakistan, 19, 72, 103, 209–217, 240, 252, 284

Palau, 37, 283

Palestinian territories, 269, 282

Panama, 159, 281

Papa New Guinea, 123, 272, 283

Paraguay, 262, 282

People's Republic of China (PRC). See China.

Peter the Great, 27, 60

Persia, 12, 29, 64, 68, 76, 78, 105, 112, 122. See also Iran.

Persian Empires, 61–62, 75, 136–137, 141, 195, 209, 237. See also Qajar Dynasty; Safavid Empire.

Peru, 98, 262–263, 282

Philippines, 37, 59, 88, 156, 219–221, 225, 231, 284

Pitcairn Islands, 283

Poland, 43, 66, 78, 83–84, 93, 98, 126, 129, 145, 249–250, 280, 287

Polish-Lithuanian Commonwealth, 22, 27, 61, 114, 138, 243

Pol Pot, 159, 222, 225

Populism, 263, 265–266

Portugal, 16, 20, 24, 58–60, 76, 82, 109, 131, 144, 147, 150, 155–155, 168, 173–174, 220, 256, 258, 286

Portuguese Empire, 16, 20, 22, 24, 59, 89, 121, 144, 155, 173–174, 261

Postscripts. See Aftermaths of empire: postscripts.

Protestant, 21, 54, 59–60, 67, 82, 110, 256

Prussia, 22–24

Puerto Rico, 37, 281

Q

Qajar Dynasty, 10, 29, 239

Qatar, 46, 151, 192, 205, 282

Qing Dynasty, 32, 34, 51, 122, 144. See also Chinese Empire.

R

Republic of China (ROC), 77, 122, 131, 228–229, 280, 287

Republic of the Congo, 183, 185, 285

Reunion, 285

Revolutions of 1848, 109

Roman Catholics, 12, 58–60, 67, 79, 82, 97

Romania, 11, 43, 126, 280, 287

Roosevelt, Franklin Delano. See FDR.

Russia, 1, 4, 20, 24, 40, 43, 67–68, 126, 134, 146, 149–150, 154–156, 163–169, 171, 191, 195, 204, 209, 214, 231, 238, 240, 244–250, 253, 269, 280. See also Soviet Union.

Russian Empire, 2, 7–8, 10–11, 15, 18–24, 27–30, 33–34, 51, 58, 63–64, 66, 74, 78, 96–97, 106, 122–123, 133, 135, 141, 153, 173, 187, 196, 204–205, 209, 227, 237–239, 243, 250

Orthodox expansion, 60–61

Diversity and discrimination, 78–82, 93, 95, 105, 107, 114–115, 118

Winners and losers, 137–139

WWI, 39–40, 45

See also Soviet Union.

Russian Orthodox, 12. See also Eastern Orthodox.

Russian Revolution, 40, 54

Russo-Persian/Iranian Wars, 10, 28

Russo-Turkish/Ottoman Wars, 10, 28

Russo-Japanese wars, 29, 34, 137

Rwanda, 285

S

Safavid Empire, 4, 10, 12, 62–63, 187, 195, 199, 209

St. Barthelemy, 281